Shamans, Housewives, and Other Restless Spirits

STUDIES OF THE EAST ASIAN INSTITUTE

Shamans, Housewives, and Other Restless Spirits

WOMEN IN KOREAN RITUAL LIFE

LAUREL KENDALL

UNIVERSITY OF HAWAII PRESS

HONOLULU

First edition 1985
Paperback edition 1987
91 92 93 94 95 96   7 6 5 4 3

© 1985 UNIVERSITY OF HAWAII PRESS

MANUFACTURED IN THE UNITED STATES OF AMERICA

Library of Congress Cataloging in Publication Data
Kendall, Laurel
  Shamans, housewives, and other restless spirits.
  (Studies of the East Asian Institute)
  Bibliography: p.
  Includes index.
  1. Shamanism—Korea (South)   2.   Shaman—Korea (South)
  3.   Women—Korea (South)—Religious life.   I.   Title.
  II.   Series.
  BL2236.S5K46   1985   299'.57   84-24138
  ISBN 0-8248-0974-2

  ISBN 0-8248-1142-9 (pbk)

Cover design: Pujŏk, or talismans, are produced
by shamans and Buddhist monks from traditional patterns. Pasted to the wall or secreted
in one's clothing, pujŏk ward off misfortune or
insure success.

To
Dr. Lee Du-hyun
from
an appreciative student

Contents

Preface   ix

ONE   A *Kut* for the Chŏn Family   1

TWO   Confucian Patriarchs and Spirited Women   23

THREE   Enduring Pine Village   39

FOUR   Divine Connections: The *Mansin* and Her Clients   54

FIVE   Wood Imps, Ghosts, and Other Noxious Influences   86

SIX   The Care and Feeding of Household Gods and
         Kindred Spirits   113

SEVEN   The Care and Feeding of Ancestors   144

EIGHT   Women's Rites   164

APPENDIXES

    Appendix 1.   The Chŏn Family *Kut*   183
    Appendix 2.   Major Concerns Expressed in
                  Divination Sessions   185
    Appendix 3.   Ancestors Appearing in *Kut*   186

Notes   189
Glossary   199
Bibliography   213
Index   223

Preface

Clanging cymbals and the steady thump of an hourglass drum draw women and children to the gateway of a Korean house. They know from the flood of sound in the alleyway that the shamans are doing a *kut,* and a *kut* is high entertainment. This account of shamans and housewives begins with a *kut.* My own interest in Korean women's rituals began with a *kut,* a boggling event in color, sound, and costume. To plunge into the *kut* means to be overwhelmed, amused, and possibly bored. Most spectators experience this gamut of responses. Women are the most numerous and enthusiastic participants, both as loquacious shamans and as delighted, slightly tipsy spectators. Sometimes the women drag their reluctant menfolk into the center of the action, tugging at their clothing or pulling them by their ears. These are the same women who, on village lanes and city streets, walk demurely behind their husbands. Why, then, do women dominate the world of *kut,* and what place do *kut* and the many other rituals women perform hold in Korean social and religious life?

This is an ethnography of Korean women's ritual realm—the rites that demarcate it, the supernatural beings who inhabit it, and the shamans who diagnose its vicissitudes and heal its ills. The rituals women perform in public and private, alone or with the help of shamans, reveal a complex system of belief and practice encapsulating significant notions of household, family, and kin. Some scholars consider these events the survivals of an ancient faith discarded by civilized men

and perpetuated by their more superstitious wives. Others suggest that
these rituals give women, as shamans and clients, cathartic release
from oppressive patriarchy. Both of these interpretations are circular.
The social subordination of the Korean woman is accepted as axiom-
atic, then proven again in her religious enthusiasm. Missing is an
appreciation of the participants and of the cultural assumptions that
motivate them. Whether as shaman or housewife, Korean women
wield positive powers. In cooperation, they perform socially essential
ritual work. Their religious activities are a measure of Korea's distinc-
tiveness within the Confucian world.

I describe in these pages the system of belief and practice I found
among women and shamans in and around Enduring Pine Village,
Republic of Korea. Since I focus almost exclusively on ritual life, I fear
that the women of Enduring Pine Village will appear obsessed with
the machinations of gods and ghosts. They are not. They make rituals
quietly on appropriate occasions, then again, more vociferously in
affliction. Ritual responsibilities occupy a small corner of village
women's busy lives, but they hold that corner. The women know
ample ghost stories for a leisure hour, but in the hurried conversations
of everyday they speak of food prices, the latest school fee, children,
and neighbors.

The ethnographer risks both melodrama and romanticism. I present the *mansin* as a professional who performs her services for pay.
Those who consider the shaman a stock type for melodrama, an avaricious exploiter of the peasantry, might find evidence for such in these
pages. That is neither my intention nor was it my impression. Those
who deem the *mansin* a fraud might pounce on such lapses as a shaman asking for her rubber shoes in the midst of trance. But the village
women who evaluate her performance have different standards of satisfactory trancing than the Western connoisseur.

More likely, I might be charged with romanticizing what I describe.
The Western ethnographer seeks exotic customs while some village
women discard rituals as bothersome, expensive, and, to their minds,
useless. I will discuss some of the considerations that inform this
choice. Risking both romanticism and melodrama, I describe what I
saw and heard, shaded by professional training and individual perception. Where possible, I provide free translations of the women's own
explanations. Eliciting these explanations was not always easy. Egged
on by kinswomen and neighbors, a woman giggled and blushed to tell

the anthropologist how the *mansin* had exorcised a ghost from her child. With the women I knew best, the response was different. They considered me an ignorant young female in need of a practical education rather than a foreign scholar who would judge them. They spoke with authority and some pride in their knowledge of gods and rituals.

I carried some anthropological assumptions to the field and held onto them through the researching and writing of this study. I assumed that the different rituals men and women perform would reveal, through their form, content, and expressed objectives, the different perimeters of men's and women's concerns and authority in households and families. I assumed that a woman's dealings with different categories of the supernatural would have corporeal parallels in different kinds of social relationships, and that stressful relations with the supernatural would provide metaphoric clues to stressful relations among the living. My interpretations, informed by these assumptions, are distinguished in the text from the quoted wisdom of shamans and other village women.

Korean expressions are romanized according to the McCune-Reischauer system. Following Korean convention, surnames precede given names. Korean scholars who publish in English as well as Korean often adopt personal romanizations for their own names, which I have also used when referring to their work. Since most American libraries catalogue Korean-language works according to McCune-Reischauer romanizations, these have been added to the bibliography where bilingual or Korean-language works are cited. For example, Lee, Kwang-kyu [Yi Kwang-gyu]; Yim, Suk-jay [Im Suk-che].

A few other conventions are my own. Koreans commonly use the term *mudang* for both shaman and hereditary priestess, and this is the term most often used in English-language accounts of Korea. Since the term is not only imprecise but also derogatory, I refer to *mudang* only when citing sources that do not make a clear distinction between shaman and priestess. I prefer the more polite and localized title *mansin* (pronounced man-shin), the term I used to address the shamans I knew.

Mansin have professional nicknames, the Chatterbox Mansin, the Boil-face Mansin, the Town Mansin. By Korean etiquette adults are not addressed by their given names. Village women are identified as the mothers of village children, Yongsu's Mother, Okkyŏng's Mother, Munae's Mother. I use these baby-mother *(aegiŏmma)* titles for the *mansin* and village women I knew best. Some women are known by where they live, the Tile-roof Auntie, the Hilltop Auntie, the Beside-the-Road Mansin, or by what they do, the Noodle Shop Auntie, the Rice Shop Auntie. Any woman is politely an aunt or a grandmother, depending on her age. All of the names given in the text are fictitious.

Throughout I refrain from such condescending qualifiers as "Korean women believe, or think, that . . ." I describe the workings of the supernatural as they were described to me, rendering a belief system in its own terms, "A god was angry because . . .," "She was possessed by her grandmother because . . ." I let the women of Enduring Pine Village present themselves in their own words. They have little enough chance to address a broader audience, and they have much to tell us.

Shamans, Housewives, and Other Restless Spirits completes a long journey from an early inspiration, through the research and writing of a dissertation, to the preparation of a book. I am indebted to the many people I encountered along the way, many more than I can mention here. My oldest debt is to Dr. Lee Du-hyun, who first introduced me to the world of shaman ritual and tempered my youthful enthusiasm with wisdom and patience. This book is dedicated to him in appreciation of his years of generosity to foreign scholars.

I am also grateful to my American teachers, Myron Cohen and Morton Fried, who guided me through graduate school, and to the other members of my dissertation committee: Clive Kessler, Gari Ledyard, and Herbert Passin. Their comments were rigorous and always constructive. The *mansin* and village women who appear in these pages also deserve thanks for all that they taught me.

My research in Korea was made possible by fellowships from the Institute for International Education (Fulbright) and the Social Science Research Council, as well as by a grant from the National Science Foundation. A fellowship from the Korean Traders' Association enabled me to write up my results as a Junior Research Associate of the East Asian Institute, Columbia University. The experience of fieldwork was enhanced by discussions with other anthropologists at work in Korea: Cho Haejoang, Roger and Dawnhee Janelli, Clark Sorensen, Yoon Soon-young, and Barbara Young. Sohn Hak-soon and Lee Hyon-suk assisted me in collecting interviews. Lucy Hwang transcribed tapes and led me to a memorable Tano Festival. Sandra Mattielli and Bea and David Liebson provided hospitality and hot showers, no small contribution to the morale of an anthropologist in the field.

My fictive Korean family nurtured me while I lived in Enduring Pine Village and were an invaluable source of information. My own parents, Henry and Ramona Kendall, not only cheerfully adjusted to their only child's wanderings but traveled out to see Enduring Pine Village for themselves.

The following persons read all or parts of this manuscript and provided me with useful comments: Jess Bell, Vincent Brandt, Martina Deuchler, George DeVos, the late Youngsook Kim Harvey, Roger and Dawnhee Janelli, Michael Kimmel, Lewis Lancaster, William Lebra, Tom Maretzki, Evelyn McCune, Clark Sorensen, and Arthur Wolf. Marie Adams of the Center for East Asian Studies, University of Kansas, processed the final manuscript. Anita O'Brian of the East Asian Institute, Columbia University, helped me to find a publisher. Nicholas Amorosi of the American Museum of Natural History designed the two figures that accompany the text. The editorial staff at the University of Hawaii Press combined meticulous editing with good humor in the final polishing of the manuscript. My husband, Homer Williams, relentlessly criticized both my prose style and arguments, and, equally relentlessly, kept me in good cheer. I alone am responsible for the shortcomings of this effort and for the sometimes controversial opinions that I have expressed.

Preliminary versions of chapters 1, 5, and 8 have appeared in *Traditional Thoughts and Practices in Korea,* edited by Yu Eui-young and Earl H. Phillips, the *Journal of Korean Studies,* and Senri Ethnological Studies, Volume II, respectively. Kim Yu-gi's poem in praise of pine and bamboo was translated by Richard Rutt in *The Bamboo Grove: An Introduction to Sijo.* The "Song of a Mediocre Woman" is quoted in *Women of Korea: A History from Ancient Times to 1945,* edited and translated by Y. Kim (EWUSP). The tale of "The Honest Witch" is from James S. Gale's *Korean Folk Tales: Imps, Ghosts, and Fairies.*

ONE

A *Kut* for the Chŏn Family

When the roof beam god is out of sorts,
The master of the house is out of sorts.
When the foundation god is out of sorts,
The lady of the house is out of sorts.
Kyŏnggi shaman chant

A cold November sun fades over rooftops of slate, straw, and corrugated metal. Shadows lengthen across fields of rice stubble. A bustle of activity resounds from behind the Chŏn house wall. There is the clatter of incessant chopping in the kitchen and the rise and fall of many voices from behind the inner room's lattice and paper doors. Women issue from the kitchen with steaming tubs of rice cake. The Chatterbox Mansin stands firm amid the flurry, shrilling out directions as women heap plates with rice cake, fruit, and delicacies to feast the household gods and ancestors. The Chŏn family is holding a *kut* to cure Grandfather Chŏn of a nagging illness.

What follows is a frankly flamboyant description of a flamboyant event. I will let the action of the *kut* speak for itself, with a minimum of introductory remarks here to set the stage and introduce the players.

For the Chŏn family *kut* one must imagine a traditional Korean country house. There are two rooms whose floors are heated by a system of flues. A broad wooden porch, polished slick, separates these two hot-floor rooms. Grandmother and Grandfather Chŏn live in the inner room, the main heated room to the left of the porch. A low-roofed kitchen, storerooms, and stock pens are all built around a mud courtyard. An elevated platform at the side of the house holds earthern storage jars of soy sauce and pepper paste. Low walls conceal the low building from the village lane. Today, however, the great front gate is open to the fields. This is the Chŏn house.

A large cast of characters will appear during the Chŏn family *kut*. It includes:

The Shamans
The Chatterbox Mansin—Grandmother Chŏn's regular shaman, and the organizer of the *kut*
Okkyŏng's Mother—The Chatterbox Mansin's apprentice "spirit daughter"
Yongsu's Mother
The Town Mansin

The Household
Grandfather Chŏn—the old man whose illness is the primary reason for this *kut*
Grandmother Chŏn—Grandfather Chŏn's second wife

The Family
The son—Grandfather Chŏn's child by his first wife
The daughter-in-law—the son's wife
Their children—Grandfather and Grandmother Chŏn's grandchildren

Kin
The daughter—Grandfather Chŏn's married daughter by his first wife
The maternal aunt—Grandmother Chŏn's own sister
The paternal aunt—Grandfather Chŏn's sister

The Women
The friend—Grandmother Chŏn's friend from her natal village, the paternal aunt's neighbor
Women who live in the Chŏns' neighborhood

The Ancestors
Parents—Grandfather Chŏn's father and mother, father-in-law and mother-in-law to Grandmother Chŏn
Wife—Grandfather Chŏn's first wife, mother of the son and daughter

Preliminaries

About a month ago Grandfather Chŏn went on an outing with his cronies. This carousing precipitated an upset stomach, which, in turn, developed into a general state of malaise. Grandmother Chŏn described Grandfather Chŏn's complaint to the pharmacist in town and brought home the pharmacist's preparation. It consisted of several packets each containing five different colored pills in white powder. When this medicine brought no relief, Grandfather Chŏn went to an outpatient clinic for the standard treatment, an unspecified shot. An expensive series of shots brought no marked change in Grandfather Chŏn's condition. Grandmother Chŏn then went to the Chatterbox Mansin, a shaman she has consulted for several years, and received a divination.

As Grandmother Chŏn suspected, her Great Spirit Grandmother (Taesin Halmŏni) was greedy for a *kut*. One of Grandmother Chŏn's ancestors was a shaman, and the dead shaman now meddles in the Chŏn household's affairs as the Great Spirit Grandmother of their pantheon. An active Great Spirit Grandmother blesses and protects the family, but every three years or so, the family must feast and entertain her with a *kut*. The Chŏns had not held a *kut* for five or six years. Grandfather Chŏn's illness is a warning that the ritual is overdue. Further misfortune might follow more delay.

Although Grandfather Chŏn was dangerously ill a few weeks ago, he is a bit better now and lounges about in pajamas, chatting with his friends. He is a small, light-framed man with white hair and a neatly clipped beard. Grandmother Chŏn is a lean woman, bent with arthritis but lively and quick to smile. The Chŏns live alone, fairly comfortably, raising pigs and rabbits. The hot-floor rooms are freshly papered and well furnished with chests and cabinets. A large television stands in the main hot-floor room. Color reproductions of traditional folk paintings cut from a calendar decorate one wall.

The Chŏns' son and his wife live in Seoul, where the son is trying his luck, not very successfully, as a shopkeeper. Son, daughter-in-law, and their children have returned today for the *kut*. The Chŏns' married daughter has also returned. Grandmother Chŏn's own sister, the maternal aunt, is here from Seoul. A plump woman with short grey hair, she wears a ready-made trouser suit. She beams, happily anticipating the festivities. Grandfather Chŏn's sister, the paternal aunt, arrives with one of Grandmother Chŏn's old friends from her natal village. Both of these women are wearing fancy Korean dresses shot with silver thread; a *kut* is a special occasion.

Four *mansin* will perform the *kut*. Because Grandmother Chŏn is the Chatterbox Mansin's own client, the Chatterbox Mansin takes charge. She has brought along her own apprentice spirit daughter (*sinttal*), Okkyŏng's Mother, although Okkyŏng's Mother is not yet trained to do much but hit the cymbals. The Chatterbox Mansin has invited Yongsu's Mother and the Town Mansin to perform this *kut* with her. The Town Mansin seldom performs for fear of embarrassing her married daughter, but as an old acquaintance of the Chŏn family, she has agreed to perform this *kut*. Yongsu's Mother has brought the anthropologist with her from Enduring Pine Village.

The *Kut* Begins

In the fading afternoon light the *mansin* set up their hourglass drum and a tray of wine and rice cake on mats outside the house gate. The wine and cake are for the spirits. The *mansin* yell for everyone to come out of the house, and women emerge, red faced, from the kitchen. Grandfather Chŏn, bundled into an overcoat for protection from the wind, hobbles out and sits far to the left of the drum with his cronies. Family and neighborhood women crowd around the drum. More women will join them once the drumming starts. Children wander among the women's skirts. A woman leads the ox out from the enclosed courtyard. Another woman yodels for the dog, who bounds out of the gate. When the *mansin* hit the drum to start the *kut,* no one dares remain inside the house, and all stand wide of the overhanging roof. With the sound of the drum, gods inside the empty house open wide their eyes. This is a dangerous moment. Like the genie in the bottle, awakened household gods seize upon whatever greets their gaze.

Yongsu's Mother hits the drum. Okkyŏng's Mother hits the cymbals. The Chatterbox Mansin declares before the gods and ancestors that the Chŏn family is holding a *kut*. The *mansin* drive unclean, noxious influences away from the house. They invite gods from mountains and distant places to enter the house and be entertained.

The Chatterbox Mansin takes a long blue vest from the top of the drum. She dances, pumping her arms up and down, jumping on the balls of her feet. She stops and scowls at the offering tray. She flings wide her vest and hisses, "There is a Great Spirit in this house, there is, there is."

One of the greedy supernatural Officials (Taegam) has possessed the Chatterbox Mansin. The Officials make trouble when they see wealth

—money and posessions—going into the house. The family should share their good fortune, give the Officials a cup of wine. This particular Official is the Soldier (Kunung Taegam), one of the worst. He prowls outside the house wall, spying on the family. The Soldier Official chides Grandmother Chŏn for the paucity of her offerings. No supernatural Official is ever satisfied with the offerings. Grandmother Chŏn promises more and better food later if the Official will make her husband well. This exchange is stereotypic, repeated throughout this and other *kut*. Grandmother Chŏn knows her part. If she did not, Yongsu's Mother and Okkyŏng's Mother would coach her from the drum or importune the god on her behalf.

With another burst of drumming and dance, the Chatterbox Mansin removes her costume. She takes up a dried fish that has been offered to the Official, breaks the head off the fish with her foot, and flings it into the fields, casting scraps of food and cupfuls of wine in its wake. Officials, ghosts, and noxious influences eat, drink, and depart. The *mansin* flings down the fish. The decapitated trunk points inward, toward the open gate of the house. Some noxious influences remain. Quickly, she pours and tosses more cups of wine, and again she casts down the fish. The trunk points out, toward the fields. This first batch of spirits is satisfied.

The women follow Yongsu's Mother, still hitting the drum, through the gate and into the courtyard to the edge of the wooden porch. At her side, Okkyŏng's Mother hits the cymbals and, over the din, the two *mansin* proclaim that the *kut* is now within the walls.

Rites within the Walls

The *mansin,* the anthropologist, and the Chŏn family eat a hasty meal. The Chatterbox Mansin performs a drum song on the porch, singing out the names and ages of all the Chŏn family, announcing them to the gods. She names the married son, daughter-in-law, and grandchildren, but not the daughter, who is married into another family.

The *mansin* expel pollutions *(pujŏng)* accumulated in the house through birth, death, and profane existence since the last ritual cleansing. While the Chatterbox Mansin sings, Yongsu's Mother waves one dipper of pure water and another of purifying agents—ash, salt, and

red pepper[1]—over the offering food and across all of the furniture in
the inner room. The house is clean.

The Chatterbox Mansin now sings long lists of household gods,
major and minor, inviting them to enter the house, Grandmother
Chŏn lights the candles on the offering trays, sets down two thousand-
won bills, and bows with her head to the floor. She bows a full dozen
bows. The Chatterbox Mansin finishes her song and smokes a cigarette.

The next sequence is for the Chŏn family's ancestors. But several
gods appear first, leading the ancestors back to the house. Each category of god has a special costume. The Chatterbox Mansin, in a jade
green robe, summons the family's accumulated distant dead. She
waves her tasseled exorcism wands across the porch and through the
inner room, then flings them down. The wands point out toward the
open courtyard. The distant dead are satisfied; their influence is gone.

Now the Chatterbox Mansin wears a broad-sleeved red robe and
carries a high-crowned red hat. The most regal gods in the pantheon
wear this costume as kings or magistrates. She faces the open courtyard with an open fan spread in front of her face. The fan trembles as
the Mountain God descends into the *mansin*. This is the Mountain
God of the Chŏn family's ancestral home (Ponhyang Sansin), the god
who reigns over and pacifies the ancestors in their hillside graves. The
Mountain God chides Grandmother Chŏn for neglect. Grandmother
Chŏn spreads a bill on the Mountain God's open fan. The Mountain
God tells her, "Don't worry, Lady Chŏn, I will make your husband
well. I will make you rich. I will help your son become rich. I will help
your grandchildren speak well and write well."

The Chatterbox Mansin removes the red robe, revealing the green
robe again underneath. Twelve suicides who serve as netherworldly
guards *(kamang)* appear. Grandmother Chŏn places another bill on
the *mansin*'s fan. Now the Chatterbox Mansin puts on a yellow robe
for the Great Spirit Grandmother, the god who will lead the Chŏn
family ancestors into the home. This is the powerful and angry god
most directly responsible for Grandfather Chŏn's illness. The Great
Spirit Grandmother picks up the *mansin*'s huge battle fork and broadsword and jabs at the tub of rice cake the family has prepared for her.
She indicates, raising her arms high, what a huge pile of rice cake she
craves. She grabs the married daughter, drags her up to the wooden
porch, and makes her bow before the offering tray. Like the other

gods, the Great Spirit Grandmother berates Grandmother Chŏn. Grandmother Chŏn retorts, "Then make us rich, and next time we'll give you more."

The Great Spirit Grandmother asks for a new yellow robe. She fingers Grandmother Chŏn's crumpled skirt and complains, "Your clothes are much nicer than mine."

Grandmother Chŏn sputters, "What do you mean, better than yours?"

Yongsu's Mother chimes in from behind the drum, "Yes, Grandmother, your skirt is much nicer." Grandmother Chŏn protests.

The Great Spirit Grandmother then extends her open fan to the daughter, who spreads a five-hundred-won bill on top demanding, "Make us all rich."

The deity offers her fan to the plump daughter-in-law, who giggles her protest, "I'm not surnamed Chŏn." But the Great Spirit Grandmother persists and the daughter-in-law contributes.

The Great Spirit Grandmother enters the inner room and demands money from Grandfather Chŏn. Grandfather Chŏn looks confused. Grandmother Chŏn bursts in yelling, "How do you expect a sick person to have any money on him?" She puts another bill on the Great Spirit Grandmother's fan. Okkyŏng's Mother pleads on behalf of the Chŏns, "Please, Great Spirit Grandmother, make Grandfather Chŏn well." The Great Spirit Grandmother beams and tells Grandfather Chŏn, "You've given me this money, so I'll make you well. Don't worry, old man, you're not going to die. Now just give me one of these [she indicates her yellow robe], and I'll be quiet." She sings a song praising herself as a "good and wonderful Great Spirit Grandmother."

The ancestors appear next, sobbing *"Aigo, aigo."*

Grandfather Chŏn, wrapped in a blanket, sits facing the wall. He does not want to participate. The Chatterbox Mansin turns to Grandmother Chŏn, clutches her shoulders, and weeps. The *mansin* is possessed by Grandmother Chŏn's mother-in-law and father-in-law.

The neighbor women demand of the ancestors, "Why have you made your own son sick? Please, please make him well."

The parental ancestors promise help.

"Will he live past ninety, then?" Grandmother Chŏn asks the manifestation of her mother-in-law.

"Ninety, that's too long," says the ancestor. There is laughter.

"Past eighty, then?"

"That may be possible, and I'll do well by my grandchildren."

The next ancestor weeps yet more violently, "Why did I die early? Why did I have to die before my time?"

Grandmother Chŏn asks bluntly, "Well then, why did you go and die?" The ancestor turns to weep over the daughter, and Grandmother Chŏn informs the anthropologist, "This is my husband's first wife. She died in childbirth." The ancestor collects a five-hundred-won bill from Grandmother Chŏn.

The much-anticipated Official's sequence is next. Yongsu's Mother's sharp-tongued humor is well suited to the comic portrayal of a greedy supernatural Official. Yongsu's Mother claims this god "plays well" when he possesses her. She wears a blue vest and broad-brimmed black hat, the costume of palace guards and low-level functionaries in films and television dramas set in dynastic times. She dances vigorously. Suddenly, unpredictably, Yongsu's Mother grabs the Mountain God's red robe from the clothesline. The Chatterbox Mansin gestures toward the yellow robe, "This one, this one."

Yongsu's Mother grabs the yellow robe and waves both costumes through the air. She throws down the red robe and puts on the yellow robe. The Great Spirit Grandmother's personal underling has come to the *kut* along with the various other supernatural Officials who hold office in the Chŏn house. The Official wears the yellow robe and again reminds Grandmother Chŏn that the Great Spirit Grandmother desires a new robe. The Official grabs Grandmother Chŏn's ears and drags her to the center of the porch. Grandmother Chŏn again protests that the yellow robe is far, far finer than her own well-worn skirt. The Chatterbox Mansin contradicts from the sidelines, "No, Grandmother, yours is ever so much nicer."

The Official continues his pantomime. He sticks a finger in his ear, twists it, and scowls, thereby indicating that the Chŏns should have hired a musician to pipe and fiddle for the Official's pleasure. The Official smears Grandmother Chŏn's face with grease from the two pig's legs piled on the offering tray. Grandmother Chŏn hands the Official a bill. The god wipes his nose with it, then casts the crumpled bank note at the drummer, who stuffs it into the collection bag tied to the drum. The Official spreads wide his arms—he wants a high pile of delicacies to satisfy his fabled appetite. The Official hobbles on all fours—the Official wants a whole pig. The Official limps, balancing on the two short pig's legs—the Offical wants two long legs from a cow. Women crowd the two hot-floor rooms and the edges of the porch, giggling at the Official's antics as they fill cups of wine.

The Official drags the son onto the porch and shakes the long ribbons that fasten the yellow robe into all of the son's pockets. The Official pours a cup of wine to give the young man luck. The maternal aunt capers around the porch, waving a bill in her hand as she dances to tease the Official. The Official pulls the maternal aunt's clothing away from her back and fans up inside with the hems of her costume, dusting the maternal aunt with auspicious forces. The Official claims money from the maternal aunt, cackling the Official's characteristic laugh, "Aha-ha-ha!"

The Official grabs the daughter-in-law and gives her a dusting of luck with the fan. The daughter-in-law draws out a five-hundred-won bill from her pocket. The Official backs away, disdainful of the small amount. The daughter-in-law hesitantly draws out her coin purse, and the Official tries to look inside. He pours cups of wine for the daughter-in-law and the daughter, then demands more money.

"Must I give you my return bus fare?" asks the daughter-in-law, holding out one of the new Seoul bus tokens.

Women giggle. The Official is indignant, "I'd have to go to Seoul to spend that."

The Official holds out the pig's legs, a gesture demanding that the women stuff bills between the hooves. The maternal aunt tries to stuff in another bus token, but the Official jerks the hoof away. Grandmother Chŏn holds out her skirt and receives both pig's legs in her lap.

The *mansin* gestures for a towel and twists it into a pad for the full tub of rice cake the women now hoist to the top of her head. In her own voice, Yongsu's Mother calls to the Chatterbox Mansin, "Give me my rubber shoes." Once shod, the Official circles the courtyard followed by Grandmother Chŏn carrying a huge kettle of wine. The Official flings cups of wine in every corner of the courtyard, in the storerooms, in the rabbit hutches, and in the pig sty. The Official strides through the whole house site within the wall, past the huge glazed jars of soy and pepper paste, around the back of the house and back to the porch, all the while spilling cups of wine. Throughout the Official's progress, Yongsu's Mother gracefully balances some thirty pounds of rice cake, meat, and terra-cotta on her head. Finally she flings down the empty wine cup and passes the tub of rice cake backward over her head to Grandmother Chŏn, who receives it on the porch.

Hat back in place, the Official indicates that Grandmother Chŏn must place bills under the crown of his hat and under his chin band at the cheeks. When only his chin remains exposed, the Official snatches the next bill from Grandmother Chŏn and puts it under his chestband. The Official again points to his barren chin, asking Grandmother Chŏn for one more bill, but this bill, too, he snatches for his chestband. The next two bills go into his chestband, front and back. The Official laughs, the women giggle. The Official finally secures a bill under his chin.

The Official sells wine to Grandmother Chŏn, the son, the maternal aunt, the paternal aunt, the daughter-in-law, and the daughter. Singing the Official's song, "Such a wonderful Official I am, so wonderful I just can't say," the Official sells cups of lucky wine to the women in the hot-floor rooms, who return the empty cups with small coins. Grandmother Chŏn follows behind the Official with a plate of soy-salted fish and a pair of chopsticks. A bite of food should follow a cup of wine; the women nibble. The drummer plays on, and out on the porch the maternal aunt continues to dance.

The Official divines the next year for all the Chŏns, advising caution for the early months and improved fortunes in the late spring. Yongsu's Mother removes her hat and vest and passes the costume to the son's outstretched arms.

"You've put yourself out," Grandmother Chŏn tells Yongsu's Mother.

"What do you mean, put myself out?" Yongsu's Mother makes a polite disclaimer.

The *mansin* pause now. Family and guests will "use the *mugam*." One by one, they put on the *mansin*'s costumes and dance in front of the drum. The *mansin* claim that good fortune follows upon entertaining one's personal Body-governing God (Momju) by dancing in the god's costume. When a woman dances in costume, her personal Body-governing God ascends, possesses her, and dances. When the god is thus entertained, the woman and her family have good fortune. Women also attest to the sheer pleasure of *mugam* dancing (see Kendall 1977b).

In a healing *kut,* like the Chŏn family *kut,* the patient dances first, the dance being part of the cure. When the patient is a man, particularly a venerable older man, he is usually reluctant to engage in abandoned public display and must be coaxed. The Chatterbox Mansin

persuades Grandfather Chŏn to dance, then leads him out to the
porch. The *mansin* clothe Grandfather Chŏn in the white monk's robe
and peaked cowl because the women in the Chŏn family pray to the
Seven Stars (Ch'ilsŏng) for the birth and health of sons. They wear the
Seven Stars' white robe when they dance *mugam* and their own personal Body-governing Seven Stars ascends.

The Chatterbox Mansin coaches Grandfather Chŏn, dancing in
front of him to show him how. She grabs his wrists and moves his
arms to the music. He smiles ever so slightly, but then drops his arms,
proclaiming his inability to dance. He returns to the inner room.
Grandmother Chŏn dances next, wearing the Great Spirit Grandmother's yellow robe. The maternal aunt dances at her side. Grandmother Chŏn is soon rapidly jumping before the drum, her personal
Great Spirit has "ascended."

The *mansin* call out the daughter-in-law next. She demurs, saying,
"You have to know how to dance."

Grandmother Chŏn yells at her, "Get out there and dance. It'll bring
you luck." The daughter-in-law's luck is the luck of the son's household.

The *mansin* dress her in the Seven Stars' white robe. She dances,
faster and faster. Now the Chatterbox Mansin throws the yellow robe
over the white costume. The Chatterbox Mansin discerns the influence of two personal Body-governing Gods, the Great Spirit Grandmother and the Seven Stars. The daughter-in-law dances to a frenzy.
Okkyŏng's Mother stands beside the dancing woman, beating the
rhythm on her cymbals, tapping her foot in time, nodding her smiling
face. The daughter-in-law finally collapses in a head-to-floor bow.
The women in the hot-floor room nod consensus, "The god ascended.
Yes, the god ascended [*sini ollatta*]."

The *mansin* call the daughter to dance. Like the daughter-in-law,
she claims that she does not know how. The Chatterbox Mansin holds
out the white robe. From the two hot-floor rooms the women shout,
"Dance and you'll have luck; wear that and you'll look pretty." The
daughter, too, goes from a graceful dance to a vigorous jumping which
she sustains for several minutes. The Town Mansin relieves Okkyŏng's
Mother on the cymbals. The daughter jumps precariously close to the
edge of the porch, but the maternal aunt stands below the edge, arms
held wide to protect the daughter from falling. When the daughter is
finished, the women tease her, "And you said you couldn't dance."

Now the maternal aunt dances in the blue vest of the Official, the robe that any woman can wear for *mugam*. The Chatterbox Mansin encourages her to put on the Great Spirit Grandmother's yellow robe. The maternal aunt refuses to wear this robe and acknowledge that the Great Spirit Grandmother is her own Body-governing God. Though she dances gracefully and with a distant smile on her lips, she cannot seem to reach the point of ecstatic jumping. The Chatterbox Mansin again urges her to put on the yellow robe. Thus attired, the maternal aunt begins almost immediately to jump. The maternal aunt stamps her feet and pounds her arms in the air; she has a strong, greedy, demanding personal spirit. Thus, the maternal aunt seizes any opportunity to dance and plunges into the gods' antics at a *kut*.

The paternal aunt dances next, then the friend from Grandmother Chŏn's old village. Thirteen neighbor women and the anthropologist use the *mugam*. I recognize some of these women from other *kut*, and they recognize me. A few of them danced at the Chatterbox Mansin's annual *kut* for her own shrine gods early in the fall.

It is well past midnight when the women finish dancing. Many of the women leave at this interlude in the *kut*. Yongsu's Mother shouts for food, and the *mansin*, the family, the anthropologist, and lingering guests eat rice and hot soup.

The Chatterbox Mansin realizes that they had forgotten to invoke the Buddhist Sage (Pulsa) at the proper time. Now they are ready to invoke the Birth Grandmother (Chesŏk).[2] Since the Buddhist Sage, Birth Grandmother, and Seven Stars are all vegetarian Buddhist spirits, who oversee birth and child rearing, the Chatterbox Mansin sees no harm in invoking them all at once. She gives rapid final instructions to Okkyŏng's Mother.

On the porch Okkyŏng's Mother invokes all of the various manifestations of the Buddhist Sage. She grabs the cymbals from the Town Mansin and performs a rapid dance to signify possession. She puts on her shoes and runs to the side of the house where the women have set offerings of rice cake, water, and burning candles for the Seven Stars on the tall earthenware storage jars. Grandmother Chŏn, the maternal aunt, the daughter, the daughter-in-law, and a small knot of women gather, rubbing their hands and bowing while Okkyŏng's Mother invokes the Seven Stars. She performs a quick divination for Grandmother Chŏn, then rushes back to the inner room where a special tray of vegetarian offerings—rice cake, fruit, and nuts—awaits the Birth

Grandmother. Like all deities, the Birth Grandmother denounces the poor quality of offering food and the delay between rituals, then waxes benevolent and promises aid. With her cymbals Okkyŏng's Mother scoops nuts and dates from the offering tray and flips them onto Grandmother Chŏn's outstretched skirt. Okkyŏng's Mother fingers the nuts and candies, divining for the son, "Someone will help him with his business. For the next two months he should be cautious in human relations and not make any decisive move, but in the second or third month of next year there will be good news."

Okkyŏng's Mother gives a divination for each of the grandchildren as she tosses more nuts and candy onto Grandmother Chŏn's skirt. Grandmother Chŏn gives the name and age of each grandchild, and Okkyŏng's Mother incorporates this information into her chant. Grandmother Chŏn forgets the age of one of her grandchildren and confers with the daughter-in-law before Okkyŏng's Mother can continue chanting.

Okkyŏng's Mother removes the peaked cowl while dancing and begins to remove the white robe. The Chatterbox Mansin and Yongsu's Mother shout to Okkyŏng's Mother that she has forgotten to invoke the unredeemed souls in Buddhist hell. Okkyŏng's Mother begins to replace the cowl but the Chatterbox Mansin tells her to leave it off. The apprentice *mansin* quickly invokes the list of unredeemed souls. Now Okkyŏng's Mother removes the white robe. She throws the red nylon skirt of her costume over her head and becomes the Princess (Hogu), a capricious dead maiden who causes domestic strife. The Princess says, "I go flutter, flutter, flutter in the inner room." Mollified with a five-hundred-won bill, the Princess departs.

The Chatterbox Mansin dresses in three layers of robes for the war gods who will appear next. Yongsu's Mother coaches Okkyŏng's Mother in the invocation for the unredeemed souls, since Okkyŏng's Mother has once again muddled the chant. The Chatterbox Mansin realizes that Okkyŏng's Mother forgot to sell nuts and candies from the Birth Grandmother's offering tray. She tells her to do it now. Singing, Okkyŏng's Mother circulates through the rooms, spilling sweets onto the women's waiting laps. They place small coins on the cymbals she carries. The older women know her song and, laughing, sing along. "Eat a date and give birth to a daughter, eat a chestnut and give birth to a son." They stuff nuts and candies into pockets and nibble them during the *kut* or hoard them for a favorite grandchild at home.

Like drinking the Official's wine and dancing the *mugam,* the women gain fortune when they purchase and consume these sweets from the cymbals *(para).*

Now the war gods appear in turn and possess the Chatterbox Mansin. The General (Changgun), in a wide-sleeved blue robe and high-crowned hat, strides majestically to the processional cadence of cymbals. The *mansin* say that the General and the Mountain God are like kings. You give them money first without their even asking; they are above the greedy, demanding antics of the Official.

The Special Messenger (Pyŏlsang),[3] in a black jacket with red sleeves and a broad-brimmed black hat, wields a broadsword and battle trident. The Chatterbox Mansin balances the sword on an overturned saucer. She jabs pig's legs onto the prongs of the battle fork and tries to balance this unwieldy object. It is a tense moment. If the trident stands on its own, the household gods have accepted the *kut* offering. If the trident continues to wobble in the *mansin*'s hands, the gods remain unsatisfied and it bodes no good for the family.

The Chatterbox Mansin calls for salt and pours it on the saucer for traction. Grandmother Chŏn sets two five-hundred-won bills on top of the meat and rubs her hands in supplication. The battle trident stands. The Chatterbox Mansin sings the Special Messenger's praises as she circulates cups of wine around the handle of the upright battle trident and passes them to the Chŏn women.

Now the Warrior (Sinjang) arrives to exorcise Grandfather Chŏn. Ghosts and other noxious influences fear the knife the Warrior wields. Okkyŏng's Mother whispers that Grandfather Chŏn has already gone to sleep in the inner room. Yongsu's Mother says that they will just have Grandfather Chŏn appear quickly on the porch and then he can go right back to sleep. Grandmother Chŏn leads Grandfather Chŏn out onto the edge of the porch, where the *mansin* ask him to kneel facing the courtyard. The *mansin* cover him with a strip of thin yellow cloth, which is an offering for wandering ghosts, as well as one of his own shirts and the Warrior's five-colored divination flags. They prop the huge battle trident and broadsword at his sides.

Yongsu's Mother kneels beside Grandfather Chŏn, banging the cymbals in close proximity to his right ear. With a series of whoops the Chatterbox Mansin pelts Grandfather Chŏn's covered form with handfuls of millet. Bits of offering food fly over his head. A metal bowl clatters to the courtyard.

Shrieking "Yaaa! Yaaa!" the Chatterbox Mansin whirls the pig's legs around Grandfather Chŏn and pokes at his back with the hooves, then casts them away into the courtyard. She circles his head with a large kitchen knife. Sitting on his shoulders, she stabs at the air all around him. She holds the tip of the blade against his back. She rips the covering from his head. Reaching her arms round his body, she tears the yellow cloth. Now she offers him the bundle of five-colored divination flags. Grandfather Chŏn taps one of the sticks and the Chatterbox Mansin draws out Grandfather Chŏn's choice, a white flag indicating the benign influence of the Seven Stars, a significant deity in the Chŏn pantheon. "All right!" the *mansin* says. The exorcism is a success, they can stop here, no further pelting is necessary.

Now the Warrior spreads the pile of divination flags on the floor, one on top of the other, and gestures for Grandfather Chŏn to cover the top flag with money. Grandmother Chŏn stands beside Grandfather Chŏn, handing him thousand-won bills. When the Warrior is satisfied with the money on one flag, he rolls it back to reveal another and yet another empty flag awaiting money. The Warrior is not easily satisfied and the daughter-in-law gets impatient. She tries to roll one of the flags back herself but is foiled by the Warrior, who snaps the flag back in place. Finally satisfied, the Warrior hands Grandfather Chŏn an apple from the offering tray and sends him back to sleep in the inner room.

The Warrior offers the divination flags to Grandmother Chŏn and the daughter-in-law, who both receive favorable colors and divinations. Twice the daughter chooses the green flag, a flag that indicates that restless ghosts *(yŏngsan)* follow her. The Warrior divines that the daughter's fate is bad. She should make a special offering to her own household's supernatural Official. The Warrior whirls the flags around the daughter's body and has her choose again. This time the flag is red, the most favorable color. The daughter gives the Warrior five hundred won, complaining, "You're taking my return bus fare," but the Warrior demands yet another bill. The Warrior turns to Grandmother Chŏn and gives her some final advice, cautioning her to be careful about Grandfather Chŏn's food.

The Warrior Official (Sinjang Taegam), the greedy official serving under the martial spirits, appears next. The Warrior Official contemptuously flings away the pig's legs, collects a few bills from the women, and sings a song of self-praise. As she has begged all the deities,

Grandmother Chŏn implores the Warrior Official to make her husband well and give her son success in business. This segment is brief. It is now three o'clock in the morning. The women spread sleeping mats in the two hot-floor rooms. Grandmother Chŏn and the *mansin* discuss the merits of various pharmacies in town before everyone falls asleep.

The next morning, everyone wakes up early. The women wash and cook the rice, and breakfast is over by nine. Some of the neighborhood women come by to watch the *kut*'s completion. A few women ask the Chatterbox Mansin for advice. She approves the direction of a contemplated residence change, cautions delay for a husband anxious to switch jobs, and gives instructions for a minor household ritual.

Meanwhile, Yongsu's Mother and the Town Mansin are having a quarrel. Yongsu's Mother complains that the Town Mansin merely drums and hits the cymbals without performing any of the segments, far more strenuous work. Yongsu's Mother insists that the Town Mansin perform the next segment for the House Lord (Sŏngju) in the roof beam. The Town Mansin tries to beg off. "I haven't done a *kut* in three years, so I've forgotten what to say. Besides, my feet hurt."

"Lies!" shrieks Yongsu's Mother.

"But I don't have a Korean dress."

Yongsu's Mother throws a parcel at her. "Wear this, you'll look so pretty."

The Town Mansin performs the House Lord's segment. She flicks drops of wine up onto the roof beam where the god dwells. She tosses up grains of rice and catches them in her hands, counting for an auspicious even number. Finally, she burns the paper *kut* announcement the family had pasted to the beam days ago to inform the House Lord of the impending *kut*.

The Chatterbox Mansin urges the women to use the *mugam* again. Grandmother Chŏn dances first in the Great Spirit's yellow robe. As Grandmother Chŏn begins to dance, the Chatterbox Mansin hands her wine from all the cups on the offering tray. Grandmother Chŏn rocks back and forth as the drum beats pick up speed. Grandmother Chŏn whirls on her feet, then grabs the pig's legs and runs into the inner room. She rubs her husband lightly with the pig's legs. There is soft chuckling from the women. Next Grandmother Chŏn picks up the battle trident and sword and whirls with them. The shaman ancestress has ascended as Grandmother Chŏn's personal god.

The maternal aunt dances again. The paternal aunt dances again. Grandmother Chŏn's old friend dances beside the paternal aunt, singing a few bars of a popular song, "Goody, goody, cha-cha-cha." The paternal aunt starts jumping but soon stops.

"Why didn't you dance longer?" the women ask.

"I had a headache."

The Chatterbox Mansin tells her that she discerns the presence of an active Buddhist Sage in the paternal aunt's home; she should make special offerings to this spirit next year.

The Chatterbox Mansin, in a green robe, invokes the Clown (Ch'angbu), god of dead actors, songsters, and acrobats. While the Chatterbox Mansin sings the Clown's invocation, the maternal aunt begins to dance again. The Clown hits the maternal aunt with a fan and tweaks her breast, then divines for Grandmother Chŏn, repeating the other gods' promises that things will improve. The god acknowledges the paternal aunt's numerous worries about health and finance and promises succor, but the paternal aunt must make the proper offerings. The Clown reassures the daughter and reminds her that she must offer rice cake *(kosa)* to the gods in her husband's home. Finally, the Clown tells the maternal aunt that she must change the date of her sixty-first birthday celebration to a more auspicious month and give feast food to the ancestors *(yŏt'am)* on the eve of the celebration. Finally, the Clown pulls the maternal aunt's clothing wide from her back and fans up good fortune. The maternal aunt again beams.

The *kut* inside the house is finished. The Chatterbox Mansin presses her brass mirror into a tub of rice grain for a final prognosis of the house gods' pleasure. None of the grains stick. She tries with one of the cymbals. No luck. "Fuck it!" she shouts, then claims that she can never perform this divination for her own regular clients. Yongsu's Mother presses the mirror into the rice. Four grains stick to the surface.[4] She spills them onto Grandmother Chŏn's skirt. The even number is the desired sign.

Moving outside the House

Women disassemble the offerings while Yongsu's Mother prepares to invoke the House Site Official (T'ŏju Taegam). With a swift invocation and dance on the porch, she puts on her shoes and runs to the back of the house, where a tub of rice cake on a tray awaits the House Site Official.

"Wine!" snaps the Official, "Wine! Wine!" The daughter-in-law rushes up with a full kettle. The Mansin puts the tub of rice cake on her head and the House Site Official makes a progress through the courtyard and around the outer wall of the house, spilling cups of wine and throwing bits of rice cake to secure the house site's boundaries. The daughter-in-law follows with the huge wine kettle, constantly filling the cup. The Official enters the courtyard and stands below the porch, demanding money from the daughter and daughter-in-law. The daughter protests that she has spent all of her money, then slowly draws out another bill. The Official divines, predicting auspicious months and urging Grandmother Chŏn to seek medicine and acupuncture treatments for Grandfather Chŏn. The Official passes the tub of rice cake back to Grandmother Chŏn.

In the courtyard Yongsu's Mother quickly invokes the Grain God (Kŏllip), the god who brings wealth into the house. She propitiates the Foundation God (Chisin) of the earth below the house with a libation of wine spilled in a circle in the front courtyard. Standing before the threshold, the *mansin* spills wine for the Door Guard (Sumun Taegam).

Back on the porch the Chatterbox Mansin divides the money collected during the *kut*. Okkyŏng's Mother and the Town Mansin receive 12,000 won each, while Yongsu's Mother receives 14,000 won for her more strenuous participation. The Chatterbox Mansin retains 18,000 won. She will also claim 2,000 won from the final segment.[5] As the *mansin* in charge, the Chatterbox Mansin claims one of the pig's legs and all of the rice grain used to prop up her brass mirror during the *kut*. Each *mansin* takes home a generous package of rice cake and some candy and fruit from the offering tray. Grandmother Chŏn also gives rice cake to the women who helped her in the kitchen. The *mansin* are pleased with the money they have collected at this *kut*; the women spent freely, and the maternal aunt was particularly generous. As usual, Yongsu's Mother feels that the Chatterbox Mansin took an excessively large share of the pay while she, herself, performed the more exhausting Official's segments.

Everyone, including Grandfather Chŏn, moves outside the gate. The *mansin* bring out bundles of costumes, props, and rice cake. They set up a small tray of offering food. The Chatterbox Mansin again invokes the Soldier Official who appeared in the first segment. She is still singing the invocation when the daughter and daughter-in-law, carrying their bundles of rice cake, rush down the road to catch the bus for Seoul. Grandmother Chŏn begs the Soldier Official, "I'll make special offerings [*kosa*], I'll give you another *kut* if you just help my son succeed in business."

The Chatterbox Mansin invokes the souls of ancient scholar-officials who were victims of political intrigues or committed suicide over thwarted careers. Next come the less-distinguished ghosts, those who died violent or untimely deaths. The *mansin* chants them as they pass before her eyes. "Those who died of fevers, those who died on the road, those who died in traffic accidents, those who drowned, those who died in childbirth."

Finally, the Chatterbox Mansin beckons Grandfather Chŏn. He kneels facing the field with his back to the house. She piles another strip of yellow cloth and Grandfather Chŏn's own shirt on his head. Grandmother Chŏn brings a bound chicken. The Chatterbox Mansin presses the chicken to Grandfather Chŏn's chest and rubs it against his back, then whirls it around his head and tosses it off into the fields. She pelts Grandfather Chŏn with millet. She dumps rice wine, vegetables, and bits of candy from the offering tray into a gourd dipper and flings some of the food over Grandfather Chŏn's shoulders. She stabs at the air around Grandfather Chŏn's shoulders and head with a kitchen knife. She reaches around his chest and rips the thin yellow cloth, breaking the hold of wandering ghosts. Carrying the dipper full of scraps, she runs into the field and sets it down, luring misfortune away from the house. The Chatterbox Mansin gives final instructions to Grandmother Chŏn. She must have someone bury the chicken on the hillside like a human corpse, and quickly burn the yellow cloth and the shirt from the exorcism.

The *mansin* politely decline Grandmother Chŏn's invitation to lunch and hasten down the road in the early afternoon sunshine to catch the bus.

Epilogue

I have described one *kut* as I came to understand it, a living and loud event with some mistakes, much skill, clumsy moments, copious wine, and considerable laughter. I have not given a proper folklorist's rendering of *kut*. One can, in any case, find precise lists of deities, costumes, and offering food elsewhere.[6] In this less orthodox presentation, I have beckoned up from field notes and memory the flavor of a particular *kut*, the Chŏns' *kut*, and there is method in this indulgence.

A *kut* honors a basic structure, a progress through the house wherein gods and ancestors appear in place and in approximate sequence (see app. 1). The house, both as setting and prime metaphor of *kut*, embraces both the living members of the "house" *(chip)* and the gods who appear as the *mansin* move through the dwelling. The *mansin* pass tubs of rice cake, costumes, and pig's legs back to the family in the direction of the porch and hot-floor rooms. The gods fan blessings into pockets and up under clothing. They fill skirts with grain, nuts, and seeds. The family catches positive influences and secures them within the house. The *mansin* cast pollutions, wandering ghosts, noxious influences, and a scapegoat chicken out beyond the gate. *Mansin* confirm the expulsion of negative forces with the cast of a knife, the tip of the blade pointing out, away from the open gate.

But a systematic diagram of *kut* necessarily ignores unscripted idiosyncrasies in the drama of an individual *kut*, those special twists that make each *kut* necessarily a shaman ritual. A family's social and supernatural circumstances—variations on some standard themes—color and shape the drama of their own *kut* and all of their dealings with shamans. The relative potency of the different household gods and ancestors varies from house to house and from *kut* to *kut*. Certain families have, by reason of family history, particularly powerful gods in their household pantheons. The Chŏns' shaman ancestress became the nagging, bantering Great Spirit Grandmother of their *kut*. During the *mugam* the Great Spirit Grandmother's yellow robe went from hand to hand as her spirit rose up in a sequence of dancing kinswomen. Another ancestress, a woman who honored the Seven Stars, assumed a dancing presence when Chŏn women wore the Seven Stars' white robe in *mugam*.

Ancestors, the family beyond the grave, hover in endless variation on a theme. The dead are dangerous simply because they are dead and do not mingle well with the living. The spectators chided Grandfather Chŏn's own parents for contributing to his illness, then secured the ancestors' promise of succor and gently but firmly sent them on their way. Of more intentionally malevolent potential was Grandfather

Chŏn's first wife, bitter at her own untimely death and jealous of her husband's second marriage. She confronted her successor, sobbed with her own children, and then, her ominous powers neutralized by a gift of "travel money," she departed.

The *mansin,* as shaman, claims the power to see the gods and ancestors in visions and to call them down to speak through her lips. The *mansin* makes a dynamic link between her clients and their household supernatural. She determines the appetites of gods and ancestors through the visions she receives in divination sessions. The Chatterbox Mansin is the Chŏn family's link to the will and appetite of their Great Spirit Grandmother. In *kut* the supernatural stand up large as life while the *mansin,* in trance, use stock characters and semi-scripted exchanges to evoke a client family's own legends. *Mansin* used the authority of Chŏn gods and ancestors to assert that Grandfather Chŏn would recover, the son would be successful, and the children would do well in school.

Another special feature of the Chŏn *kut* was that it was a healing *kut (uhwan kut),* distinguished from a *kut* for good fortune and prosperity *(chaesu kut)* or a *kut* to send off the dead *(chinogi kut).* Grandfather Chŏn reluctantly claimed center stage at crucial moments. The *mansin* exorcised him twice with a flourishing of cymbals and a pelting of grain. Kinswomen and neighbors importuned the gods and ancestors on his behalf. Gods and ancestors issued optimistic prognostications. In a ritual process that would transform Grandfather Chŏn from sick to cured, the *mansin* finally shifted the lingering vestiges of his illness to the body of a white chicken that she cast out and had buried like a corpse.

But one is also struck by Grandfather Chŏn's minimal participation in events performed ostensibly on his behalf. The *kut* was a women's party. Grandmother Chŏn made the initial arrangements and led the bantering with the gods and ancestors. The gods also made heavy demands on the daughter-in-law since the son's household would also draw luck and blessings from the *kut.* More surprising in a patrilineal, patrilocal Korean village, the Chŏns' married daughter was linked to her parents' household gods. She danced *mugam* inspired by the Great Spirit Grandmother, and this god's influence went with her to her husband's household just as Grandmother Chŏn, before her, had carried the Great Spirit Grandmother's influence from her own natal home when she married into the Chŏn family.[7]

Other non-Chŏn women traveled to the *kut*. Grandmother Chŏn's own sister, the dancing maternal aunt, was an avid participant and generous financial contributor. Grandfather Chŏn's sister, another out-married Chŏn woman, danced *mugam* and received divinations. Often at the thick of the action, these women received blessings from the gods in proportion to their financial contributions.

Some benefit from the *kut* also reached the neighbors and friends who spent small amounts of cash on divinations, lucky wine, and sweets from the Birth Grandmother's tray, and who danced *mugam* and savored the *kut*'s inebriated gaiety. Not passive spectators, these women formed a concerned chorus. They importuned the gods and commented on the unfolding drama. They found almost everything funny that did not make them weep. They approached the gods and ancestors much as they approach life—with a sharp tongue, a sense of humor, and a good cry.

TWO

Confucian Patriarchs and Spirited Women

> Korean folk-tales frequently have to deal with a situation
> where a gentleman is ill, but will have nothing to do with
> the spirits. His wife, however, holds the opposite opinion,
> and unknown to her lord, smuggles in a *mudang* [shaman]
> or *pansu* [exorcist] to exorcise the demon of disease.
>
> Homer B. Hulbert, *The Passing of Korea*

East Asian philosophers and some contemporary anthropologists tell
us that darkness defines light by contrast—dark *ŭm* to bright *yang,*
female to male. Women's assumptions, actions, and experiences qualify men's self-defined social cosmos. Through a female prism, the Chinese family or a Mount Hagen pig exchange or an Amazon hunter's
braggadocio assumes another dimension (Murphy and Murphy 1974;
Strathern 1972; M. Wolf 1972). In Korea cosmology sets men and
women and much else besides in complementary opposition.[1] Women
and their gods beg a reconsideration of the male-defined Korean family. In the following pages, we will reconsider Korean society through
women's ritual.

The costumed gods of the Ch'ŏn family *kut* appear in a woman's
world. As professional *mansin,* some women summon and speak for
the gods. Other women implore, bargain, and argue with the gods.
When the household gods fall silent, the women put on the *mansin's*
costumes and dance into a state of mild euphoria, possessed by their
own Body-governing Gods. Korean women's enthusiasm for divine
possession follows upon numerous other ethnographic examples of
what I. M. Lewis calls "this sexual bias of the spirits" (Lewis 1966,
309). In 1907 Bogoras wrote that most of the Chuckchee shamans
were women, but since the Chuckchee believe that women fall into
trance more easily than men, male shamans enjoy greater prestige
(Bogoras 1907, 414). Nearly fifty years later and on the other side of

the world, Mischel and Mischel wrote that in the Shango cult of Trini-
dad, fully 75 percent of those cultists who achieved possession were
women (Mischel and Mischel 1958, 251). Women are the targets of
saka spirits among the Wataita of Kenya (Harris 1957), *zar* spirits in
Ethiopia (Messing 1958), and *bori* spirits among the Hausa in West
Africa (Onwuejeogwu 1969). Japanese shamans and Lango diviners
are women, and Burmese *nat* mediums are almost invariably women
(Fairchild 1962; Curley 1973; Spiro 1967).

Discarding the alleged hysterical propensity of women, the mysteri-
ous powers of their yin-dark nature, and other magico-scientific
explanations, the anthropologist looks instead to social relations for
the source of women's supernatural attraction. Synthesizing the volu-
minous ethnographic literature on spirit possession, I. M. Lewis suggests that like witchcraft accusations,[2] instances of spirit possession
can be shown to run in particular social grooves (Lewis 1969, 27–28).
Where female shamans and possession cult devotees dramatize role
reversals in male clothing, Lewis finds tacit acknowledgment of men's
status and power and of women's concomitant deprivation, "is not
imitation the sincerest form of flattery?" (ibid., 109). For Lewis this is
more than a cyclical ritual rebellion (cf. Gluckman 1954). Women use
possession as a strategy; in trance, they speak the unspeakable. Possession, institutionalized in healing rites, becomes a "means by which
women, and sometimes other subject categories, are enabled to protect their interests and profer their claims and ambitions through . . .
affliction" (Lewis 1966, 322). While this assumption underlies much
of the ethnography of spirit possession, Lewis issues the boldest statement. Possession cults are front organizations for a "feminist subculture" wherein women pitch oblique barbs of protest at a man's world
(Lewis 1969, 89).

Lewis' characterization of the possession cult as a subculture follows upon his dichotomization of "main morality possession religions" and "peripheral cults." The former appear in simple, homoge-
neous societies lacking clearly demarcated political authority. Here,
the shaman holds sway and the shaman's spirits support the moral
order. By contrast, "peripheral cults" exist outside the main morality
religions of complex societies. Cult spirits are often the officially dis-
credited survivors of an ancient faith, now left to the women in compensation for their own "peripheral" social status (ibid., 34, 148). The
seeds of this dichotomy sprout from the work of Durkheim, who dis-

tinguished "Church," the supreme expression of the aspirations of the community, from "cult," the particularist application of magic to individual circumstances and needs (Durkheim [1915] 1966, 59–62). Women are "peripheral" where men "hold a secure monopoly of the major power positions and deny their partners effective jural rights" (Lewis 1966, 321). Peripheral women are afflicted by peripheral spirits who "play no part in upholding the moral code of the societies in which they receive so much attention. Full of spite and malice though they are, they are believed to strike entirely capriciously and without any grounds which can be referred to the moral character or conduct of their victims" (Lewis 1969, 30–31).

Some of the material presented in this study suggests that in Korea ritual and trance provide the aggrieved with a supportive environment for a therapeutic venting of spleen. Are these rituals and the women who perform them also peripheral to Korean society? I shall argue the contrary position, that the gods and ghosts of the Chŏn family *kut* are integral components of Korean family and village religion. Within this religious system, women and shamans perform essential ritual tasks that complement men's ritual tasks.

The study of Korean women's rituals has been clouded by both the Korean literati's long-standing discomfort with indigenous custom and by the Korean Confucian's ideological devaluation of women. That the elite should disdain women's rituals is a consequence of Korea's complex religious experience but so too is the fact that women's activities remain a vital component of Korean ritual life. We need, then, to consider the social and historical basis of these attitudes, and their manifestation in contemporary scholarship.

Two Traditions under One Roof

Anyone familiar with China reads Korean ethnography with a smothering sense of déjà vu. Families are patrilineal, marriage, patrilocal. Ancestor worship adds an ethical imperative to the birth of boy children, who will work on and eventually inherit the family's lands and sustain the family's ancestors. Extrafamilial kin groups, patrilineages, hold higher-order commemorations of prestigious agnatic ancestors. In lineage organization, Koreans honor the primacy of the senior line, harking back to an older Chinese pattern (Janelli and Janelli 1978).

The most obvious contrast between Korean and Chinese social organization is in the way each society organizes inheritance and succession. While Chinese households have partible wealth and brothers are equal coparceners in the division of a single household's property, Koreans acknowledge the primacy of the first-born son, who inherits the house and the largest share of the family property. Secondary sons and their wives leave the family when they are ready to establish independent households. The contrast between Chinese and Korean domestic cycles suggests that Chinese and Korean women enter domestic politics with different expectations. These differences color the ways Chinese and Korean women behave, the strategies they adopt, and the manner in which Chinese and Korean men perceive them. All of this is reflected in the different symbolic constraints imposed on women and in the different ritual tasks accorded them in these two overtly Confucian societies.

Social historians remind us that "Confucianization" was, in Korea, a recent and self-conscious process. In the early fifteenth century, Neo-Confucian reformers in the government of the newly established Yi dynasty (1392–1910) sought a thoroughgoing transformation of Korean society, attempting to impose changes from the top upon a very different social order (Deuchler 1977, 1980). The social patterns now associated with "traditional Korea" did not take firm root until the sixteenth or seventeenth century, a scant three centuries ago. Until this fairly recent era Korean kinship was most likely collateral rather than patrilineal. Gentry daughters inherited land and slaves, and sometimes the right to worship a father's ancestor tablet. Ancestor worship was not yet a rigorously Confucian rite. Daughters' children appeared in the genealogies of a woman's natal as well as affinal family. Husbands were longtime residents in the wife's natal home. A woman joined her husband's kin as mother and matron, succeeding a mother-in-law or establishing her own household (Pak 1974, 323–354; Deuchler 1977; K. K. Lee 1977, 289–292; Peterson 1983; Wagner 1983). Koreanists have begun to question the extent and pervasiveness of Confucianization. Korean women's un-Confucian rituals offer a promising but little-considered vantage point on the Confucian/Korean compromise.

Early ethnologists described the "dual organization" of Korean household religion. Men worship the ancestors in solemn, dignified rites. Women honor the household gods and expel ghosts. Some women's rituals require an ecstatic shaman, a pounding drum, and a *kut*'s raucous gaiety (Akamatsu and Akiba 1938, 1:192–194; Akiba 1957; T. H. Kim [1948] 1969, 409). Men's rituals are usually described as Confucian. Women's rituals have been called spirit worship, shamanism, folk beliefs, and superstition. The form and content, indeed the very mood of men's and women's religious actions pose contrasts, but these contrasts are fluid, never absolute. Men sometimes perform community-level rituals that include, in combination with more sober elements, some loud, flamboyant, "shamanistic" frolicking (Dix, n.d.), and women's rituals sometimes include silent, reverential acts and a bit of asceticism. Nuances shift, but there remain rituals appropriate to men and rituals appropriate to women.

Koreanists inevitably wonder at the prominence of female shamans and priestesses in a society where expressed ideology and social forms otherwise constrain women. Most *mansin* are women, and all *mansin* minister directly to women. The rare male shaman in Korea *(paksu mudang)* performs *kut* wearing women's clothing, down to the pantaloons that hide beneath his billowing skirt and slip. A woman (or man) becomes a shaman through traumatic possession sickness, initiation, and apprenticeship to a more experienced shaman. Thereafter she performs in public the songs, dances, and comic antics of the gods who possess her. In addition to performing *kut,* she provides divinations and executes numerous small rituals at her own shrine or in her clients' homes. Sometimes she leads a client on a pilgrimage up a sacred mountain.

A study of Korean women's ritual necessarily draws in shamans,[3] and an understanding of shaman ritual is incomplete without the ordinary woman who seeks the shaman's services. A woman's relationship with her own household gods and ancestors underpins most shaman ritual, much as filial sons worshipping virtuous ancestors provide the basic building blocks of male ritual. Shamans appear in these pages as the specialists women consult for a range of advice and for ritual expertise in all dealings with the supernatural. Accustomed to articulating the lore of gods and ghosts, to patiently explaining procedures, and to telling cautionary tales, shamans provided much of the information contained in this study.

The term shamanism and the adjective shamanistic have been broadly, indeed sloppily, applied to a vast spectrum of Korean religious activity. They have been used to characterize rituals of the professional shaman, rituals of the housewife, communal rituals performed by professional shamans and women, and communal rituals performed by men. Indeed, any practice that is not explicitly Buddhist and not directly attributable to Confucian literary sources tends to be labeled shamanistic. Non-scholars in Korea call these same activities *misin*, "superstition," literally "false belief." The term *misin*, like the more scholarly and less prejudicial *musokchŏk*, is of relatively recent coinage and probably dates from the introduction of Christianity and reformist ideology into East Asia at the end of the last century. Originally *misin* was a term of derision for all traditional practices, ancestor worship as well as shaman rites. Presumably it retains that usage in the People's Republic of China and in the Democratic People's Republic of Korea today. In the Republic of Korea, however, only the most zealously orthodox Christian would apply this term to ancestor rites. For lack of an indigenous label, *mansin* use the term *misin* to describe women's rituals. Shamans and their clients often asked me, "Do you have this sort of *misin* in America?" A *mansin* might praise her clients as "a household that observes well the practices of *misin*" *(misinŭl chal chik'inŭnjip)*.

Some religious historians use the term shamanism to indicate a single and ancient tradition diffused from Siberia (see Eliade 1956). In the tradition of religious history, scholars do speak of Korean shamanism as a discrete religion and a historical stratum. Yim Suk-jay and his students have discussed the limitations of this approach. In Korea the term *mudang* indicates both the hereditary priestess and the inspirational shaman. As in Okinawa, shaman and priestess perform many of the same ritual functions, a distinction ignored by the blanket use of the term shamanism. The term shamanism, when used to designate an ancient faith, obscures the historical development and contemporary complexity of Korean religious traditions (Yim 1970, esp. 215–217; Ch'oe 1978, 12–13).

In anthropological literature shamanism indicates a cross-culturally comparable religious phenomenon, not a regional or historical religion. William Lebra provides a useful working definition of shamans. Shamans wield recognized supernatural powers for socially approved ends and have the capacity to enter culturally acknowledged trance states at will (William P. Lebra n.d., cited in Harvey 1979, 4). By this criterion the *mansin* who performed the Chŏn family *kut* have a solid claim to the title. The Chatterbox Mansin, Yongsu's Mother, and their colleagues actively engage the supernatural. They summon down the gods and ancestors, they bear the gods and ancestors in their own persons, and they issue supernatural commands. They lure gods into dwellings, exorcise malevolent beings, and cajole and bargain with a variety of spirits. For comparative purposes these activities may be dubbed shamanism, although some of the *mansin*'s gods step down from a Buddhist pantheon and some of the *mansin*'s rituals express a Confucian concern for the family's ancestors. Since Korean housewives perform many mundane rituals by themselves without a *mansin*'s aid, I see no reason to call these activities shamanistic, especially when the term carries intimations of romantic archaism.

Designated Confucian, men's rituals are at least loosely anchored in a corpus of written text and orthodox ritual. In the early years of the last dynasty, Neo-Confucian reformers urged the Confucianization of ancestor worship in the households of the office-holding elite. For the Neo-Confucian a well-tended ancestral shrine and scrupulously performed rituals of homage demonstrated and perpetuated propriety *(ye)*, ethical and orderly behavior in a harmonious society. Statutes specified the form and content of ancestor rites and discouraged, but did not eradicate, other rituals performed to placate the family ancestors (Deuchler 1980; n.d.). Koreans consider *chesa* a Confucian (Yugyo) ritual, although the ancestors were a part of Korean folk religion long before their Confucianization. In some Korean villages a pot of grain, basket, or nest of paper representing the house ancestors suggests pre-Confucian traditions (Chang 1974, 164–165; Guillemoz 1983, 150–151; MCBCPP "Kyŏngbuk," 158). For the residents of Enduring Pine Village and for most contemporary Koreans, honoring the ancestors means *chesa,* the formal offering of wine and food by filial sons and grandsons. This ritual is described in ceremonial manuals, expounded upon by scholars, and carefully reviewed by the officiant's most venerable male relatives.

As a consequence of ancestor worship's prestige and ethical import, social scientists working in Korea have delved into the form and social significance of the male ritual realm.[4] They have shown less enthusiasm for women's rituals. Ancestor worship commands attention for good reason. These rites bare the bones of social structure, revealing Korean society as Koreans themselves define it. Sons offer wine, rice, and delicacies to dead parents and grandparents and thereby dramatize patrilineal principles that underpin the family, the lineage, and, by

an analogous relationship of ruler and subject, the state. Not a demonstration of structural principles alone, the rites of ancestor worship
exemplify the ethical content of proper human relationships. Through
ancestor worship men demonstrate filial piety *(hyodo)*, the attribute of
virtuous sons and loyal subjects. Their actions are lauded in philo-
sophical treatises, household etiquette manuals, classroom lectures,
and government propaganda. Mens' rituals represent the most articulate, codified, and commendable aspect of the Korean religious experience. Men's rituals are therefore the most accessible aspect of the
Korean religious experience.

Contrasting the pride men take in explaining ancestor worship to
anthropologists and children, village women were frankly confused by
this ethnographer's interest in their rituals. "What do you want to
know about that for?" they would ask. "What's the use of knowing
that?" In vain I tried to explain the value of comparative studies. I
tried to tell them that American women were interested in the lives of
Korean women. It was only when I said, "They sent male students to
Korea to study the *chesa*. Since I'm a woman, they sent me to study
what you do," that I at last received a nod of understanding. Honoring
a social and ritual division of labor in their own lives, they deemed my
research interests appropriate to my sex.

The Scholar and the Shaman

In his discussion of contradictory motifs in Korean society, Vincent
Brandt juxtaposes the "serene tranquility . . . exemplified in the dignified scholar and the violent, emotionally charged activity of the
ecstatic shaman." This opposition, he suggests, "is a constantly recur-
ring theme of Korean history, folklore, and literature" (Brandt 1971,
28). The scholar and the shaman carry between them three related
oppositions: man versus woman, elite versus commoner, and bearer of
Chinese learning versus bearer of indigenous custom. Throughout the
last five hundred years, "dignified scholars," elite men versed in Chinese learning, have declared themselves the shaman's adversaries. Also
through the centuries, the wives of dignified scholars have continued
to patronize shamans.

The scholar-official of old held women's rituals doubly suspect. A
woman was an unpredictable entity outside the moral order of filial

sons and virtuous fathers. Her offerings to the household gods and the female shaman's zesty performances were not the correct rituals ordained in the classics. Ch'oe Pu, a Korean official who visited China in 1487, was asked, "Does your country worship gods and spirits?" Putting Korea's best face forward, he answered, "All my countrymen build shrines and sacrifice to their ancestors. They serve the gods and spirits they ought to serve and do not respect unorthodox sacrifices" (Meskill 1965, 83). This was wishful thinking on Ch'oe's part, but his statement nevertheless reveals both what a Korean official of the fifteenth century considered proper and what he felt Confucius' countrymen would consider proper. His Chinese hosts, of course, indulged in a similar hypocrisy.

Confucian reformers of the Yi period tried to stifle the activities of *mudang*, both shamans and hereditary priestesses, on the grounds that these women coveted wealth, deceived people, and were licentious. *Mudang* were accused of conspiring with ambitious palace women and dabbling in sorcery. The government attempted periodically, and with scant success, to ban *mudang* from the capital. Indignant officials repeatedly memorialized the throne, fulminating against wicked shamans *(yomu)* and their lewd rites *(ŭmsa)* (N. Yi 1976). But women on all levels of traditional society, palace women and queens no less than peasant wives, summoned professional shamans (ibid., 45–56; Allen 1896, 193; T. H. Kim [1948] 1969, 409).

As a principle of harmonious administration and a practical consequence of his limited authority, the local magistrate respected local customs (Kawashima 1980; Palais 1975, 12–13). Tales are told of zealous reformers who exposed *mudang* charlatans, banned their activities, and taught the people to honor the local tutelary god with reformed, Confucian-style rites (Gale [1913] 1963, 125–129; Hulbert [1906] 1970, 420–421; N. Yi 1976, 223–224, 233, 242). In many other communities, magistrates not only countenanced shaman rituals but were expected to supervise community offerings to the tutelary gods. In many county seats *(ŭp)*, including my field site, Bright County Town, shamans were hired to make an annual offering to the community tutelary god, to exorcise the yamen of malevolent forces, and to petition the rain dragon during droughts (see chap. 2; N. Yi 1976; Akamatsu and Akiba 1938, 1:148; Akiba 1957, 2–9). According to Jones, "every prefect is also compelled to maintain worship at the shrines of the local spirits and . . . tithes of rice for the Confucian worship also include rice for the official worship of these Shamanite gods" (Jones 1902, 39). Today some rural communities hire their own shamans to honor the local tutelary god. The Tano Festival (lunar 5.5) in Kangnŭng is, to my knowledge, the only surviving celebration that still draws in the local administration. At the Kangnŭng Tano Festival, a huge county fair with a tent full of *mudang* at its core, local functionaries appear in the regalia of an antique magistrate and his retinue.

Early Christian missionaries in Korea readily accepted elite perceptions of *mudang* as "the lowest of the low," for "in addition to an entire lack of morals, she is supposed to have commerce with evil spirits" (Hulbert [1906] 1970, 358). These early observers were confounded by the inconstancy of their informants. To Moose's missionary dismay, "The religious feeling of the people is so strong that even the highest and best educated classes do not hesitate to call for the *mudang* when they are in trouble. There is probably no other class of women in the land that makes so much money as do the *mudangs*" (Moose 1911, 192).

It was Hulbert's perception that, "Most Korean gentlemen will scoff at the idea that the spirits have any control over human destiny, but they put nothing in the way of their wives' adhesion to the lower cult." Hulbert reveals that even the gentleman's expressed cynicism was not absolute. "There are also many men who in ordinary life would laugh the imps to scorn and yet when laid upon a bed of sickness or subjected to some other painful casualty are willing enough to compound for their previous scepticism by the payment of large bribes to these same imps" (Hulbert [1906] 1970, 406). From another early account, "If a sick man has reason to believe that his distemper is caused by a spirit, he will send his wife to a *mudang* to describe his symptoms and learn if possible what spirit is doing the mischief" (Korean Mudang and Pansu 1903, 147).

In the field I heard similar anecdotes. One tells of the husband who, thinking himself at death's door, contradicts his earlier intransigence and begs his wife to seek out a shaman and sponsor a *kut,* another is of the husband who, barely rescued from the jaws of bankruptcy, thanks his wife's favorite *mansin* in person. Some women do visit the *mansin* in secret rather than confront a peevish spouse. An early observer noted that "there are many people who wish to make use of the *mudang*'s services and are still ashamed to have it known; so they have her perform the ceremony at her own place and no one is the wiser, probably not even the patient" (ibid., 204). On the eve of her daughter's wedding in 1977, my landlady went to Yongsu's Mother's shrine with special offerings *(yŏt'am)*. Although Yongsu's Mother's house was just down the lane, my landlady managed to conceal her actions from her husband. He had been grumbling for days at the daughter's wedding expenses, and my landlady feared a fresh tirade. All of the daughters of the household, including the "American daughter," shared her secret and were coached what to say.

Sometimes male opposition is merely a pose before the world. One of the Clear Spring Mansin's clients, a policeman's wife, came to the Clear Spring Mansin because her husband's legal problems were jeopardizing his career. The Clear Spring Mansin told her to worship her household gods. The policeman objected. As a minor official, he must oppose "superstition." His wife was emphatic, and the Clear Spring Mansin performed the ritual with clanging cymbals throughout the policeman's house.

That year, things went well for the policeman and his wife. In the tenth month, the wife said, "We should worship the household gods again." Her husband instructed her, "Just do it quickly and finish before I come home." Running behind schedule, the Clear Spring Mansin was still noisily invoking the gods when the policeman walked in the door. Yongsu's Mother, there to help, quickly poured the policeman a cup of wine with a show of politeness. "You've done a lot for us," the policeman said. "Just make me lucky and rich." When she told me the tale the very next day, Yongsu's Mother cackled with glee.

The humble policeman follows in the footsteps of a turn-of-the-century magistrate, one Jung Hunsi, who donned ordinary costume, took a few strings of cash, and went to observe a famous shaman. The shaman, in trance, discovered his identity and "scolded him very sharply saying that it was exceedingly impolite on the part of an official to present himself to the spirit of the war god with so little ceremony. The magistrate, scared out of his wits, went away only to come back in full court dress with $60.00 for an offering" (*The Independent,* 7 June 1898).

With a kindred baggage of decorous posing, Korean studies might profit by developments in the study of Chinese religion. Sinologists suggest a distinction between a member of the elite's expressed adherence to proper or orthodox behavior and the diverse beliefs and practices he sanctioned in private (Welch 1970; Yang 1961, 275–277;

Freedman 1974, 38). In Korea the fact that un-Confucian rituals are women's rituals intensifies elite discriminations between proper and improper religious behavior.

The Scholar and the Shaman in the Twentieth Century

The missionaries who gave the West its first glimpse of Korea stood the Confucian moralizer on his head. A woman's dabbling in superstitious practices was one more indication of her depressed and miserable state under the tyranny of Confucian patriarchy. Even her gods were the sorry product of her victimization and the further instrument of her oppression. Gifford lamented, "In what a narrow world do they pass their lives! And then the women are universally spirit-worshippers and live in constant dread of evil spirits. In view of these facts, can we wonder that the habitual thinking of Korean women is petty, or superstitious, or vulgar? Poor things!" (Gifford 1898).

Modern-day progressives echo these sentiments, expressing frustration at what they see as the backward perspective of the Korean wife and mother. According to one study sponsored by the Korean Institute for Research in the Behavioral Sciences, "for most women, a process of regression starts with marriage as far as modernizing influences are concerned." Women are thus "an easy prey to superstitious beliefs" (Chung, Cha, and Lee 1974, 270, 184). Another scholar suggests that centuries of ignorant, if well-intended, country women have trivialized a proud religious heritage—shamanism—into a petty preoccupation with good and bad fortune (Chang 1974, 137–138). Theologians, on the other hand, blame women for "shamanizing" Korean Christianity (H. Lee 1977; EWUWSP 1977, 208).

Some writers attribute the Korean housewife's continuing enthusiasm for the household gods and her patronage of shamans to her continuing vulnerability within the Korean family. Women leave their own kin and villages to enter their husbands' families as suspect strangers. They have been told that infertile brides might be sent back home in shame. The birth of a son is a woman's first success, insuring that she will not be cast out. But a woman must raise up healthy children to anticipate a secure old age and an ancestor's immortality. Thus, we are told, women under duress will resort to all manner of bizarre practices to secure, through mystical means, the conception, safe birth, and long life of sons (Akamatsu and Akiba 1938, 2:193; T. H. Kim [1948] 1969, 145–146; Chung, Cha, and Lee 1977).

Despite the combined disdain of genteel conservatives and impatient progressives, Korean and Japanese folklorists have recorded a wealth of descriptive material on women's and shaman's rituals. The zeitgeist contemporary Korean folklorists imbibe recalls the zeitgeist that inspired folklore's European progenitors. In the wake of Korea's rapid postwar development one finds now the luxury of nostalgia. Abstract issues of national identity and the preservation of a Korean cultural heritage infuse intellectual discourse. Customs once taken for granted become folklore. The folklorist would record the not-so-distant past ere it vanish away. To this end researchers seek out the most distant hamlets and oldest informants, who thereby hold the purest and truest custom. Ironically shaman rituals are now avidly recorded precisely because they were never Confucianized. Intellectuals hail shamanism as the vestige of a uniquely Korean religious experience. At the extreme nationalist side of this spectrum, one scholar considers shamanism the source of the Korean people's spiritual energy (*chŏng-sin enŏji*) (T. G. Kim 1972a, 76).

When the folklorist enters women's ritual realm, cultural preservation assumes top priority. The field is active, the practitioners dedicated. Korean folklorists have recorded vast quantities of material, and anyone who presumes to do fieldwork in the Korean countryside will profit from an acquaintance with this corpus.[5] In addition, several folklorists have actively campaigned for official recognition and government support of folk arts that might otherwise have died out or succumbed to the reformist zealotry of local functionaries.

The gleanings of the folklorist do not always serve the needs of the social anthropologist. Recorded custom falls under typological headings: "shaman practices," "Buddhist practices," "household gods." An organizational typology facilitates regional comparisons, but it does not yield an appreciation of the complex integration of belief and practice in the religious life of a Korean village. Villagers cross categories. The same informant might worship at Buddhist temples, visit shaman shrines, and set down rice cake for the household gods. The folklorist considers the shaman, preferably an older shaman, a living repository of indigenous religion and literature. It is through such informants that old customs are salvaged, sometimes from memory. One finds in the records of the folklorist detailed and precise descrip-

tions of the mechanics of ritual but little about the women who perform them today and less about their reasons.

The Korean past also inspires religious historians. Historical chron-
icles of the early Korean Three Kingdoms[6] speak of lavish state-spon-
sored shaman rituals and "shamanistic" warrior cults. Archaeological
evidence suggests that ancient kings—or perhaps ancient queens[7]—
wielded shamanic powers. A number of Korean scholars consider
present-day shamans the heirs of this bygone era, their influence dilut-
ed by infusions of Buddhism from the sixth and seventh century and
Neo-Confucianism most emphatically from the fifteenth century
(T. K. Kim 1963, 15–104; Chang 1974, 134–139; et al.). At this
point some scholars clutch their volumes of Eliade and leap into
archaic time when "true" shamans flew between two worlds and
Korean shamans were men. On the strength of the male *paksu
mudang*'s pantaloons and with a liberal interpretation of mythology,
some religious historians suggest that women became shamans only
after men had discarded archaic religion for the more prestigious foreign faiths. Women then trivialized archaic shamanism into the superstitious practices they perpetuate today (J. Lee 1981, 1–21; Yu 1975,
164–169). These theories bespeak a dim view of women.

Korean psychiatrists encounter shamans and shamans' clients in
their own practice. By the immediacy of their concerns psychiatrists
differ from folklorists and religious historians. With more than a
touch of professional condescension, two therapists evaluate the shaman's techniques against their own notions of a working therapy for
living people. Rhi Bou-yang (1970) describes the ancestors' appearance in *kut* as effective psychodrama. Kim Kwang-iel (1972b) acknowledges various psychotherapeutic elements at work in *kut*:
catharsis, abreaction, suggestion, hypnotism, and transference. A *kut*
is good "group therapy," well suited to Koreans' "basic orientation of
mutual cooperation and interdependency" (K. Kim 1973, 45). Both
Kim and Rhi fault the shaman for encouraging a "vicious cycle of pro-
jection" with no possible resolution. They do concede, however, that
the shaman's therapy addresses the needs and understandings of "traditionally oriented" patients (ibid., Rhi 1970; 1977). Here again the
authors assume that women indulge in traditional practices because
women themselves are more traditional or, without the euphemism,
backward. Rhi goes one step further into the mysticism of Jungian
dichotomy. He characterizes Korean shamanism as a "vessel contain-

ing things irrational and female, which were oppressed on the surface of male consciousness in society" (Rhi 1970, 15).

Studies of Korean shamanism from various disciplinary perspectives have overwhelmingly emphasized the shaman's intrapsychic experience over her therapeutic efficacy as a professional healer. Folklorists carefully record a thumbnail sketch of the informant's career. The Korean shaman's initiatory experiences are of a pattern, and Korean scholars describe the syndrome from their own disciplinary perspectives. Folklorist Kim T'ae-gon lists the symptoms of the destined shaman as "persistent illness for no apparent reason, appetite loss, unwillingness to eat meat and fish, cravings for cold water, weakness or pain in the limbs, dreams, hallucinations, and crazed wandering." He considers this experience typical of pan-global shamanism and interprets the initiatory illness as a religious experience rather than a psychological malfunctioning (T. G. Kim 1970, 1972a, 1972b). Kim Kwang-iel uses the vocabulary of psychiatry to classify the same phenomenon. He suggests that the cases of initiatory illness he has encountered may be divided into a "prodromal phase" and a "depersonalization phase." In the prodromal phase, the would-be shaman exhibits "hysterical or psychosomatic symptoms such as anorexia, weakness, insomnia, indigestion, and/or functional paralysis of the extremities." In the depersonalization phase, symptoms are aggravated and "hallucinatory experiences, dreams of revelation or prophecy, confusion, with or without psychomotor excitement, are common additional symptoms" (K. Kim 1972a, 233). Korean psychiatrists use the term *sinbyŏng,* or "god sickness," for the shaman's initiatory illness. Kim Kwang-iel describes *sinbyŏng* as a "culture-bound depersonalization syndrome," a regressive state wherein subjects seek infantile wish fulfillment. He does acknowledge that shamanism provides a means of working through inner conflicts (ibid.).

Harvey's (1979, 1980) portraits of six Korean shamans are by far the most detailed and respectful life histories of Korean shamans to date. Harvey has interviewed each woman in the shaman's own home amid the shaman's clients and family, slowly building rapport over several months. Harvey is therefore able to render each woman's accounting of her own life. The six shamans defy easy generalization. They represent diverse class backgrounds, different degrees of exposure to traditional and modern influences, a variety of experiences in childhood, marriage, war, and migration, as well as an age span of several decades. For each woman Harvey finds a high level of intelligence, verbal skills, perceptiveness, and a strong sense of self. She suggests that these women seized possession sickness and the *mansin*'s career as a way out of the impasse "between social expectations of them as women and their personal goals and interests as individuals" (Harvey 1979, 237). Harvey's work welds social-structural explanations—possession is a woman's ecstatic compensation for social deprivation—and a long tradition of life history analysis—distinct personality traits make some but not all members of a society successful shamans.

Anthropologists writing in English have only recently begun to describe and analyze the content of Korean shaman rituals and the matrix of belief and circumstance surrounding them. Harvey (1976) describes the shaman as a "household therapist" giving divinations and advice to her female clients. Janelli and Janelli (1979; 1982, 148–176) discuss soul-raising in the shaman's ritual *kut*. Dix (1980) analyzes the relationship between shamanistic belief in spirits and scholarly cosmological explanations of fate contained in the scholar's almanac. Soon-young Yoon (1976), Kim and Sich (1977), and Sich (1978) discuss clients' use of shamans in the health-seeking process. I have discussed the symbolic content and social implications of a healing rite, trance dancing *(mugam)*, conception rituals, and exorcism (Kendall 1977a, 1977b, 1977c, 1981). Writing in Korean, Ch'oe Kilsŏng (1978) describes the social structure of hereditary *tanggol mudang* teams. Writing in Japanese, Shigematsu Mayumi (1980) describes stressful relationships between in-marrying women as they are reflected in women's participation in *kut*. Writing in French, Alexandre Guillemoz (1983) describes the household gods' cult in the context of a village ethnography.

In sum, there exists a wealth of pure description, some analysis of shaman personalities, and some focused analysis of specific rituals. What is lacking is a systematic ethnographic appreciation of the who, why, what, where, and when of women's rituals, a gap that precludes generalization on the role of women and shamans in Korean religious life.

THREE

Enduring Pine Village

Peach and plum of springtime
    do not flaunt your pretty blossoms;
Consider rather the old pine
    and green bamboo at year's end.
What can change these noble stems
    and their flourishing evergreen?
Kim Yugi (late 17th century)

Let us follow the *mansin* Yongsu's Mother home from the Chŏn family *kut*. From the window of a country bus Enduring Pine Village resembles any of the numerous rural settlements on the northern periphery of Seoul. The thatched roofs of a few years past are gone, replaced by corrugated metal or slate tile roofs. Television antennas sprout from many house tops. The headquarters of the New Village Movement (Saemaŭl Undong), an imposing concrete structure with its loudspeaker tower and bulletin board, stands on elevated ground just off the road, flanked by a small white church. On the other side of the paved road a painted sign proclaims that Enduring Pine Village is a "rabbit-raising village," producing pelts for export with official encouragement.

Also visible from the road is the red gate of the old Confucian academy *(hyanggyo)*, where country scholars offer semiannual libations to the sages enshrined within. The caretaker and his wife maintain the grounds with a subsidy from the main shrine in Seoul. In summer women sew under the shade trees in the courtyard.

Off, away from the main road, one finds more traces of an older Korea—broken memorial stones beside a village lane, a lone old-fashioned tile-roofed house with its mud walls buckling under the weight of the curved roof, and stone guardians beside a grave mound on a hillside overlooking the rice fields.

Further up the hillside back behind the village stands the tree where the village Tutelary God (Todang) dwells. Strips of thin paper knotted on the lower branches and the burnt stubs of candles and incense sticks bespeak a recent offering, scant evidence of an enduring but almost invisible realm of ritual and belief. More obvious is Yongsu's Mother's house just beside the bus stop on the main road. Frequent cymbal clanging and telltale chanting spill out to the road, evidence of a *mansin*'s shrine within. Noise is the only hint. The house looks like any other village house. This roof, too, bears its television antenna.

The Village in History

Enduring Pine Village, though no traditional village, is nevertheless a village rich in tradition. During the last dynasty Enduring Pine Village was not a village at all but the bustling seat of Bright County where the local magistrate held court. Bright County Town was a place of some repute in the Koryŏ and Yi kingdoms, but tradition holds that the Buddhist temple on the hillside dates from the ancient days of Silla[1] (Ch'oe and Chang 1967, 6). Destroyed and rebuilt several times over the intervening centuries, the present temple is but a pale reflection of the splendid monastery bombed by American planes during the Korean War. Leftist activists shot the abbot.

Located at a significant crossroads a day's journey from Seoul, the town market prospered and the roadside wine houses were famous during the last century. The 1911 count revealed a flourishing community of 540 households with a total population of 2,600. Village tradition holds that the town once boasted more than a thousand tile-roofed houses (ibid., 4; K. Lee 1967, 15–16, 28; D. Lee 1969, 205).

As in other administrative centers, the founders of Bright County Town heeded geomantic principles. Geomantic dictum states: "Establish an administrative center under a protective mountain and auspicious forces will accrue." The public buildings and private dwellings of Bright County Town nestled at the base of an imposing granite hillside once thick with pine trees. The magistrate's court *(kwana, amun),* perched on elevated ground above all other buildings, inspired awe and fear of officialdom (K. Lee 1967, 11–12).

An abundant and elaborate ritual life reflected the town's prosperity and stature. Up on the protective mountain, behind the magistrate's court, stood the Altar to Land and Grain (Sajik), where the magistrate made offerings when the king offered the royal sacrifice at the main shrine in Seoul. Similarly, local literati from throughout the county made spring and autumn offerings at the Confucian shrine when literati at the national academy held their rites in the capital.

Each year the men of the town honored the Mountain God at his hillside shrine (Sansin Kak), and every three years the women held a *mansin*'s *kut* at the Tutelary God's shrine. Villagers observe both of these rites today, supported now, as then, by public subsidies collected from each household.

Another *mansin kut* exorcised and purified the public buildings *(kwanch'ŏng kut)*. The *mansin* who organized the *kut* at the Tutelary God's shrine and the *mansin* who exorcised the public buildings received this charge from the magistrate and with it the title Appointed Mansin (An Mansin). In time of drought each household contributed money or grain to hire a *mansin* and hold a *kut* at the rain dragon's well by the Tutelary God's tree *(kiu che)* (ibid., 21; Ch'oe and Chang 1967, 4; Murayama 1938, 319–320). Within living memory a *kut* for rain was interrupted by a freak summer hailstorm. When the summer rains were late in 1977, the elders said that the village would not sponsor a *kut* since the community is now equipped with pumps.

Absent from ritual life in Bright County Town is the elaborate communal worship of lineage ancestors so prominent in the ethnography of single-lineage *yangban* communities (M. Lee 1960; T. K. Kim 1964; Biernatzki 1969; Janelli and Janelli 1978, 1982; Pak and Gamble 1975). Students of Korean society have yet to reach consensus on a working definition of the term *yangban*. However, by even the broadest definition of *yangban* status—membership in a recognized branch of a lineage demonstrating genealogical proximity to a titled officeholder and sustaining its claim through the performance of corporate lineage rites and periodic genealogy maintenance—Bright County Town was not a *yangban* community in dynastic times. Asked in a survey, "Are you of *yangban* stock [*yangban ch'ulsin*]?" contemporary villagers most often answered, "I am not baseborn [*sangnom*]." My landlady and fictive mother was a refreshing exception. Answering for her absent husband, she said, "*Yangban*? Him a *yangban*? [*Yangban? Musŭn yangban?*]" Most villagers claimed that their families maintained genealogies *(chokpo)* or, at very least, that their written record was destroyed during the war. The village elders frankly distinguished themselves from recognized *yangban* in other communities down the road.

Yangban were appointed to the town as officials, but the local elite were *ajŏn*, low-level functionaries at the magistrate's court as clerks and men-at-arms. According to the local elders, *ajŏn* who managed to amass wealth through high land rents and extortionate loans held sway as the local elite *(yuji)*, "those who acted like *yangban*." More cynically, the old men told me, "They used to call those who had money *'yangban.'* "

Superficial though this picture is, it squares with Korean historiographic portraits of the *ajŏn* as a petty official who took good advantage of his ample opportunities for extortion and graft. Indeed, the *ajŏn* of popular imagination struts about in the *mansin*'s portrayal of the Official (see chap. 1). Like the *ajŏn* who serves a magistrate, the supernatural Official serves a more regal deity, a Mountain God, General, or Great Spirit. These high gods would not deign to demand tribute, and merely extend a fan and claim their due. The underling Official suffers no such constraints. His greed is legendary.[2]

The three surnames Ha, Yi, and Na were the most renowned *ajŏn* families in Bright County during dynastic times. The Ha were skilled in music, the Na at calligraphy, and the Yi in literary accomplishment. Today the village abounds with Yi households. Relatives up to the eighth degree of relationship *(tangnaegan)* take part in each other's household ancestor rites. These occasions, combined with weddings, birthdays, and casual visiting, give members of Yi households ample opportunity to visit relatives at far corners of the village. Yi households now living in Seoul return for ancestor rites and graveside worship with their close kin.

The Ha and Na have all but dispppeared from Enduring Pine Village. The main house of the Na family moved to Inch'ŏn forty years ago and broke ties with the few Na households remaining in the village, four at the time of this study. In 1977 only one Ha household remained, and outside of the immediate family no one in the village seemed to remember the Ha family's place of origin *(pon'gwan)*. Villagers attribute the dispersal of the Ha and Na families to their economic tribulations during the Japanese colonial period, when Bright County Town lost its geographic prominence and entered a period of decline.

A railroad line linking the capital to the north bypassed Bright

County Town and undermined its strategic position on the old road junction. In the twenties the county office was relocated in Righteous Town on the new railroad line. The market followed. Many old county seats shared a similar fate. Lee Kisuk describes this process of decline. The large landowners moved to the new administrative and commercial centers. Tenants deserted the land to seek fortunes elsewhere. Abandoned building sites became fields or lay fallow (K. Lee 1967, 28–29, 46).

Bright County Town fared better than some of the "old county seats." The town remained the administrative center of the *myŏn,* a lower-order administrative unit introduced by the Japanese. Now, townspeople tasted institutional changes and the trappings of modernity introduced into Korea during the colonial period in the form of a post office, grammar school, printing company, and police station (ibid., 28). By villagers' estimates there were three hundred houses in the town before the wartime bombing, a decline of less than half from 1911. Despite the loss of official status, people still called the place the county seat *(ŭmnae)* in common parlance. Indeed, they still do.

The town preserved something of its former pomp. The daughter of a prosperous Righteous Town family told me that she had been pleased and excited when she learned that she would marry into Bright County Town. "Even though it's nothing but a village now, everyone knew of Bright County Town back then. When the district office was here, you could see all of the Japanese women in their kimono with the wide sashes tied around their waists. And when someone shouted 'The district chief approaches!' everyone would bow down low beside the road." This was Bright County Town during the 1930s.

Situated just south of the demilitarized zone, Enduring Pine Village was shattered by the first battles of the Korean War. As one survivor tells it, "The sound of guns burst out all at once, and we ran. All of a sudden, we just had to run. What do you think happened?" The town was reputed to be a leftist stronghold. After the Inch'ŏn landing, American planes rained bombs on Bright County Town. By now villagers were perennial refugees. "Some went to Pusan, some to Ch'ungch'ŏng Province. All of the houses were burning here. There were so many hardships in the refugee's life. When you flee with only your skin, how do you eat and survive?"

But of those who fled the farthest and stayed away the longest, most were men. Some feared conscription, others, reprisal. When the Chinese army entered Enduring Pine Village only women and small children remained. One village woman told me, "Excuse me for saying so, but we liked the Chinese soldiers better than the American soldiers. The American soldiers were always shouting for women, women, women. The Chinese soldiers weren't like that." When American soldiers entered the village, the younger women hid. One woman, an adolescent during the war, recalls, "Once when an American soldier came into the house, my two friends and I hid under the porch. The porch was built low and there was a lot of bumping around. We had no idea the soldier was standing right on top of us. When he was gone, someone said, 'The Americans will think that we have earthquakes in Korea.' We were lucky; we always escaped."

After the war some returned, some settled elsewhere. Refugees from the North settled in the area, married local women, and began new lives, not knowing if wives, children, and kin left in the North were living or dead. Uncertainty, and some measure of guilt over lost relatives, pours out when the *mansin* evokes and propitiates their dead in *kut*.

During the war, the district office and police bureau were bombed. After the war, they were permanently relocated. In the villagers' words, Enduring Pine Village was, "just a country village now." Even the name was changed.

Enduring Pine Village Today

One hundred thirty-six village houses, less than half of the prewar number, are divided between six hamlets. The total population has remained fairly constant over the last decade or more: 880 according to the 1965 county yearbook (*YTY* 1965, 10), 896 in 1978 according to the village chief's figures. But stable size does not mean a stationary population. Villagers move to Righteous Town or to Seoul. Soldiers and employees at nearby military installations settle their families in the village. Retiring military men buy land or livestock with their severance pay and take up residence in the village.

During my own residence it seemed as if some household was always moving out of the village and another household moving in. Sons established households near urban employment. Commuting husbands wanted to be closer to their jobs and moved their families to town. Some newcomers, unable to clear a profit on a store or live-stock-raising enterprise, left to try their luck elsewhere. Some former residents returned to the village. One man brought his family back to take over a village store abandoned by newcomers from another province. A repentant son patched up a quarrel with his father and step-mother and urged them to return. Facing bankruptcy, a woman brought her children to her natal village while her husband worked as a traveling salesman. A son gave up his factory job to join his father in a rabbit-raising enterprise.

Rice production for cash and subsistence is no longer the most significant means of livelihood in Enduring Pine Village. Seventy households, more than half the total of 136, are registered as nonagricultural. Nonagricultural households do not cultivate rice, although most of these households own or rent dry fields for vegetable cultivation, and some raise livestock. Some of the men work at the local military installations, some work in the market town as semiskilled laborers—taxi drivers, factory workers, carpenters, and stonemasons. Two men from the village accepted contracts as drivers for a Korean construction project in Saudi Arabia.

Modern techniques of food and livestock production and paved roads connecting the town and the capital brought new money-making opportunities to the village. The market has always been a marginal source of cash for the housewife, but today some village households are exploiting new commercial opportunities. Twenty village families are cultivating unseasonal and specialty vegetables in vinyl greenhouses. Thirty households raise poultry for the market, and fifteen raise rabbits. A major commercial livestock enterprise, its stock-barns filled with pigs and poultry, relocated to the village a few years ago. Wage workers employed in the barns live in Enduring Pine Village with their families. Two other households of outsiders recently settled in the village and embarked upon single-family pig and poultry-raising enterprises. These new ventures require a substantial initial investment and a certain amount of risk. It costs twenty-five thousand won to construct a vinyl greenhouse. Pedigreed rabbits with the most desirable fur cost one hundred thousand won or more.

The village chief of Enduring Pine Village and his wife are typical of the new villagers, outsiders attempting to capitalize on innovations in the rural economy. The village chief's wife told me, "We're originally from North Kyŏngsang Province. We traveled around for several years while my husband was in the army. When he retired we settled here because we hadn't gotten rich and were ashamed to go back home. With his five hundred thousand-won severance pay, we settled here and tried to raise chickens, but we had no luck. Then we tried raising cows, but that didn't work either." The village chief works at the district office where he trains the local militia. His wife cultivates vegetables in a vinyl greenhouse and tends the family's two pigs. The eldest son and daughter work in factories in Seoul and sleep in the factory dormitories. Another son is still in school. It is a comment on changing times and needs that the village chief's military background and his association with the district office, rather than a longtime familiarity with village affairs, qualifies him for leadership in Enduring Pine Village.

Children's school fees and the rising cost of living make women increasingly anxious to supplement the household income, but they have limited access to cash earnings. When the private garden yields a surplus, the housewife bundles the produce off to the Righteous Town market. Most women wholesale their produce to an established market vendor rather than hawking it themselves. A few women acquire an occasional windfall by hawking sundries on consignment from Seoul factories. One woman peddles ready-made clothing through the surrounding villages. Another woman manufactures bean curd for the village shops and the town market.

By far the most steady and widespread source of women's cash is piecework quilting, the local cottage industry. A factory in Seoul that manufactures hand-quilted kendo robes for export to Japan supplies pieces to a central distribution point in the village. Working on her own time, a woman may earn five or ten thousand won a month. The most avid quilters, a group of women who quilt together each afternoon, earn an average of twenty thousand won a month. The most productive quilter is a young wife living with her own parents for the duration of her husband's military service. Liberated from the most time-consuming domestic tasks, she earns twenty-five thousand won a month. Quilting is alienated labor rather than a traditional handicraft, in that the women know that the finished product is worn for some form of martial art, but are unable to visualize just what part of the completed robe the piece they are quilting comprises.

Women also receive small cash payments of one or two thousand won, as well as food and gifts when they help in the kitchen during a wedding, funeral, or *kut*. Some women work as day labor in other households' fields, but they do this reluctantly. Their tanned faces are an open admission of poverty.

Women do not like to discuss their own earnings. In interviews women claim that the amount of money they earned from quilting or marketing vegetables was insignificant. Household needs, cosmetics, or the children's school expenses swiftly consume it. Women do seem, however, to amass enough cash to invest in rotating credit associations *(kye)* and to lend lump sums at interest. Many a significant household purchase or daughter's wedding transpires at the housewife's initiative when her *kye* money falls due.

Like other rural Korean villages, Enduring Pine Village has a New Village Movement. The village decides on public works projects using materials subsidized by the government. Each household contributes one person's labor for one day a week for the duration of a project. New Village work ceases during the hectic transplant and harvest seasons.

In Enduring Pine Village villagers have replaced all of the straw roofs with tile or corrugated metal. They have built a New Community Movement Hall, rebuilt two bridges, improved the irrigation channel, and constructed three laundry spigots and cement drainage areas for washing clothes. As a future project they plan to roof over the drainage areas to protect women from the rain.

In an older form of village cooperation each household contributes to the annual offering for the Mountain God (Sansinje) and to the *kut* at the Tutelary God's shrine (Todang Kut). Households also contribute small amounts of rice, rice wine, or cash to families holding a wedding or funeral.[3] All of these contributions are officially solicited by the hamlet chiefs *(panjang)* and recorded.

Four small shops within the village vend alcohol, soft drinks, sweets, vegetables, bean curd, and household sundries. They also double as wine shops, common gathering places for village men. The village has its own barber shop. Children from neighboring villages attend the local elementary school. Several children from Enduring Pine Village make the fifteen-minute bus ride to middle school and high school in Righteous Town. On their way home from school children can pick up food or sundries in the market or report a parent's illness symptoms to a pharmacist, returning home with diagnosis and prescription. The family saves an additional bus fare.

Village women visit the town once or twice a week for the market. They turn to the pharmacies in town as their first recourse in time of illness. For more serious complaints they visit several small private hospitals or a Chinese-style doctor who gives herb and acupuncture treatments. The beauty parlor, bathhouse, Chinese restaurants, movie theater, tearooms, and a plethora of fortune-tellers are occasional indulgences. Most village sons and daughters are married new style *(sinsik)* in one of the town's two wedding halls *(yesikchang)*.

Well over half of the village houses have television sets and television is now the prime form of evening entertainment. Things seen or heard on television are recurrent topics of conversation. Variety shows and serialized historical dramas are particularly popular.

Seoul is an hour and a half away by bus, with one transfer from the country bus to the intercity bus. A family with parents, siblings, or married children in the capital considers birthdays, death anniversaries, and the New Year occasions for a visit. Children sometimes spend part of a school vacation with married siblings in the city. Sons and, more recently, daughters of village families find employment in Seoul factories and shops. Some village children meet their future spouses while working in the capital. Others return to their country families and ask them to arrange a match.

Shamanism in a Not-So-Typical Korean Community

Enduring Pine Village is no pristine traditional village where inaccessability and social conservatism buffer the onslaught of modernization. As a county seat during the last dynasty, the community was never far removed from the cultural mainstream flowing along the road to the capital. Even in the Japanese period, a time of relative decline, the town, as district center, got a taste of modernization. The Korean War was an immediate nightmare.

Commercialization of agriculture and increasing reliance on wage income are transforming rural communities throughout the Korean peninsula today. In Enduring Pine Village the vicissitudes of history and proximity to the town and capital accelerated the process of dissolution. But Enduring Pine Village was not, even in the last century, what might be called a typical agrarian community with a traditional round of life circumscribed by the cultivation of rice and the transfer of rice land. Pomp, politics, and the market informed the local world view.

Even so, northern Kyŏnggi Province carries the epithet, "Seoul's conservative backside" (Lee Du-hyon, personal communication). Enduring Pine Village and its environs were known from long ago and are still known today for an abundance of shamans and shaman ritual. Korean and Japanese folklorists made profitable forays here. The villagers' enthusiasm for "superstitious practices" is the eternal frustration of the New Village Movement chief and the local minister. The complex of ritual and belief described here is no relic of the past, preserved in isolation, but part of the fabric of life in a changed and still changing community. Here, television sets are exorcised of wood imps while a shaman masters her long chants with the aid of a portable tape recorder.

Koreanists will inevitably wonder if the absence of homegrown *yangban* in Enduring Pine Village accounts for its rich tradition of nonelite ritual. According to the traditional elite perspective, echoed in more contemporary scholarship, "shamanism" and "superstition" find adherents only among the less-educated and much-victimized lower classes. I consider this issue a red herring on two counts. First, although there were never any "real *yangban*" among village families, the local *ajŏn* boasted education and some refinement. Even without the presence of *yangban,* the townspeople might yet have been urbane. Their flourishing crossroads community permitted a lavish ritual life, including community shaman rituals sanctioned by the magistrate in a working compromise of Neo-Confucian principle and community custom.

Second, like some turn-of-the-century observers, I observed several full-dress shaman *kut* in the homes of avowedly *yangban* families in other northern Kyŏnggi villages. One new client from a *yangban* family made elaborate postures of reluctance, declaring that only the urgency of illness and misfortune brought her to sponsor a *kut*. Reluctance does not imply a separate "elite" religious tradition. The *mansin* were delighted when the woman's father-in-law delved into his cosmology texts and emerged from his studio to set an auspicious hour for the *kut* to begin. The hesitant daughter-in-law became a regular client at Yongsu's Mother's shrine.

When a *mansin* performs a *kut* in a *yangban* household, she deals with the household gods, ancestors, and ghosts as she would deal with the supernatural denizens of any home. These beliefs are held in common. As with any household, a *yangban* household's particular supernatural history is reflected in minor variations in the household pantheon. Yongsu's Mother has several clients whose households belong to a local branch of a *yangban* lineage. The lineage's apical ancestor and an early descendant who held high office appear with their consorts when these households hold *kut;* they are special King (Taewang) deities in the pantheons of lineage households. The local lineage also sponsors periodic *kut* (Taewang Kut) to honor the Kings and promote harmony among the kinsmen.

The Janellis' work in a *yangban* community south of Seoul also suggests that shamans minister to clients across traditional class boundaries. While villagers in Twisöngdwi claim only infrequent recourse to shamans, *kut* do occur when the need arises (Janelli and Janelli 1979; 1982, 148–176). Their study of "ancestral malevolence" reveals conceptualizations of ancestral and ghostly activity akin to descriptions I received in Enduring Pine Village (Janelli and Janelli 1982).

The strength of shamanism in Enduring Pine Village and its environs may neither be attributed to the absence, in traditional times, of cultural refinements usually associated with the *yangban* class, nor to isolation from modernizing influences in the present. Enduring Pine Village hardly fits the ethnographer's romantic vision of an isolated community with its traditional life-style still intact, if, indeed, such a village survives anywhere on the Korean peninsula today. It was nevertheless an intriguing place to begin this study. Where a rapidly suburbanizing village is at once a hotbed of shaman activity, the *mansin*'s work reflects the flesh-and-blood concerns of contemporary people.

The Village, the *Mansin,* and the Anthropologist

My first acquaintance with the northern Kyŏnggi countryside dates back some five years before I began this study. As a Peace Corps volunteer working in Seoul, I indulged an interest in Korean folk drama. In 1971 Dr. Lee Du-hyon (Yi Tu-hyŏn) of Seoul National University introduced me to a group of masked dancers living in a village north of Seoul and not far from Enduring Pine Village. The mask dance, once performed at festivals in the old town, survives today as a government-designated Intangible Cultural Property. Dancers receive a small stipend for perpetuating the art and training successors. The drama portrays monks, *yangban,* shamans, and common folk with cartoon masks and bawdy humor (D. Lee 1969, 201–276).

I visited the dancers many times to watch performances and, insofar as my then-limited Korean permitted, to ask them about the mask dance tradition. When I returned to Korea in 1976, and with Dr. Lee's encouragement, I again sought out the masked dancers who, happily, remembered me. I explained that I had returned to study shaman ceremonies and talk to village women. They suggested I meet the young *mansin* of Enduring Pine Village who occasionally danced minor parts in the mask dance drama.

One cold December afternoon, the maskmaker brought me to the home of the *mansin* whom I call here Yongsu's Mother. She was at work in her shrine, chanting as she waved a struggling white chicken over a tray of offering food while a tiny gray-haired woman rubbed her hands in supplication.

Having just read Ch'oe's and Chang's (1967) description of shaman practices in Kyŏnggi Province, I suspected the ceremony underway was a *p'udakkŏri,* a minor exorcism, and whispered the question to my guide. My use of the term surprised and pleased him; he later relayed my words to Yongsu's Mother like the proud parent of a precocious child. Koreans in the Seoul region have had passing acquaintance with foreigners, most often the American military, and assume, with considerable justification, the foreigner's total ignorance of Korean life. The burden of proof rested with me, and my question turned out to be an auspicious fluke that indicated a little knowledge and a capacity to learn.

Relieved of her ritual duties, Yongsu's Mother suggested a game of flower cards with a round of cheap rice wine as the stake. She proceeded to coach me, peering over my shoulder, telling me which card to set down, and cautioning me in a stage whisper that the other players were peeking at my hand. The card game set the tone of our working relationship, a relationship characterized by Yongsu's Mother's nonstop flow of information and advice, her patience, her well-intended but occasionally overbearing desire to protect and coddle me, and her mischievous sense of humor.

Yongsu's Mother told me later that when she first heard about me, she had been filled with pity for a woman who must wander alone, away from her family and her native land. Yongsu's Mother's own life had been wretched and she was now, at forty-one, a lonely widow. She claimed that misfortune was a bond between us, and out of compassion she wanted to help me complete my research.

Whatever tangle of motives might have underlain these sentiments, Yongsu's Mother was an eternally cooperative informant, perceptive, articulate, and with a knack for rendering even her most complex explanations into clear, simple Korean syntax. These are, of course, attributes of a successful *mansin,* particularly one who must deal with young town matrons unfamiliar with the lore of gods and ghosts. She was also a warm-hearted friend, who coached me in etiquette, advised me on the sort of man I should marry, and once shoved a packet of medicine from the pharmacy down my throat when I was sick.

I had originally assumed that most of a *mansin*'s cases would come from her own village, that my residence in a rural community would provide an intimate day-to-day knowledge of clients, their households, and relations between households, kin, and neighbors. I soon found that a *mansin*'s sphere is far more wide-ranging than a single village. Many of Yongsu's Mother's clients came from Righteous Town, a sizeable number of regular clients *(tan'gol)* came from the next district, near Yongsu's Mother's former home. Five other *mansin* in the area frequently asked Yongsu's Mother to assist them in performing *kut.* I traveled with Yongsu's Mother down the road to *kut* in country villages, up the road to houses in the narrow alleys of Righteous Town, to a public shrine in Seoul, and by subway to a burgeoning urban center south of the capital. My observations and interviews necessarily came from a variety of far-flung sources.

First, I spent many hours in Yongsu's Mother's house observing divinations and minor ceremonies and traveled with her when she performed *kut.* When she wasn't busy, I would ask Yongsu's Mother long lists of questions based on what I had seen. Her explication of a particular spirit or cosmological concept called forth accounts of other clients or people she had known in the past, illustrations of the dire consequences of supernatural manifestations or the efficacy of an appropriate ritual cure. As *mansin,* she would use this same anecdotal approach when explaining a diagnosis to a client. Her "case material" helped me sort out the relationships between perceived supernatural causation, social manifestation, and ritual resolution. At Yongsu's Mother's house, I also interviewed her clients and followed their cases through repeated visits.

Another source was my contact with village women. I asked them about the ritual traditions of their households and about their own experiences with divination, exorcism, and *kut.* Some of these women were Yongsu's Mother's clients; many were not. A few were Christian; some others claimed that they had no dealings with *mansin* and "superstition." Some claimed that they had broken a relationship with a *mansin;* others claimed that they had recently established a relationship with a *mansin.*

Finally, there were the occasional invitations to *kut* performed by other *mansin* in the area. I also witnessed *kut* characteristic of other geographic regions in Seoul and on short trips to other parts of the peninsula, and read descriptions of other regional traditions. This remains, however, a study of women's beliefs and practices as I observed them in and around Enduring Pine Village and not a definitive statement of Korean shamanism throughout the peninsula.

I may be faulted for my heavy reliance on the perceptions and explanations of one *mansin,* albeit balanced by outside interviews and my own experience and observations as participant observer. I opted for the advantages of close cooperation with one *mansin* and the chance to move within her realm, to explore it on its own terms. My friendship with Yongsu's Mother implied loyalty, symbolized by the gradual process whereby I assumed the ritual responsibilities of a client, establishing a special relationship with the "grandmothers and grandfathers," the gods of Yongsu's Mother's shrine.

I used the *mugam* at *kut* and eventually dedicated a robe to my personal spirit. I made offerings at Yongsu's Mother's shrine in the seventh lunar month and at the lunar New Year. I sponsored a *kut* to enlist the spirits' aid in my pursuit of a degree, worshipped at the Tutelary God's shrine, and made a mountain pilgrimage. When I left the village, I made a final offering to the grandmothers and grandfathers of Yongsu's Mother's shrine. When they possessed her and spoke to me, the Buddhist Sage Grandmother cried.

FOUR

Divine Connections:
The *Mansin* and Her Clients

This order is recruited from among hysterical and silly girls
as well as from women who go into it for a livelihood or for
baser reasons.
                    H. N. Allen, *Some Korean Customs*

The magistrate said, "Alas! I thought *mutangs* were a
brood of liars, but now I know that there are true *mutangs*
as well as false." He gave her rich rewards, sent her away in
safety, recalled his order against witches, and refrained
from any matters pertaining to them for ever after.
                    Im Bang, from "The Honest Witch"

The *mansin*'s house is much like any other country residence. She
hangs no sign outside. Women seek out the *mansin*'s house by word of
mouth or on the recommendation of kinswomen or neighbors. Once
inside, a client makes herself comfortable, sitting on the heated floor.
She should feel at home in the *mansin*'s inner room, for the place
resembles her own. The room where Yongsu's Mother divines could
be the main room of any prosperous village home, crammed with the
stuff of everyday life. Here are cabinets full of clothes and dishes, a
dressing table with a neatly arranged collection of bottled cosmetics,
an electric rice warmer, and a television set decorated with an assortment of rubber dolls and pink furry puppies.

The Gods and Their Shrine

Yongsu's Mother's shrine, tucked away behind the sliding doors of the
one spare room, resembles a rural temple. Gilt-plaster Buddha statues
sit on the front altar. Bright printed portraits of Yongsu's Mother's
gods hang on the walls. Incense burners, brass candleholders, alumi-
num fruit plates, water bowls, and stemmed offering vessels clutter the
main and side altars. Each utensil and the three brass bells above the
altar all bear the engraved phrase "Grant the wish of," followed by the

name of the client. These are clients' gifts. The *mansin* advises a client to secure a particular god's good offices with appropriate tribute. One incense burner and water bowl bear my name. Yongsu's Mother told me, with some embarrassment, that the Buddhist Sage and the Mountain God requested gifts since I was doing my research through their will. She told a soldier's wife worried about her husband's fidelity and a young wife worried about her husband's job prospects to dedicate brass bells. She told another young wife to dedicate a water bowl because the Mountain God has helped her husband. Other clients gave the *mansin* her drum and battle trident, her cymbals and knives, her robes and hats, all the equipment she uses to perform *kut*. She stores this equipment out of sight under the altar. Like the shrine fittings, each of these accoutrements bears a client's name. A shrine littered with bells, water vessels, and incense pots advertises a successful *mansin*. In the early morning the *mansin* burns incense, lights candles, and offers cold water inside the shrine. Clients leave incense and candles, and the *mansin* echoes their requests in her own prayers.

A *mansin*'s shrine is called a god hall *(sindang)* or hall of the law *(pŏptang)*, a Buddhist term. In casual conversation Yongsu's Mother calls her shrine the grandfathers' room *(harabŏjiŭi pang)*. When I first visited her, I mistook the unmarked plural and thought she was renting a spare room to an older man. "Grandmother" and "grandfather" are honorific, but not excessively formal, terms. In Korea all old men and all old women, by virtue of the status white hair confers, are politely addressed as grandfather and grandmother. Gods also carry a faint connotation of kinship. Although both power and position set gods *(sillyŏng)* above ancestors *(chosang)*, some gods, like the Chŏns' Great Spirit Grandmother, are also known ancestors. They are grandfathers and grandmothers writ large. Whether venerable distant kin or generalized venerable elders, Yongsu's Mother owes her gods respect and good treatment. Her gods are not distant, awesome beings; with a common term of address, she brings them close. She dreads their anger and anticipates their will, but she also expects them to help her, as a Korean child looks to a grandparent for small indulgences.

Standing before the gods in her shrine, Yongsu's Mother assumes the self-consciously comic pose of a young child, head slightly bowed, eyes wide with pleading. Speaking in a high, soft voice, she says, "Grandfather, please give me some money. I'm going to the market." She takes a bill from the altar and stuffs it into her coin purse. "I'll be right back," and she brings her hands together and nods her head in a quick bow.

Yongsu's Mother originally kept her gods in a narrow storage alcove off the porch and rented her spare room. She began to suspect that the gods disliked the alcove when she, her son, and her roomers' child were all sick at the same time in the middle of winter. One night her dead husband appeared in a dream. He boldly marched into the spare room while its occupants were in Seoul. Yongsu's Mother yelled at him, "You can't go in there when people are away. They'll think you're going to take something." Her husband answered, "This is my room. I'll give you the rent money." Yongsu's Mother continued to quarrel with her husband until she woke up.

The very next day, her roomers announced that they were moving to Seoul. Someone else wanted to rent the room immediately, but Yongsu's Mother said that she would have to think about it. That night she dreamed that all of the grandmothers and grandfathers in her shrine left the alcove and followed Yongsu's Father into the spare room, calling as they passed, "We'll give you the rent money, we'll give you the rent money."

She told her dream to the Chatterbox Mansin who agreed that Yongsu's Mother must make the spare room into a shrine. Thereafter, she prospered as a *mansin*. Her grandmothers and grandfathers gave her the rent money.

This incident is typical of Yongsu's Mother's ongoing tug-of-war with her grandmothers and grandfathers. Her gods do well by her, but they are even more demanding than her clients' gods. She intended to give a *kut* every three years for their pleasure, but after a prosperous early spring, they made her ill to let her know that they wanted an annual *kut*. The next year, in the fall, she gave the grandmothers and grandfathers special feast food (*yŏt'am*) before her stepdaughter's wedding. The gods were angry because she hit the hourglass drum and roused them but did not give them a *kut*. Her luck was bad for several months. She purchased fabric to make new robes for the General and the Warrior, and gave another *kut* the following spring.

Like many children from Enduring Pine Village, her son Yongsu goes to the private Christian middle school in Righteous Town. The fees at the school are minimal and admissions relatively open, but pressure to convert is high. The gods in the shrine do not like Yongsu's daily brush with Christianity. They make his thoughts wander in school. He says he feels an urge to rush home. Yongsu's Mother told the principal that Yongsu's family had "honored Buddha from long ago," and asked him to understand that Yongsu cannot become a Christian. Then she went to her shrine, hit the cymbals, and implored her grandmothers and grandfathers: "Please understand, please forgive. Yongsu has to get an education. Let him go to that place until he's gotten his education."

The Descent of the Gods

A *mansin* engages in a battle of wills with the gods from the very beginning of her career. A woman is expected to resist her calling and struggle against the inevitable, but village women say that those who resist the will of the gods to the very end die raving lunatics. Strange, wild behavior marks a destined *mansin*. Yongsu's Mother describes the struggle:

> They don't know what they're doing. They yell, "Let's go, let's go!" and go running out somewhere. They snatch food from the kitchen and run out into the road with it. God-descended people swipe things and run away. They strike at people and shout insults.
>
> If I were a god-descended person and my husband were hitting me and calling me crazy woman, I'd shout back at him, "You bastard! Don't you know who I am, you bastard?" That's what the Clear Spring Mansin did. Then she sat beside the road talking to the chickens. So funny!

The destined *mansin*, or god-descended person *(naerin saram)*, can experience a variety of symptoms. According to Yongsu's Mother,

> It's very difficult for them. They're sick and they stay sick, even though they take medicine. And there are people who get better even without taking medicine. There are some who can't eat the least bit of food; they just go hungry. There are some who sleep with their eyes open, and some who can't sleep at all. They're very weak but they get well as soon as the gods descend in the initiation *kut*. For some people the gods descend gently, but for others the gods don't descend gently at all. So they run around like crazy women.

Although the destined *mansin* acts like a "crazy woman," Yongsu's Mother makes a distinction between the god-descended person *(naerin saram)* and someone struck temporarily insane *(mich'ida)* by angry household gods or ancestors. "You just have to see them to tell the difference. Insane people look like they're in pain somewhere. The god-descended person wanders here and there singing out, 'I'm this god, I'm that god.' " The *mansin* exorcise insane people as swiftly as possible in a healing *kut* for fear that the possessing spirits will torment their victims to death. The *mansin* flourish knives and flaming torches, threatening, cajoling, and pleading with the offending spirits, urging them to depart (Kendall 1977a). In the initiation *kut* for a god-descended person *(naerim kut),* the initiating *mansin* invites the gods to complete their descent and allow their chosen one to dance and sing as a *mansin.*

A woman often endures considerable anguish before her initiation. The Chatterbox Mansin's story is typical. She was a young matron when the gods descended, a first son's wife living with her mother-in-law. She had already produced two healthy sons. Her husband was away in the air force when she began to exhibit bizarre behavior. She would wander about, talking in a distracted fashion. Worried, her mother-in-law sent for Chatterbox's sister, but when the sister arrived, Chatterbox was sitting in the main room, calmly sewing. She said that every night an old woman—a grandmother—came and asked her to go wandering about with her.

Her sister thought that if Chatterbox was normal enough in the daytime and only behaved strangely at night, she would be all right soon enough. But a few days later, Chatterbox came back to her natal home, clapping her hands together and shrieking like a lunatic. She looked like a beggar woman in torn clothes. Her hair was a tangled mass down her back and her face was filthy. When her mother-in-law came to take her back home, she just sat on the porch and screamed. They tried to pull her up, but her legs stuck fast to the wooden boards of the porch. She asked for some water and poured it all over her body. That night she wandered away. She went into a house and stole a Buddha statue. When her family asked her why she did this, she said, "I was told to do it." For two weeks she went about clapping her hands and pilfering small objects. Then she disappeared completely.

Her family thought she was dead. Much later they heard that she had become the apprentice spirit daughter of the Boil-face Mansin, a great shaman *(k'ŭn mudang)* in the next county. The Boil-face Mansin had taken her in, initiated her, and was training her to perform *kut.* Over the years she learned chants, dances, and ritual lore.

During Chatterbox's distracted wanderings her mother-in-law began divorce proceedings. The woman never lived with her husband again and was forbidden to see her children. But when sorrow overwhelmed her, she would go to the school and, from a safe distance, watch her sons playing in the school yard. A quarrel with his stepmother prompted the oldest son to search out Chatterbox in the countryside. After the boy's flight her sons visited her every summer.

Chatterbox prospered as a *mansin* and built up her own clientele. She broke with her spirit mother after a bitter fight, claiming the shaman overworked and underpaid her. Today, some twenty years after the gods' initial descent, no trace of the haunted young matron remains. Well dressed in Western-style clothing, Chatterbox walks through the streets of the county seat where she has just purchased a new house. Today people in the area consider her a "great shaman" and her own spirit daughter accuses her of stinginess.

By her own admission, Yongsu's Mother had an easy experience as a god-descended person. Widowed after only two years of marriage, she was left with two stepchildren and her own small son. She worked as a peddler, one of a limited number of occupations open to a woman who must support a family. At the end of the mourning period, she went to a *kut* at Chatterbox's shrine.

During an interlude in the *kut,* women danced the *mugam* in the Chatterbox Mansin's costumes to amuse their personal guardian gods and bring luck to their families. The Chatterbox Mansin told Yongsu's Mother to use the *mugam* and dance for success in her precarious business ventures. As Yongsu's Mother remembers it,

> I said, "What do you mean 'use the *mugam?*' It's shameful for me to dance like that." But the Chatterbox Mansin kept saying, "It'll give you luck. You'll be lucky if you dance." So I put on the clothes and right away began to dance wildly. I ran into the shrine, still dancing, and grabbed the Spirit Warrior's flags. I started shouting, "I'm the Spirit Warrior of the Five Directions," and demanded money. All of the women gave me money. I ran all the way home. My heart was thumping wildly. I just wanted to die like a crazy woman. We talked about it this way and that way and decided there was no way out. So the next year I was initiated as a *mansin.*

Although Yongsu's Mother's possession was sudden and unique in its relative painlessness, there had been suggestions throughout her life that she would become a *mansin*.[1] In her early teens during the Korean War, she was fingered as a member of a right-wing youth organization and arrested by North Korean soldiers just before their retreat. Taken on the march north, she made a bold escape on the same night that the Mountain God appeared to her in a dream and said, "It's already getting late."

In late adolescence she had frightening hallucinations. The little Buddha statue a friend brought her from Japan burst into flames in the middle of the room. She watched her mother's face turn into a tiger's face. She wandered about at night, drawn to the stone Buddha near a neighborhood temple. Her mother held a healing *kut*. During the *kut* the girl fell asleep. A white-haired couple appeared and gave her a bowl of medicinal water to drink. When she woke up, she told her dream to the *mansin,* who was pleased. The *mansin* asked her to become her spirit daughter and be initiated as a *mansin,* but she and her mother refused.

Years later, on her wedding night, her sister-in-law dreamed that the new bride was sitting in the inner room hitting a drum. Overhead, on a rope line, hung all of the gods' clothes, as if a *kut* were in progress. Later, when her husband was fatally ill, Yongsu's Mother went to a *mansin*'s shrine for an exorcism. She set out her offerings and the *mansin* began to chant, but when Yongsu's Mother went to raise her arms over her head and bow to the ground, her arms stuck to her sides as if someone were holding them down. She could not budge them. It was destined that her husband would die and she would become a *mansin*. There was nothing she could do about it.

Yongsu's Mother was a young widow awash in economic difficulties when the gods descended. The Chatterbox Mansin was separated from her husband but living with her mother-in-law, the woman who would later insist on divorce. I am reluctant to speculate on the two initiates' subconscious motivations, but Harvey (1979, 1980) suggests that severe role stress propels women like the Chatterbox Mansin and Yongsu's Mother into god-descended behavior. It is true that, as *mansin,* such women stand above the social and economic constraints imposed on a proper Korean wife, and as *mansin,* they wear the gods' costumes and speak with the gods' authority. But whatever personal and economic gratification she enjoys, the *mansin* and her family pay a price. Shamans were listed, under the occupational classification system of the Yi dynasty, among the despised "mean people" *(ch'ŏnmin)* along with butchers, fortune-tellers, roving players, monks, and female entertainers. According to one early missionary, "Sometimes the daughter of a genteel family may become a Mootang, though this is rare, as her people would rather kill her than have her madness take this form" (Allen 1896, 164).

Like the female entertainer, the *kisaeng,* the shaman engages in public display, singing and dancing. An element of ambiguous sexuality wafts about the *mansin*'s performance. In folklore and literature *mudang* are portrayed as "lewd women," and so they are often perceived (Wilson 1983). The *mansin* Cho Yŏng-ja told Ch'oe and Chang that the county chief had come to her home on the pretext of having his fortune told and had then insisted on sleeping with her. Disgusted, she contrived an escape. Thereafter all was coldness between the *mansin* and the county chief (Ch'oe and Chang 1967, 32–33).

The *mansin* play to their female audience, but when the supernatural Official sells "lucky wine," the costumed *mansin* roams through the house seeking male customers. The men have been drinking by themselves in a corner of the house, as far removed from the *kut* as possible. Now they emerge, red faced, and the bolder of their company dance a few steps on the porch. Men buy the Official's wine and tease the *mansin,* flourishing their bills in front of her face before securing the money in her chestband. An audacious man may try to tweak the *mansin*'s breast as he secures his bill.

The *mansin* is caught at cross purposes. By her coy, flirtatious performance, she encourages the men to spend more money on wine. But as a woman alone, she must defend herself from harassment and protect her reputation. Yongsu's Mother was resourceful.

> It doesn't happen so much anymore, but when I first started going to *kut,* men would bother me. We were doing a *kut* at a house way out in the country, and I was going around selling the Official's wine. Some son-of-a-bitch grabbed my breast. I put out my hand so the drummer would go faster, then brought my arms up quick to start dancing. I knocked that guy against the wall. Afterwards, he asked me, "What did you mean by that?" I said, "Oh, that wasn't me, it was the honorable Official who did that." Other times, I'd be drumming and some guy would say, "Auntie, where is Uncle? What is Uncle doing now?" and go on like that. I'd reach out to beat the drum faster and slap the guy with the drumstick.

At the *kut* for the dead, performed outside the house gate, men gather off to the side. They gaze at the *mansin* garbed like a princess who sings the long ballad tale of Princess Pari, rapping the drum with elegant flicks of her wrist. My landlady told me of a famous *mansin,* now aged, who was once a beauty. "When she did the *kut* for the dead, it would take forever. This one would carry her off on his back, and that one would embrace her."

To the exemplar of Confucian virtue, the *mansin* offends simply because she dances in public. When an officer from the district police station tried to stop a *kut* in Enduring Pine Village, he threatened to arrest the *mansin* because "they were dancing to drum music and students were watching." The moral education of the young was thereby imperiled. An envelope of "cigarette money" finally silenced this paragon.

It would be a distortion to paint the *mansin* I knew in northern Kyŏnggi Province as social pariahs. Since she has no husband, Yongsu's Mother's house is a favorite gathering place for village women. In their leisure moments they drop by to chat about the latest school fee, the inept village watch system, the new neighborhood loan association, or simply to gossip. Even the wife of the progressive village chief, though she disdains "superstition," seeks out the company of the articulate, loquacious *mansin*. Yongsu's Mother is a favorite guest at birthday parties. She gets the singing started and makes people laugh. She can sometimes be persuaded to bring her drum so the women can dance.

But Yongsu's Mother lives under the shadow of potential insult. Village people say, "Not so many years ago, even a child could use blunt speech [*panmal*] to a shaman."[2] Although this is no longer true, when tempers flare Yongsu's Mother's occupation is still flung in her face. Yongsu's Mother and the widowed Mr. Yun were great friends. Village gossips expected them to marry. Mr. Yun's daughter-in-law rankled at the possibility. She finally exploded in a fit of rage, shrieking at Yongsu's Mother, "Don't come into my house! I don't want a shaman to come into my house! It's bad luck if a shaman comes into your house." Pride wounded to the quick, Yongsu's Mother avoided the Yun family and there was no more talk of marriage.

After her stepdaughter's marriage Youngsu's Mother was anxious lest the groom discover her occupation. She did only one hasty New Year Rite for a client on the second day of the New Year since she expected a visit from the newlyweds on that day. She dreaded the thought of them walking in and catching her banging her cymbals in the shrine.

The Chatterbox Mansin's sister-in-law found her own children dancing in time to the drum rhythm during a *kut*. She slapped them soundly, then howled at her miserable fortune to have married into a shaman's house. Since this was all in the family, and the Chatterbox Mansin is never at a loss for words, whatever the circumstance, she snapped back, "Well then, you knew this was a shaman's house. You didn't have to marry my brother and come to live here."

The *mansin* shares in the ambiguous status of other glamorous but morally dubious female marginals, the actress, the female entertainer, and the prostitute. Like the others, she makes a living, often a comfortable living, by public performance in a society where so-called good women stay home. But the *mansin* is neither an actress nor a courtesan. She is the ritual specialist of housewives. The good women who stay home need her. She came from their midst, lives like them, and speaks to their anxieties and hopes.

The gods who have claimed a woman as a *mansin* leave her one lingering shred of respectability. It is well known that only by virtue of divine calling is she a shaman, and that is a compulsion fatal to resist.[3] Her neighbors assume that she did not want to become a *mansin*. She tells her story to clients, describes how she resisted the call with the last ounce of her strength and succumbed only after considerable suffering and in fear for her very life.

Like most respectable matrons, Yongsu's Mother had to be coaxed even to dance the *mugam* at a *kut*. She thought abandoned public dancing was shameful. Yet once she put on the *mansin*'s costume, instead of simply dancing to exhaustion like the other women, her gods descended. There was nothing to be done. After years of avoiding the warnings, Yongsu's Mother had to become a *mansin*.

The shaman also suffers the onus of charlatanry and greed. The *mansin* makes her living by interpreting the gods' will and manifesting their presence. Divine ultimatums fill her pockets with cash. Much of a *kut*'s comedy revolves around the tug-of-war between greedy, extortionate gods who demand more and more money and the housewife who stubbornly resists, argues, and then grudgingly capitulates. The gods peer into pockets and lift skirts, looking for cash. The women shout that they have spent everything. Then, giggling, they run and hide inside the house, only to reemerge, pockets bulging with more bills for another round with the greedy gods.

This is play and the rules are understood. In northern Kyŏnggi Province the *mansin* and her client settle the price of the *kut* far in

advance, and the client brings the money in a bundle to the *mansin*'s
shrine a few days before the *kut*. On the day of the *kut* the *mansin*
retains a basic fee in a cloth bag tied to the drum. She returns the rest
of the money to the housewife, who doles it out throughout the *kut,*
paying off the eternally demanding gods and ancestors. When the
housewife does not enter into the combative spirit of the event, the
mansin say the *kut* "tastes flat." Yongsu's Mother told me with disgust,
"We did a *kut* in Tranquil Spring the other day, and the lady of the
house didn't even know as much as you, Tallae. We'd ask her for
money and she'd just hand the bill over with a blank expression on her
face."

Still, the *mansin*'s ceremonies cost money. A *kut* takes a significant
lump of the family's budget, equivalent to a child's hundred-day party
or a first-year birthday, occasions when the family provides an elaborate breakfast and wine for a vast array of neighbors and kin. By
divine authority the *mansin* urges the family to spend money on exorcisms, shrine prayers, and *kut*. She advises them to dedicate robes,
brass bells, knives, and musical instruments for demanding gods.
There's the rub. The possibility of divine possession coexists with the
potential for fakery, especially when the gods' demands enhance the
shaman's income and prestige. The *mansin* must make a living, but
she knows that she cannot push her clients too far. Her gods are
demanding, but the *mansin* fears for her own image. Yongsu's Mother
tries to disassociate herself from the greedy gods she serves. She gives
back a portion of the fruits and candies her clients bring to the shrine.
She stuffs money for a treat of wine into the pocket of a household
patriarch to stifle potential grumbles over the cost of a *kut*. She complains,

> Sometimes I hate all my grandfathers. They should cherish the unfor-
> tunate but instead they scorn them. When someone is poor, I tell them to
> come to the shrine for a ritual and bring only a small offering. I tell them
> it's all right. Then I go to the grandfathers' room. When the grandfathers
> speak they say, "What's this? This person has set down so little," and yell
> at them. It goes against my own feelings to talk like that, but I can't do
> anything about it. It's the grandfathers who make me say those things.

The false and greedy *mudang* is a common butt of satire in both folk
literature and in contemporary Korean television dramas. Gale's

translation of the seventeenth-century literati tale "The Honest Witch" provides a unique twist. A reforming magistrate issues a ban, on pain of death, against the activities of all false *mudang* under his jurisdiction. One plucky *mudang* challenges him, claiming that his decree only applies to "false *mudang*." She demonstrates the veracity of her profession by summoning the magistrate's deceased friend who, speaking through the *mudang,* recalls intimate details of their past friendship. The magistrate, convinced, rewards the *mudang* and withdraws his decree (Gale [1913] 1963, 125–129). This magistrate is akin to some cosmopolitan Koreans who have confessed to me that although they had never before believed, they were confounded by a dead kinsman's appearance in a *kut*.

If the women of Enduring Pine Village accept that there are real shamans, they also assume that charlatans and sloppy performers gather where there is money to be made. The *mansin* level accusations among themselves and the village women make their own evaluations. The dramatic descent of the gods and the god-descended woman's tor- ✓ tuous resistance enhance the individual *mansin*'s legitimacy. Although shamanism is one of few potentially lucrative women's occupations, the woman who willingly or easily becomes a shaman would be suspect. Her extreme reluctance and suffering testify to those who will judge her that her calling is sincere and her gods are strong.

Initiation and Training

When the *mansin* do an initiation *kut (naerim kut),* they dress the initiate in costumes for all of the gods of *kut,* segment by segment. A *mansin* stands beside the initiate and implores the gods to descend. The drum throbs. The initiate dances wildly, shouting out the gods' presence as they possess her. "I'm the Mountain God Buddhist Sage, the Monk Buddhist Sage, I'm Buddhist Sage Maitreya," or in the Spirit Warrior's garb, "I'm the Spirit Warrior Who Rides the White Horse, the Spirit Warrior Archer, the Honorable Buddha Spirit Warrior . . ." *Mansin* scrawl long lists of deities as the initiate chants them. They hang the strips of paper on the walls to show the new *mansin* the myriad deities in her pantheon, the gods she can summon to *kut*.

The one initiation *kut* I observed was, in the *mansin*'s view, a fizzle. The gods never completed their descent into the initiate, they just "came and went." The *mansin* dressed the god-descended woman in the Buddhist Sage's costume and prayed. The initiate started to dance, grabbed the Spirit Warrior's colored flags, and stood on the water jar. From the water jar she told Yongsu's Mother that she had a message for her; the gods said that Yongsu's Mother was heavy-hearted because she had gone up a sacred mountain with her querulous sister. After this half-hearted effort at divining, the god-descended woman gave up, removed the costume, and the *mansin* continued the *kut* themselves.

This was the Clear Spring Mansin's second attempt at initiating this same god-descended woman. A *kut* the year before had also failed. Yongsu's Mother thought the effort and expense were premature. The gods were not ready to descend. Yongsu's Mother contrasted this woman's failure to the performance of a properly god-descended initiate.

> She should have been dancing like crazy. Descended people wave their arms and dance whenever they hear the hourglass drum. They shout out, "I'm this god, I'm that god." She should have said things like, "You're filthy with menstruation, why have you come here? Ugh, dirty person from a house of mourning!" but she didn't say anything like that. She might have said, "Here's woman who fights with her husband," but she didn't. And she carried the Spirit Warrior's flags when she was the Buddhist Sage. She shouldn't do that. The Spirit Warrior Buddhist Sage comes later. She told me I went to the mountain with my sister. What's the big deal about that? She could have heard about that from the Clear Spring Mansin. It wasn't the Buddhist Sage descending. Some ancestral grandmother [*chosang halmŏni*] in the house just rose up, that was all.

The ancestral grandmother rose up as a Body-governing God, a minor deity who might possess anyone. The initiate's behavior resembled an ordinary woman dancing *mugam* at *kut*, not a professional *mansin*.

After a successful initiation *kut* the *mansin* can invoke at will the visions the gods send her. She can now divine with coins and grains of rice. Three days after Yongsu's Mother's initiation *kut,* a woman came to her for a divination. Yongsu's Mother was so ill-prepared for her new role that she had to run to a kinswoman's house and borrow a tray for the divination rice and coins. Thereafter, clients kept appearing at her door. While her peddling business dribbled away to nothing,

Yongsu's Mother began to derive a satisfactory income from divinations.

When women hear of a new *mansin*, they come to her shrine out of curiosity. Some, struck by the clarity of her diagnosis and the success of her ritual advice, remain her regular clients. Others, their curiosity satisfied, stay with their own regular *mansin* or continue to shop around. Yongsu's Mother described the hectic first New Year season after she became a *mansin*. "The house was jammed with people. Everyone wanted to have their fortune told. I didn't eat. I couldn't even go outside to piss. I got weak, and that spring I was sick for a long time."

The initiated *mansin* still has much to learn. She must master the long invocations, songs, and procedures of *kut*. The *mansin* who initiated her, her spirit mother *(sinŏmŏni)*, brings her to *kut* where she hits the cymbals, sets up food offerings, and receives a few thousand won for her trouble. The new *mansin* invites more experienced *mansin* when her own clients hold a *kut*, but here she claims several measures of rice grain and more than a token share of the take.

A *mansin* begins manifesting the gods at *kut* by performing the Birth Grandmother and the Buddhist Sage. Okkyŏng's Mother, three years after her initiation, still has trouble with these relatively simple segments. She forgets to pick up a fan, misses whole portions of an invocation, or uses incomprehensible words from the dialect of her native Kyŏngsang Province.

After mastering the Buddhist-inspired spirits, a *mansin* manifests the Official and House Site Official, and gradually gains confidence, eventually summoning all of the gods of all the segments of *kut*. I have seen only the oldest and most experienced *mansin*—the Chatterbox Mansin, the Clear Spring Mansin, and the Bell Mansin—perform the long drum song to expel pollutions and invite the gods into the house. At the time I left the field, Yongsu's Mother was trying to learn the Death Messenger's "Song of Lament" (Hoesimgok) from a paperbound book of shaman songs. If she could invoke and be possessed by the Death Messenger, she would be much in demand when *mansin* organize *kut* to send off dead souls.

A *mansin* develops her performing arts with practice, and she does homework. Her spirit mother instructs her and has her watch several *kut* before pressing her to do more than hit the cymbals. Yongsu's Mother likened this learning process to my own slowly expanding knowledge of *kut*. But the *mansin* consider their skilled performance a blend of talent, effort, and divine will. Yongsu's Mother told me, "When I started going to *kut*, I thought 'How can I do all that? Won't I be embarrassed to stand up in front of everyone?' But the grandfathers told me, 'This is the right way, do this next.' "

Ultimately a *mansin* masters a particular skill only through the will of her grandfathers. Yongsu's Mother sat at home practicing the *kut* drum rhythm over and over, and often threw down her drumstick in frustration. One night she heard the right rhythm in a dream. She was a strong drummer from then on. A *mansin* must not claim divine assistance prematurely. Okkyŏng's Mother installed an image of the Buddhist Sage in her shrine before she received any indication in her dreams that she should do so. Her luck was bad. Clients did not come to her home for divinations. She quarreled with her parents-in-law, who went back to the country. Her husband had to look for a new job. On Yongsu's Mother's advice, Okkyŏng's Mother removed the image from her shrine and kept only a paper marker bearing the god's name.

Some *mansin* acquire additional gods and talents later in their careers. When Yongsu's Mother first became a *mansin*, the Clear Spring Mansin had been shamanizing for over ten years, but she was still poor and lived in a rented shack. Once when the Clear Spring Mansin was ill, she asked Yongsu's Mother to perform an exorcism. During the exorcism, Yongsu's Mother saw the Clear Spring Mansin's dead father as the Twelfth Spirit Warrior in her pantheon. In life the father had been a doctor of Chinese medicine, skilled in herbalogy and acupuncture. As the Twelfth Spirit Warrior, he is the special patron of acupuncture in his daughter's pantheon. After learning of her own father's divine influence, the Clear Spring Mansin kept a special image of the Twelfth Spirit Warrior in her shrine. Yongsu's Mother attributes the Clear Spring Mansin's current prosperity to the powerful Spirit Warrior. Through her physician father's divine influence, the Clear Spring Mansin can read pulses, although she has had no special training.

Because she originally divined his presence, the Twelfth Spirit Warrior "plays well" when he possesses Yongsu's Mother in *kut* at the Clear Spring Mansin's shrine. She claims that he is fond of her, but he also makes demands. At the Clear Spring Mansin's *kut*, Yongsu's Mother drank some expensive wine and almost immediately felt severe stomach pains. Although she felt terrible, the other *mansin* insisted that she perform the sequence for the House Site Official. When she stood up to manifest the House Site Official, the Twelfth Spirit Warrior appeared out of sequence instead. He scolded her for not offering him wine before drinking some herself. Yongsu's Mother's pain was punishment but also an acknowledgement of a relationship, a public reminder of the Clear Spring Mansin's debt to her younger colleague. Yongsu's Mother's stomach pains stopped immediately after she purchased wine for the Spirit Warrior and asked his forgiveness.

Mansin Teams at Kut

As a *mansin* gains experience, her reputation for performing *kut* grows, and other *mansin* include her in their teams when they do *kut*. I have seen a minimum of three *mansin* perform cheap, quick *kut* in crowded rented rooms. Six *mansin* performed a *kut* to dispatch a dead bachelor's restless soul and cure his cousin's debilitating headaches. The family spared no expense, the house was full of guests, and the final send-off of dead souls lasted until the late afternoon of the second day.

A *mansin* makes from ten to fifteen thousand won per *kut*. The number of invitations she receives from other *mansin* depends on her known skill and her ability to work well with other *mansin*. Because the Officials and the Spirit Warrior "play well" with Yongsu's Mother, other *mansin* invite her to perform these exhausting but highly entertaining and lucrative segments at *kut*. The Death Messenger plays well with the Mansin from Within the Wall, so well that her performance scared me. Yongsu's Mother invites the Mansin from Within the Wall when she does a *kut* to send off dead souls.

Kut teams form and reform following subtle rules of reciprocity. One *mansin* invites another, but if the favor is not returned, she invites someone else. If a *mansin* feels that she has not received fair recompence for her efforts at a *kut* organized by another *mansin,* she does not invite her to perform in her own *kut* and is reluctant to participate in future *kut*.

According to Yongsu's Mother, the Chatterbox Mansin is excessively greedy. When she performs the drum song at the start of a *kut,* she always claims the two thousand-won bills the housewife fastens to the drum strings at the start of the song. The money does not go into the common bag tied to the drum. When she does the final send-off, the Chatterbox Mansin also takes that money for herself. She is tight-fisted when she divides the common take among the *mansin* she has invited to a *kut*. Yongsu's Mother says that other *mansin* used to invite the Chatterbox Mansin far and wide to do *kut,* but they avoid her now. But the Chatterbox Mansin is successful in her own career and does not have to depend on the good graces of other *mansin*. She has collected numerous regular clients in her twenty years' practice and claims the grudging loyalty of Okkyŏng's Mother and Yongsu's Mother, the two *mansin* she initiated. Between *kut* for her own clients and *kut* for the other two *mansin*'s clients, she is sufficiently busy and prosperous. During the time I knew her, she moved from Willow Market to a new house she had purchased in Righteous Town.

Yongsu's Mother performed in thirty-five *kut* in the lunar year that began in February 1977. She organized eight of these *kut* herself for her own clients and invited other *mansin* to join her. In the spring she entertained her own shrine gods with a *kut* and asked three other *mansin* to help. She went to eleven of Okkyŏng's Mother's *kut*. The inexperienced *mansin* was enjoying a rush of business in a working-class neighborhood in Tranquil Spring, a new town on Seoul's periphery. The *mansin*'s sister lived in this neighborhood and sent for Okkyŏng's Mother when neighbors, mostly recent migrants, needed divinations.[4] Okkyŏng's Mother, Yongsu's Mother, and the Chatterbox Mansin did many *kut* in the tiny rooms of Tranquil Spring houses.

The Chatterbox Mansin and the Clear Spring Mansin each included Yongsu's Mother in five of their *kut,* and she went to six others organized by a variety of *mansin*. When Yongsu's Mother organizes her own *kut,* she invites the Chatterbox Mansin, the Clear Spring Mansin, and Okkyŏng's Mother. When she does a *kut* to send off dead souls, she invites the Mansin from Within the Wall. Early in the year she was disgusted with Okkyŏng's Mother's novice performance and excluded her from a few *kut*. Okkyŏng's Mother improved and the two women were drawn together by their mutual dissatisfaction with the Chatterbox Mansin. They also shared a lively sense of humor. Giggling like school girls, they would tease each other, "Tallae, when you go back to America, find a nice widower with a big nose for Yongsu's Mother." They asked each other for divinations when they were heavy-hearted, since a *mansin* cannot divine for herself.

In the same year Yongsu's Mother also drew closer to the older Clear Spring Mansin. The Clear Spring Mansin advised her to break with the Chatterbox Mansin and divined that Yongsu's Mother's gods would be happier if she did. Yongsu's Mother performed an exorcism for the Clear Spring Mansin's son when his injured leg would not heal. The Clear Spring Mansin read Yongsu's Mother's pulse when she was ill and recommended an herb doctor. In the same year the Clear Spring Mansin broke with her own spirit daughter in a bitter quarrel that arose when Yongsu's Mother caught the spirit daughter secreting away some of the money she had collected during a *kut*.

The *mansin* teams at *kut* are open and flexible. They form and reform from *kut* to *kut,* and a *mansin* works with a variety of other *mansin* during a year. Yet a *mansin* tends to favor certain of her colleagues out of longtime loyalty or to maintain reciprocity. *Mansin* who work often and well together develop close ties. They divine for each other and summon up each other's gods. But these are also potentially volatile professional relationships, formed around an arbitrary division of cash for services rendered. There is ample ground for jealousy and backbiting.

Women Who Come to the *Mansin's* House

A shaman's divination *(mugŏri)* is the first step in any ritual therapy. Women like Grandmother Chŏn come to the *mansin's* house when they suspect that malevolent forces lurk behind a sudden or persistent illness or domestic strife. In Yongsu's Mother's shrine I heard reports of inflamed lungs, an infected leg, fits of possession "craziness," alchoholism, and dreamy, wandering states of mind. One woman, afflicted with this last complaint, feared that she was god-descended, but Yongsu's Mother laughed off her worries and divined more commonplace godly displeasure as the source of her problems. Other women who came to the shrine worried about their husbands' or sons' career prospects, or about sudden financial reverses. Should the husband switch jobs? Would the son receive his security clearance to work in Saudi Arabia? Thieves had broken into the family rice shop, what did that presage? Other women were anxious that adulterous husbands might abandon them. Some had only the vaguest suspicion that their spouses had "smoked the wind," but one young woman was certain that her husband took the grain his mother sent up from the country and shared it with his mistress. One woman, caught in a compromising position by her enraged spouse, had fled to the *mansin* in fear of life and limb. And still other women asked about wayward children, stepchildren, or grandchildren whose transgressions ranged from mild rebelliousness to Christian zealotry, petty theft, and delinquency. A mother-in-law asked how she should deal with a runaway daughter-in-law. A daughter-in-law who had fled home asked if she should divorce her husband. An older woman wondered if she should join a married son's household (see app. 2).

The *mansin* chats with the women before fetching the divination tray. Sometimes the women begin to discuss their anxieties before the actual divination, but these are usually long-standing clients. Clients who come to the *mansin* for the first time tend to hold back and see how much the *mansin* can uncover in the divination.

The *mansin* brings in the divination tray, an ordinary low tray of the sort used for meals in any Korean home. The tray bears a mound of rice grains, a handful of brass coins (imitations of old Chinese money), and the brass bell rattle a *mansin* uses to summon up her visions.

"Well now, let's see," says the *mansin,* settling down to a kneeling posture behind her tray. The client places a bill under the pile of grain on the tray. At Yongsu's Mother's shrine in 1977 and 1978, this fee was usually five-hundred or a thousand won. Now the *mansin* shakes the brass bells beside her own ear and chants, asking the gods to send "the correct message." She receives a message for each member of the client's family, beginning with the client's husband if he is alive. She announces each subject's name and age to the gods, tosses her coins on the tray, and spills handfuls of rice grains until the Great Spirit Grandmother speaks and sends visions.

Coin and rice configurations hint at the client's concerns. A broad spread of coins bespeaks quarrels between husband and wife or parent and child, or betrays financial loss. A long line of coins broken by one or two solitary coins at the end tells of someone leaving home, a change of employment, a death, or the inauspicious influence of an ancestor who died far from home. A few grains spilled on the floor caution financial prudence; the client should postpone switching jobs or buying a house.

The *mansin* describes a situation and asks for confirmation. "Your husband has a cold or something, is that it?" "Your thirteen-year-old daughter doesn't get along with her father, is that right?" The *mansin* develops the theme, weaving her visions together with her client's information. With more tosses of coins and grain, the Great Spirit Grandmother sends more specific visions. "I see a steep embankment. Is there something like that near your house?" The woman and her neighbor nod affirmation. "Be careful of that place." To another woman, "Your daughter has two suitors. One is quite handsome. The other is extremely clever but also very meticulous. Since your daughter isn't especially clever herself, she'll have a better life if she marries the second suitor, but she must watch her step and scrupulously manage her house."

Sometimes she sights the discontented gods and ancestors of her clients' households. "Is there a distant grandfather in your family who carried a sword and served inside the palace?" "Did someone in your family die far from home and dripping blood?" She circles in on the supernatural source of her client's problems and suggests an appropriate ritual to mollify a greedy god's demands or send a miserable and consequently dangerous soul "away to a good place."

For a housewife to evaluate the skill of an individual *mansin* and trust her diagnosis, she must know the supernatural history of her husband's family and of her own kin. And if the *mansin* is convinced that there was "a grandmother who worshiped Buddha," or "a bride who died in childbirth," she tells her client, "Go home and ask the old people, they know about these things."

A foreigner, I was hopeless as a client. When Yongsu's Mother asked me if I had "an aunt or uncle [*samch'on*] who died young," I wrote home, half hoping to unravel a bit of family history. No such ghost, my mother wrote, "unless one of your grandmothers had a secret life." The *mansin* said, "We don't know how you foreigners do things in America." When I brought a Chinese-American friend for a divination, this same *mansin* acknowledged their affinity as East Sea People (Tongyang Saram), and would not let unclaimed ghosts slip by. Yongsu's Mother asked if there was someone in my friend's family who had died away from home or someone who died in childbirth, an ancestor who was an official perhaps. My friend explained that her father had been kidnapped as a boy in China and raised by foster parents, that he knew nothing at all about his own family. The *mansin* would not accept a dead end. "When you're home for a visit, ask your mother. When the two of you are sitting around chatting, she'll tell you these things." My friend again explained that her mother had already told her all she could about the family. Her father's origins were a mystery. Now the *mansin* grew concerned, appalled that a Chinese mother could send her married daughter off to set up housekeeping in a foreign land without telling her about the family ghosts and ancestors.

Seeing the Year's Luck

During the first two weeks of the lunar year, women crowd the *mansin*'s house to "see the year's luck" *(illyŏn sinsurŭl poda).* The New Year marks a fresh, auspicious start for each household. A woman therefore gets a prognosis on each member of her family. If noxious influences threaten someone in her charge, she can "make them clean" by performing simple rituals under the first full moon.

This is the peasants' winter slack season and the women are in a holiday mood when they come to the *mansin*'s house. Most arrive in groups. Waiting their turn, they bunch together in the hot-floor inner room. If the wait is long, they play cards, doze, or listen to other divinations. They sigh sympathetically for the woman whose divination reveals an adulterous husband, unruly child, or pitiable ghost. They coach the young matron who does not yet know the vocabulary of women's rituals. Not for them, the confidential atmosphere of the Western doctor's or analyst's office. The confessional's anonymity is missing here. The women enjoy each other's stories and accept each other's sympathy.

A woman, as a matter of course, receives divinations for her husband, herself, living parents-in-law, sons, unmarried daughters, sons' wives, and sons' children. Many women, however, pay an extra hundred or two hundred won for the fortunes of those whose ties stretch outside the woman's "family," the family she enters at marriage and represents in the *mansin*'s shrine. Some women ask about a married daughter, her husband, and their children, or about other natal kin. During New Year divinations in 1978, one woman asked about her own mother, brother, and brother's wife, another about her own elder sister. Yongsu's Mother teased, "What do you want to know about them for?" but provided the divinations. Women acknowledge their concern for mothers, married daughters, and siblings, but it costs more, an extra coin or two.

In the New Year divination the *mansin* predicts dangerous and advantageous months, warns against potentially dangerous activities, and suggests preventive ritual action. The following condensation of Yongsu's Mother's New Year divination for a seventy-year-old widow is an example.

My seventy-year-old lady, you shouldn't go on long trips; you must be careful now. Your children will receive succor; someone will come with aid in the seventh or eighth month. You will have some good news in the third or fourth month.

Your thirty-nine-year-old son should not visit anyone who is sick [since in this horoscope year, he is vulnerable to noxious influences]. His thirty-five-year-old wife should be heedful of things other people say about her. Their twelve-year-old son should be exorcised with five-grain rice left at the crossroads and by casting out a scarecrow stuffed with his name [because he has acquired an accretion of noxious influences and his year fate is bad]. The eight-year-old daughter will be lucky but you should burn a string of pine nuts, one for each year of her life, and address the moon on the night of the first full moon.

Your thirty-five-year-old son is troubled with sorrow and regret, but his luck is changing. There is no trouble between husband and wife, nothing to worry about there. Their seven-year-old child has a cold or something. This is a dangerous time for him so they must guard him carefully. Your unmarried thirty-year-old son doesn't even have a girl friend, but next year his prospects will improve. He should marry when he's thirty-two. He'll succeed in life when he's thirty-five or thirty-seven.

The scarecrow, five-grain rice left at the crossroads, and pine nuts burned under the moon are minor rituals performed on the fifteenth day of the lunar year. The first full moon marks the end of the New Year holidays, a time when women immunize a threatened family member, usually a child, against noxious influences lurking in the year's fortune. When the *mansin*'s visions reveal a swarm of noxious influences on the road, a growing splotch of red, she tells the child's mother or grandmother to leave five-grain rice at a crossroads, then wave it over the child's head and cast it out. A mother must warn her child to be especially mindful of traffic. When the *mansin* sees swimming fish, she tells the woman to write the child's name, age, and birthdate on a slip of paper and wrap the paper around a lump of breakfast rice on the morning of the fifteenth. The woman throws the packet into a well or stream saying, "Take it, fish!" She substitutes the rice for a child with a drowning fate.

The *mansin* also cautions that children should not swim, go fishing, or climb mountains in certain months. Here the women sigh, "How can I do that?" The *mansin* tells the housewife which family members, according to the particular vulnerability of their year horoscope, must disdain funerals, feasts, or visits to sick friends. She advises switching a sixty-first birthday celebration to a more auspicious month. She predicts the compatibility of a son's or daughter's lover or a matchmaker's candidate. She determines when "the ancestors are hungry and the gods want to play," and advises these families to hold *kut* early in the new year. The early spring is a busy season for the *mansin*.

In divination sessions a client receives a mingling of ritual information and common-sense advice. A soldier's wife, living in a rented room in Enduring Pine Village, worried about her husband's fidelity. A sympathic neighbor brought her to Yongsu's Mother. The *mansin* suggested she dedicate a brass bell in the shrine for her husband's career success, then lectured her on prettying up and serving tasty food lest home life be as unappealing as "rice cake that's already been chewed on."

A melancholy young woman came to the shrine with her maternal grandmother. The woman had married for love, but now her husband was in America and had not written a letter for several months. In a nightmare the woman had seen her husband in a room full of women. Yongsu's Mother divined that a restless ghost, the husband's unmarried aunt, was disrupting the marriage out of jealousy. Yongsu's Mother exorcised the ghost, then suggested the woman go to her husband's parents in the country. She could cook and clean for them during the spring planting and establish herself as the distant son's acknowledged wife by building up a debt of gratitude in her favor. To the woman caught in adultery, she said bluntly, "Burn incense and light candles in the shrine. Then go home and ask forgiveness. That's all you can do."

A woman goes to the *mansin* with some ambivalence. She assumes the *mansin* will discern a supernatural problem and suggest ritual action. Rituals, be it an inexpensive exorcism or an elaborate *kut,* require cash. Hangil's Mother told me, "I don't go to the *mansin*'s house anymore. They always tell you to do things that cost money, and I can't afford to do that. I'm just like a Christian now, only I don't believe in Jesus." Though some women are cynical, Hangil's Mother is not. She advised me on the rituals I should perform for my own spirits and was almost invariably among the women watching a *kut* in Yongsu's Mother's shrine. A divination is the essential first step in a *mansin*'s treatment, but the whole process may stop here. Whenever Yongsu's Mother counseled a woman to dedicate a brass bell or sponsor a ritual, the client would almost always say, "I'll have to talk it over with my husband," or "I'll have to see what the old people say." At home she weighs the potential benefits against the household budget. A woman told me, "They say we ought to do a *kut* because a grandmother of this house was a great shaman, but it takes too much money." Some women decide to wait and see if their problems will improve over time. There was, for example, the woman who said,

> Years ago, I went to a *mansin* in Righteous Town. Someone told me she was good, so I went to her by myself. My husband was losing money and I felt uneasy. The *mansin* said, "Do a *kut*," but I didn't.

Others are satisfied with the *mansin*'s actions on their behalf:

> I was sick last year. I felt exhausted and my whole body ached. I went to the hospital for treatment and that took a lot of money. . . . After the exorcism I got better.

or:

> We did a *kut* two years ago for my eldest son. He drank too much and had pains in his chest. He took Western medicine, but that didn't work. The Brass Mirror Mansin did a *kut* and he got better, so he didn't have to go to the hospital.

Some of the women were reluctant to attribute a successful cure directly and exclusively to the *mansin*'s efforts. "The *mansin* did an exorcism and my daughter took medicine; she recovered." There are also clients who claim total dissatisfaction with the *mansin*'s cure. Everyone in the Song family's immediate neighborhood knew that the entire household of the minor line became Christian when their heal-

ing *kut* did not cure the son's acute headaches. He recovered slowly
over the next few months. Another woman said that she stopped
believing when she learned that she had cancer of the womb. On the
other side of the ledger was a young woman who, years ago, had
prayed to the Christian god to spare her ailing parents. They died and
she stopped believing. Now she was sponsoring a *kut*. Other women
wonder if the *kut* the *mansin* advised might have saved an afflicted
family member:

> Three years ago, I went to a *mansin* I'd heard was good. I went for my
> husband who was paralyzed. The *mansin* did an exorcism and told us to
> do a *kut*. We didn't do the *kut,* and my husband died.

or:

> My son died when he was sixteen years old. We should have gone to a
> *mansin,* but we didn't. There was something wrong with his thigh. It
> seemed fine from the outside. We couldn't see anything wrong and nei-
> ther did the hospital. We went to the Western hospital and the hospital
> for Chinese medicine.

Some women who delay return later, and some do not. Some
women visit other *mansin* who might confirm the diagnosis or provide
a more impressive divination.[5] There are women who return the next
day and hire Yongsu's Mother to take on their gods, ancestors, and
ghosts. I found the *mansin*'s clients to be neither docile nor passive.
They did not fit the pervasive Korean stereotype of naive country
women cowed by a crafty shaman.

Of the forty-four divination sessions I recorded in my field notes
during the lunar year 1977–1978, twenty women had no reason to
return. They were women who lived far away and were only in the village for brief visits, women who went regularly to other *mansin* and
wanted only a fresh perspective, and women who required only the
year's luck or simple advice with no suggestion of supernatural malaise. Two were recent college graduates, friends of my assistant, who
were curious about their marriage prospects. The *mansin*'s visions
indicated wrathful household gods or restless ancestors and ghosts in
the households of twenty-four women. She told them to sponsor *kut*
or minor rituals, make offerings in the shrine, or dedicate bells or cos-

tumes. How seriously did they take her advice? I can say with certainty that of the twenty-four clients only fourteen had Yongsu's Mother perform additional rituals. She went to exorcise the infant of a fifteenth client, but by the time she reached the house the baby was dying and the family decided it was no use. A few of the nine lost clients may have returned to Yongsu's Mother without my knowledge; the *mansin* may have performed a minor ritual that slipped by me. I suspect that most of these nine women decided against ritual expenses or went on to consult other *mansin*.

Six of the fourteen clients who followed Yongsu's Mother's advice had come to her house for the first time to receive divinations. I saw most of them at the shrine on several occasions thereafter. They appeared on Chilsŏng nal (lunar 7.7), made offerings in the shrine, and stayed to sing and dance in the late afternoon. They also came for New Year divinations and made New Year offerings in the shrine. When Yongsu's Mother held a *kut* for her own gods, these clients attended and bought divinations, drank lucky wine, and danced *mugam*. They have all become *tan'gol*, regular clients, at Yongsu's Mother's shrine.

The *Tan'gol*

The term *tan'gol* means "regular customer." In Seoul people call themselves the *tan'gol* of a particular coffee shop, music parlor, restaurant, or tailor. The *tan'gol*'s face is known and the *tan'gol* receives special treatment. In return the *tan'gol* is loyal and brings in additional customers.

The Rice Shop Auntie was one of the women who became a *tan'gol* in the lunar year 1977–1978. When the Rice Shop Auntie first came to Yongsu's Mother for a divination, Yongsu's Mother threw down the coins with a show of frustration and disgust and scolded her, "You've been going around all day, having your fortune told in seven different places. You've been wasting your money here and there when what you really need is a *kut*." The Rice Shop Auntie confirmed that this was how she had spent the day, her rationale being, "If all seven people say the same thing, then I'll do a *kut*. Otherwise, I won't."[6]

Yongsu's Mother continued her divination. The Rice Shop Auntie claimed that Yongsu's Mother's analysis of her situation was the best she had heard all day. The Rice Shop Auntie had Yongsu's Mother organize a *kut* and thereafter became one of Yongsu's Mother's most enthusiastic clients. After the Rice Shop Auntie's *kut* three of her neighbors came to Yongsu's Mother for divinations. Within the next few months one sponsored a *kut* and two had Yongsu's Mother invoke their household gods *(kosa)*. The Rice Shop Auntie and her friends visit the shrine in a laughing group. Whatever their expressed purpose, their visits always end in a round of wine. They invite Yongsu's Mother to their birthday parties since they are all of an age. The Rice Shop Auntie and her friends are Yongsu's Mother's best *tan'gol*.

The *mansin*'s *tan'gol* enjoys a special relationship not just with the *mansin* but with the grandmothers and grandfathers of her shrine. Yongsu's Mother counts twenty-four women as her *tan'gol,* and every year the number grows. They live in Enduring Pine Village, down the road in Willow Market, in Waterfall Valley, where she used to live, and in Righteous Town. Two of her Waterfall Valley *tan'gol* have moved to Seoul, but they come to her shrine every New Year. *Tan'gol* come to their *mansin*'s house to see the year's luck. They come during the year when they feel heavy-hearted. The *mansin* knows all of the ancestors, ghosts, and gods of her longtime clients' families. A powerful *mansin* dreams of her clients and anticipates their questions before they enter her house.

At the New Year *tan'gol* bathe, put on clean clothes, and carry rice, candles, fruit, and incense to the *mansin*'s shrine for the New Year ritual called Hongsu Megi.[7] The most powerful gods in their households and the most restless ancestors and ghosts appear when the *mansin* invokes them in her shrine. Endangered members of the family can be "made clean" with an exorcism when ghosts and noxious influences are sent away at the end of Hongsu Megi. Finally, the *mansin* burns twists of thin paper, one for each member of the woman's household and one for each member of her married sons' households. The ashes waft high in the air, a good omen.

Tan'gol "sell" children to the Seven Stars when the *mansin* divines that a son or grandson has a short life fate. The client dedicates a length of cloth *(myŏngdari)* with the child's name, birth date, and address. The *mansin* keeps the cloth in the shrine and jokingly calls the child "my son." If the child comes to her house with his mother during the New Year, he bows to the *mansin* as if she were an honored relative. She gives him fruit or candy and tells him to study hard.

Women who have sold their children come to the shrine to worship the Seven Stars on the seventh day of the seventh lunar month in a ritual called Ch'ilsŏng Maji.

When a *mansin* holds a flower-greeting *kut* or a leaf-greeting *kut*—spring or autumn celebrations for her own shrine gods—she invites all her *tan'gol*. She uses all of the equipment the *tan'gol* have provided and wears the robes that bear their names. The *mansin* piles on several layers of robes so that all of the *tan'gol* gods can feast and dance at the *kut*. She displays all of the cloth *myŏngdari* that tie *tan'gol* children to the Seven Stars. When this god appears, the lengths of cloth are wafted through the air to bestow additional blessings on the children.

The *mansin* asks several *tan'gol* to provide some of the food consumed by the living and supernatural revelers at her annual *kut*. At Yongsu's Mother's last flower-greeting *kut* before I left Korea, I supplied several measures of grain for rice cake. I gave because I have an active Body-governing Official and, "All the houses with [active] supernatural Officials are giving rice cake." I also provided a pig's head. Another *tan'gol* contributed an impressive assortment of entrails to feast her own supernatural Official.

Household Traditions and Women's Work

Women go to *mansin*'s shrines and to Buddhist temples as the ritual representatives of their families and households. They sponsor *kut* in the shrine and in their own homes, but never in other houses. Other houses have their own house gods. A bond like an electrical connection links the *mansin*'s house to the housewife's own dwelling. When clients leave after making offerings in the shrine or sponsoring a *kut* there, they give no farewell salutation. The *mansin* carefully reminds new clients of this necessary breach of etiquette, and tells the women to go straight home. A woman brings blessings from the shrine directly to her own house lest they be lost along the way. The woman leaves the shrine without a farewell and enters her own home without a greeting. Salutations mark boundaries and transitions; they are inappropriate here.

Any woman, old or young, married or single, can visit the *mansin*'s house and receive a divination, but the *tan'gol* who make seasonal offerings in the shrine and sponsor *kut* are female households, the senior women in their households. Commensurate with their temporal responsibilities, they come to the shrine on behalf of husbands, children, and retired parents-in-law. Some *tan'gol* are young matrons, but others are grandmothers whose concerns stretch beyond their own households to their married sons' households. They pray on behalf of sons, daughters-in-law, and grandchildren. Sometimes a worried mother brings her own daughter to the *mansin*. Occasionally mothers press their married daughters to hold a *kut* or perform a clandestine conception ritual, and mothers often pay an extra fee to include a married daughter's household in their divinations. A mother's concern for her own daughter might suggest pity for the suffering shared by all women, but it also suggests a mother's assumed ability to aid all of her children, even those who have left the ritual family she represents in the shrine.

My own relationship with Yongsu's Mother and her shrine was anomalous because, though as old as the younger *tan'gol,* I was a single woman. I therefore made offerings in the shrine for my natal family in America. Another anomaly was a young man who came to Yongsu's Mother's shrine for a divination and who subsequently dedicated his own brass bell. He was worried about his job, but his Christian wife refused to consult a *mansin* on his behalf. A neighbor woman and her husband brought him to Youngsu's Mother, everyone giggling a little at the incongruity of a man visiting a *mansin*'s house. It was as though he had cooked his family's evening rice or pickled their winter kimchee. Korean men are not inherently unqualified for these tasks, but it is the women who perform them, save in exceptional circumstances.

In the ideal flow of tradition, a daughter-in-law continues her mother-in-law's relationship with a particular *mansin*. The *mansin*'s spirit daughter inherits the shrine and the old *mansin*'s clients or her clients' daughters-in-law. In practice, the relationship is far more flexible. The daughter-in-law sometimes favors a *mansin* close to her own age over the white-haired *mansin* her mother-in-law patronized. A spirit daughter may not enjoy the rapport her spirit mother had with clients. Some women switch *mansin* when they are dissatisfied with a diagnosis and cure. Other clients, like the Songs who converted to Christianity, stop visiting *mansin* altogether out of disappointment or because of diminishing returns. Other women said they stopped going to the *mansin*'s shrine because their present lives were "free of anxiety" *(uhwani ŏptta)*. Yongsu's Mother said, "When things are fine, people don't do anything. When someone is sick, when they lose money, or when there's trouble with the police, then they do things like Hongsu Megi and *kut*."

New clients come to the *mansin* from a variety of sources. During the New Year a group of neighbor women decide on impulse to have their fortunes told by the nearest *mansin*. Visiting their own families for the holiday, brides take their worries to their mother's *mansin*. Kinswomen and neighbors recommend a particular *mansin*. Neighbor women in a village hamlet or town alleyway know each other's worries. Older women take a maternal interest in young brides and sometimes bring a heavy-hearted woman to their own *mansin*. *Mansin* recommend kinswomen and neighbors to other *mansin* since they know these women's affairs too well to provide a convincing inspirational divination.[8] The East Town Mansin and the Clear Spring Mansin bring neighbors and kinswomen to Yongsu's Mother.

Apart from the gods' and ancestors' verbal presence, the rituals *tan'gol* perform in the *mansin's* shrine parallel the offerings that women make in Buddhist temples. The officiant invokes and addresses divine beings with a flourishing of cymbals while the supplicant prostrates herself again and again before the altar. Some of the rice and delicacies she has placed on the altar are served again to the worshipers. At temple and shrine the women's prayers are the same: "Make the children turn out well." "Make the house peaceful." Women in temples and shrines advised me to "ask for a good husband and a baby."

The *mansin* calls her actions in the shrine Pulgong, a term usually glossed "Buddhist mass." The women of Enduring Pine Village themselves consider seasonal offerings at the *mansin's* shrine and seasonal offerings at the Buddhist temple analogous practices. On Buddha's Birthday I went to the local temple with instructions from my landlady. "It's just like going to a *mansin's* house. You set your money down on the altar and you bow. You take two measures of rice, some fruit, and candles, just the same. They do it on Buddha's Birthday [lunar 4.8] at the temple and on Seven Star Day [lunar 7.7] at the shrine."

In Enduring Pine Village I found "houses that visit the Buddhist temple," and "houses that visit the *mansin's* house," and a few "houses that visit the Christian church." The Christians stand outside the folk religious system, but shamanism and Buddhism blur. Yongsu's Mother and her clients called their shrine worship Pulgyo, "Buddhism," and the *mansin* often introduced me as "a student of Buddhism."

In houses that visit the Buddhist temple, women go up the mountain path once during the first two weeks of the new year and on lunar 7.7, when other women go to the *mansin*'s shrine. Women also go to Buddhist temples on Buddha's Birthday, and some women pray there on their own children's birthdays. And women visit the temple or the *mansin*'s shrine in adversity. According to my landlady, "You go when someone is sick or when a son can't find work." City families often visit temples before a child takes the university entrance examination.

Like women who visit the *mansin*'s shrine, women who make offerings at temples must bathe themselves and be free of menstrual pollution when they carry their offerings up the hillside. One woman recalls, "We would bathe clean and wash our hair before we went to the temple. Then we'd put on clean clothing and wash all of the rice clean. When we got to the temple, we would pray for the whole family." Okja's Mother says that she is too poor to make seasonal offerings at a temple, but she squeezes some of her limited resources to make a small offering when she is anxious. "I couldn't afford to go this year on lunar 7.7, but I went on Buddha's Birthday because my husband was having so many difficulties at work. I didn't have any money to set on the altar, and I didn't bring any fruit, just a small measure of rice, some incense, and candles. They recited prayers and I bowed."

From the perspective of women worshipers, shrine and temple do not represent discrete religions, but rather the different traditions of separate households. One household made seasonal offerings at both the shrine and the temple, but other women claim, "It takes a lot of money to do both." In her own shrine, Yongsu's Mother has enthroned gilt-plaster images of Pulsŏk Buddha (Pulsŏk Puch'ŏnim), Kwanyin Buddhist Sage (Kwanseŭm Pulsa), and Healing Buddha (Yaksa Puch'ŏnim), all borrowed from the Buddhist tradition. The Seven Stars and the Mountain God are honored in both shrine and temple. Some of the services *mansin* and monk perform are identical; a partial list includes performing masses (Pulgong), lettering paper charms *(pujŏk)*, dedicating children *(myŏngdari)*, and divining.

A daughter-in-law is expected to follow her mother-in-law in temple or shrine worship, but there are easy compromises and crossovers. Yonghui's household is emphatically a house that visits the Buddhist temple. Yonghui's Mother pressed the backs of her hands together to impress upon me the incompatibility of Buddhist temples and *mansin*'s shrines. Yonghui's Grandmother warned me against spending so much time in a *mansin*'s house lest I be exploited. But other households are less rigid. When her husband was sick, my landlady prayed at the Buddhist temple; she also sponsored a *kut*. Yangja's Mother followed the traditions of her husband's family and bought a Buddhist talisman to protect her taxi driver husband. After her husband's second traffic accident, her mother brought her to the *mansin* and she became Yongsu's Mother's *tan'gol*. Other women told me that they used to go to the local temple but went to the *mansin* during a family crisis and thereafter transferred their allegiance. Some women, though they make seasonal offerings at temples, consult *mansin* for divinations. The daughter-in-law in a household of temple worshipers lowered her voice and told me that she periodically seeks out a *mansin*'s divinations for "peace of mind." She did not want her mother-in-law to hear this revelation. The women I interviewed who had broken with the traditions of their mothers-in-law happened also to be less accountable to the husband's house than women trained to succeed a mother-in-law. They were either the wives of secondary sons, living at a distance from the husband's kin, estranged from the husband's kin, or had never known a living mother-in-law.

Having outlined the basic structure of the housewife's and *mansin*'s working relationship, it remains for me to present the gods and ancestors that infuse these events with drama and personality. Restless spirits emerge from commonly held beliefs. The *mansin* uses her shamanic powers to conjure the particularly strong and dangerously discontented spirits of client households from assorted supernatural possibilities and to devise therapeutic rituals that bring past family history to bear on present anxieties.

FIVE

Wood Imps, Ghosts, and Other Noxious Influences

The evil spirits are a sort of impersonation of ill-luck. They are forever wandering about, and seeking a baneful intimacy with frail mortality. . . . One of their most common noxious pursuits is as the bearers of disease. In fact, one is tempted to style the worship of bacteria—bacteria of the mind, body, and estate.

Percival Lowell,
The Land of the Morning Calm

I'm not a doctor. I only know how to jump up and down.
Yongsu's Mother

The Patient Who Shouldn't Have Died

Mr. Pyŏn was reclining on the hot floor of the inner room when his wife brought Yongsu's Mother. Mr. Pyŏn was a gnarled man, tanned nut brown; his narrow moustache and iron gray hair betrayed an overdue dye job. He coughed and spat into an empty beer can. He was seventy years old, and seventy is not an auspicious year.

Mr. Pyŏn had suffered bouts of congestion and chest pain throughout the summer. He had taken the pharmacist's preparations, recovered a bit, and gone back to work. His irregular income from odd jobs and his wife's earnings from her vegetable plot had supported the couple and three adolescent children. This year the Pyŏns had not done badly. They had been able to renovate the house and buy a television set.

By early September, though, Mr. Pyŏn was again too ill to work. His wife went to Yongsu's Mother, and the *mansin* divined that Mr. Pyŏn was in extreme danger. The *mansin* urged a hasty exorcism. She also hinted that the family should later perform a more expensive and elaborate ritual, a *kut*. Yongsu's Mother considered the situation desperate. Mr. Pyŏn's death would leave his wife, a full twenty years his junior, the single support of their three children, all still in early adolescence.

A *mansin* tells her clients to hold an exorcism *(p'udakkŏri)* when she divines that ghosts and noxious influences lurk behind a persistent illness. Exorcism is a relatively simple process. Many housewives perform simple exorcisms by themselves without consulting a *mansin* if, for example, a child runs a high fever for a couple of days. Both Yongsu's Mother and my landlady told me how to perform exorcisms for the time when I would be on my own again in America.

In preparation for this simple exorcism the housewife places a dipper of cooked millet by the afflicted person's pillow and leaves it there for three days. Millet is coarse, unsavory fare, a proper offering for beggarlike wandering ghosts. The woman performing the exorcism whirls the dipper of millet over the patient's head and presses it against the patient's chest, asking aloud, "I implore, take so-and-so's pain away." She pelts the patient with grain and scraps of food. She casts away a piece of the afflicted person's clothing, often only a small collar guard, to lure out the possessing ghost. When the *mansin*'s divination reveals that the afflicted person has a "death fate," she has the housewife wrap the piece of clothing around a bound chicken. The *mansin* circles the chicken about the patient's body and casts it out the door as a scapegoat. The chicken is buried on a hillside like a corpse.

If the situation is so dire that the Death Messenger has already come to claim the soul, the *mansin* tells the family to prepare a tiny straw doll to fool the emissary from hell. They stuff the doll with a paper bearing the name, age, and birth date of the afflicted person, dress it in a piece of the patient's clothing, and bind it seven times like a corpse. Neighbors perform the grave diggers' chant around the patient, who lies flat, clasping the doll. The "grave diggers" carry the doll away and bury it "on the mountain" as if they were burying a corpse. The patient is carried back into the house through the back entrance because, as Yongsu's Mother explained, "A dead person goes out the front door; they can't go back in that way again, can they?" In this way the sick self dies and is buried with the straw doll. A new self, embarked now upon the process of healing, is smuggled back into the house by a different passage.

Where the offending shade is a restless ghost from the afflicted person's own family, the client provides long strips of cloth, ghost bridges *(yŏngsandari)*. The restless soul must cross one of these bridges to pass out of hell and another to pass into paradise. The *mansin* reaches around the afflicted person's body and rips the length of cloth to mark the soul's progress over the bridge. Tearing cloth bridges is considered a benevolent act, whereby the living project the dead into a better existence. But tearing cloth also dramatizes breaking the unquiet dead's hold on the living.

Baleful forces are also graphically cut away. The *mansin* or woman of the house waves a kitchen knife over the afflicted person's head, waves it around the afflicted person's body, and touches the tip to an inflamed chest or a swollen limb. As a final gesture the woman flings the knife down. If the blade points out, away from the house, the exorcism is a success; ghosts and noxious influences have been drawn away. If the tip points in, toward the house, they remain. The woman throws more millet, slices again at the air over the afflicted person's head, and casts the knife down. She repeats this process until she receives the desired prognosis. Now she picks up the dipper and runs out of the house, luring away any lingering baleful forces. A safe distance from the house, she tosses away the final scraps of food in the dipper.

The essential ritual actions of exorcism, then, dramatize drawing inauspicious forces away, casting them out, and cutting or ripping away their hold on the afflicted. Many women perform simple exorcisms in their own homes, without a *mansin*'s aid. "If someone is sick, I just do it myself with no fuss," a woman said, "I set down cooked grain and rub my hands." My landlady performed an exorcism when her middle-school-age daughter had a cold and ran a fever for a couple of days. The daughter had taken some of my aspirin but, to my knowledge, no other medication. My landlady put a dipper of millet by her daughter's pillow with a piece of the daughter's discarded clothing on top. Then, in her words, "I waved the dipper over her head five times and waved a kitchen knife over her head five times. I threw the grain away in the stream. I took it and threw it in a lucky direction. How did I know which direction? My children's father knows those things. Parents have to be half shamans to raise up their children."

A woman performs an exorcism herself either because she cannot afford the *mansin*'s more costly rite, or to be on the safe side when a child has a high fever or a nagging cough. Women who had performed their own exorcisms told me:

> Our household is peaceful these days so I don't do it anymore, but a woman my age, of course I've done it in the past. Whenever someone

was sick, I'd do an exorcism, even though I don't do a lot of superstitious practices.

or:

The last time I did it? Well, grandmother was sick. She couldn't eat. I cooked grain and threw it out. I got her some medicine from the pharmacy. She took the medicine and I did the exorcism, then she got well.

In Enduring Pine Village women tend to consult the shaman and hold an exorcism on the second or third day of a child's illness where the child has a sudden, high, or lingering fever. They consult the *mansin* almost immediately after a fit, but wait until a cold, congested chest, or body malaise has lingered through long weeks or months of treatment. One exorcism may be sufficient to expel a malevolent ghost or a throng of noxious influences. Or the exorcism may be one step in a longer curing process. Where the *mansin*'s divination reveals that individual illness is one symptom of a house beset by angry gods and restless ancestors, a slight improvement in the patient's condition after an exorcism confirms the *mansin*'s diagnosis of a grievous supernaturally engendered malaise. The family should sponsor a *kut,* wherein costumed shamans will call down the ancestors and ghosts to feast, play, and make peace with the living family.

With this background, let us return to that autumn morning in 1977 when Yongsu's Mother went down the road to exorcise Mr. Pyŏn. As they walked, Yongsu's Mother told the wife about a home tonic her own mother had used to good effect for a congested chest. It consisted of turnip shavings and a piece of taffy kept in a covered pot on the hot spot of the floor. The patient was to drink the liquid every few hours after the turnips had fermented. When Yongsu's Mother asked the wife if she had been to the pharmacy yet that morning, the woman replied, no, that she had told her daughter to pick up some medicine on her way home from school in the market town. Yongsu's Mother scolded her, "It'll be late by the time your daughter gets home. You should have gone yourself." The *mansin* was vexed at her client's carelessness.

Mr. Pyŏn's wife had prepared for the exorcism before she went out to call for Yongsu's Mother. A large plastic dipper full of millet stood beside Mr. Pyŏn's pillow. A live white chicken wrapped in one of Mr. Pyon's undershirts was bundled on the floor beside the dipper.

Chanting away restless ancestors, ghosts, and various noxious influences, Yongsu's Mother pressed the dipper of millet against Mr. Pyŏn's chest. She rubbed the chicken against his chest and back and, holding the fluttering bird by its bound legs, whirled it all around his body. She cast the bird out the door. Its neck snapped as it fell in the courtyard. She next pressed the flat side of a common kitchen knife against Mr. Pyŏn's chest. She wandered through the room, slashing with her knife at the air around the storage boxes and dressing table. She opened the storage cabinet and waved the knife through the air above the piled quilts inside the cabinet. She spent a long time slicing at malevolent forces around the television set.

Mr. Pyŏn's dead first wife appeared, speaking through Yongsu's Mother. She moaned that she was hungry for rice. Yongsu's Mother claimed that she saw a vision of someone who had drowned when she spoke for the dead wife. Mr. Pyŏn's wife confirmed that the first wife and one of her children had drowned many years ago.

Yongsu's Mother had Mr. Pyŏn draw the Chinese characters for king (*wang*) and child (*cha*) on two small squares of paper. Yongsu's Mother pasted the characters to the television set as an exorcism talisman. The Pyŏns had recently purchased the set and brought it into the house on an unlucky day. Wood imps entered the house with the television and were compounding Mr. Pyŏn's trouble. Yongsu's Mother had driven them out; the talisman would hold them at bay.

Yongsu's Mother went to the courtyard and burned lumps of moxa and red pepper at the base of each newly erected fence post and along the foundation of the cinder block storage shed to drive out wood imps and earth imps from the new construction. She told Mr. Pyŏn's wife to paste another "king" character outside the gate and a "child" character inside. She boiled water in a huge rice pot in the kitchen and cast in handfuls of red pepper. She set a porcelain bowl, turned upside down, afloat on the bubbling water and covered the pot with an iron lid. Tapping on the lid of the rice pot, she chanted to lure all malevolent earth imps and wood imps inside the steaming caldron. When all the water had boiled away in the closed pot, she checked under the bowl and judged the house successfully fumigated of wood imps and earth imps.

Yongsu's Mother left the house, shouting back over her shoulder to Mr. Pyŏn's wife, "Be sure you buy medicine."

"Which medicine?" the woman yelled back.

"Any medicine. They'll tell you which one at the pharmacy."

She turned to me when we were out of hearing and muttered, "That woman isn't very bright." Yongsu's Mother felt that Mr. Pyŏn's wife grasped neither her husband's extreme peril nor her own dire situation should he die before the children were grown. Widowed early, Yongsu's Mother knew the consequences. On several other occasions, I saw her urge clients to spare no medical expense for an ailing husband.

When I interviewed the Pyŏns a few weeks later, Mr. Pyŏn was outside resting in the sunshine. He still clutched an empty beer can for sputum. He told me that the exorcism had not improved his health, that he was ill because he was old. His wife, however, told me that she thought he was a bit better. She attributed his difficulties to his first wife's malevolent shade.

In early November Yongsu's Mother reported that Mr. Pyŏn had entered the hospital with an advanced lung inflammation. "He's too old; he has no strength," she sighed. "It'll be a disaster for that house if he dies. That woman can't support herself. If he lived for just ten more years, then the daughter would be old enough to work and bring money home." In January Mr. Pyŏn was released from the hospital. The doctor judged his case hopeless and sent him home to die surrounded by his family.[1] In a few days he was dead.

Yongsu's Mother felt called upon to explain why, despite the exorcism I had witnessed, her patient died. She provided ample reasons: Mr. Pyŏn's year horoscope was bad. The house had a full battery of restless ancestors and ghosts. Wood imps and earth imps entered the house when the family brought in wooden furniture and lumber and when they had moved earth for construction on an inauspicious day. But Yongsu's Mother considered Mr. Pyŏn's condition a medical as well as a supernatural problem. He was old and weak and his lungs were bad. She called him a cheapskate because of his unwillingness to pay for sufficient medicine and take proper rest early in his affliction. When he entered the hospital in November, she was already resigned to his death. "What do you expect when someone coughs all the time and brings up so much phlegm? Even if you do an exorcism, it's useless if its his fate [su] to die. He's seventy years old. Even younger ones who cough like that die. It's so pathetic."

The *mansin* attributed Mr. Pyŏn's demise to an interlacing of supernatural causation, medical and ritual neglect, and the vicissitudes of fate and old age. The diverse strands of causality in Yongsu's Mother's explanation of Mr. Pyŏn's demise are not a confused tangle. The several strands are woven together into a more-or-less cohesive fabric, and our task now is to unravel them, carefully, to retrieve the underlying pattern.

The *Mansin* and Medicine

The *mansin* functions within a plural health system. She provides one of many contrasting, but not necessarily contradictory, therapies. She does not, in her capacity as *mansin,* provide medicine, massage, or any other directly physical treatment. Yongsu's Mother did recommend a homemade concoction, but so too might any concerned neighbor provide advice and share a recipe. Far from being hostile to cosmopolitan medicine, Yongsu's Mother urged her patient's wife to consult the pharmacist immediately and faulted her patient for neglecting his health. The *mansin* assume that when their clients fall ill, they will consult pharmacists, herbalists, acupuncturists, and hospitals. The *mansin* themselves patronize pharmacists, herbalists, acupuncturists, and hospitals.

In Enduring Pine Village the first recourse in illness is the cosmopolitan pharmacist. Fevers, dizzy spells, digestive trouble, and body weakness are common complaints. A family member, often a child on the way home from school in the market town, describes the symptoms to the pharmacist and receives the medicine with simple instructions. If the pharmacist's treatment does not soon bring noticeable relief, the family may consider other pharmacists or perhaps a Chinese-style herbalist. With a debilitating, extremely uncomfortable, or prolonged illness, the patient goes to a hospital. A hospital *(pyŏngwŏn)* may be no more than a private outpatient clinic in the doctor's own home. It may be a single ward, or one of the large general hospitals in Seoul.

For the Korean family, prolonged illness means prolonged expense, money drained out of the house. Prolonged illness also implies the loss of an able-bodied family member's labor. Anxious to preserve the life and strength of the afflicted, the family also desires the cheapest, quickest, most effective treatment. When an illness lingers over weeks and months, as did my landlady's dizzy spells, the patient grows impatient with a daily dose of expensive pills. Neighbors suggest another druggist. Kin provide a box of alternative medicine as a holiday gift. Family members might even agree that this illness merits a trip to the hospital. Sometimes families terminate treatment because they do not have enough money to continue to completion.

When the *mansin* divines supernatural influences as the root cause of affliction, she offers a way out of a cycle of illness and expense, a means to the root cause underlying affliction. Yongsu's Mother describes the process. "In the countryside, if people are sick for a long time and keep taking medicine, that just wastes money. If you are sick and don't get better, you should do a *kut*." A woman at a healing *kut* took it upon herself to explain the event to me. "We Koreans, when we are sick we take medicine and go to the hospital. If that doesn't work, we do like this."

Yongsu's Mother and her clients expect that medical treatment—assuming one locates the appropriate treatment and can afford to follow it through—will solve medical problems. Speaking through the possessed *mansin,* the gods themselves sanction medical expenditures where the family is reluctant or the afflicted person embarrassed. But the gods give only the most general medical advice, this not being their area of expertise. "Buy medicine," they say. "Get acupuncture treatment." "Get a packet of Chinese medicine and sweat out your body aches." Occasionally the gods initiate a new direction in the health-seeking process. Speaking for the Spirit Warrior, a god who exorcises baleful forces, a *mansin* told a young man with nagging digestive trouble, "Buy medicine in the west. I see a medicine shop in that direction and a pharmacist with a thin face. If you buy medicine from him, you will get well."

There are at least two instances in which Yongsu's Mother discourages medical treatment. She considers the doctor's tranquilizing shots inappropriate therapy for sudden and violent possession—fits, frothing at the mouth, and other crazy *(mich'in)* behavior. The problem, in her view, is clearly supernatural and can only be dealt with through ritual. A sudden fit is symptomatic of a dangerous possession. The afflicted person's life is at peril and they need immediate ritual attention. According to Yongsu's Mother, "With an injection, the person just sleeps; they don't get better. The medicine just makes them weak."

I know of one other situation where Yongsu's Mother advises her clients to suspend medical treatment. She told a woman suffering from a generalized body malaise to stop going to the hospital for expensive daily treatments. The *mansin* divined that restless ancestors were the cause of both the woman's physical affliction and of her son's rebellious Christian zealotry. She told the woman to boil and cast out millet grain, to perform a small exorcism. If her son's behavior improved and if she herself felt a bit better, the client would know beyond all doubt that her problems were supernatural and could now justify the expense of a *kut* to cure them. Yongsu's Mother added the provision, "If you feel like you're going to die and your son's behavior is worse, go back to the hospital." Suspended medical treatment tests the truth of the *mansin*'s diagnosis, but a break in treatment can have deleterious consequences, a point brought home to me when Yongsu's Mother suggested I stop taking a daily prescription of antibiotics while she exorcised me of wandering ghosts. Impatience with extended treatment and abrupt breaks and switches in therapy characterize overall medical strategy in the Korean countryside, whether the client consults doctors, pharmacists, or *mansin*. The *mansin* gives her advice within a broader realm of health-seeking behavior where interruptions of treatment are common (see Kim and Sich 1977; S. Yoon 1977b).

By the *mansin*'s model of causation, a serious or prolonged illness is symptomatic of deeper malaise within the household, of angry gods and restless ancestors. That certain people are struck ill, that illness persists even with treatment, and that wealth goes out of the family to pay for medicine and hospital visits, these are the workings of the supernatural. While the *mansin* concedes the efficacy of medicine for herself and her clients, medical expense is another aspect of household affliction.

Adrift in an Ordered Cosmos: Horoscopes and Personal Vulnerability

Like medical treatment, horoscope divinations are technically the realm of another specialist, traditionally a scholarly gentleman steeped in the lore of Chinese cosmology texts (see Dix 1980). But *mansin* weave notions of horoscope, fate, and the individual's relationship to an eternally shifting cosmos into their own schema of affliction. Individual fate is determined by the eight characters *(p'alcha)*, properties of the year, month, day, and hour of one's birth. Since divination texts were, until recently, written only in classical Chinese, professional horoscope readers boasted at least the rudiments of a classical education.[2] Even so, everyone cites bits and pieces of popularized horoscope lore. Village women will comment, "It's bad for someone to be born late at night in a tiger year, but this child was born in the day. That's all right, because you can go around in the daylight and be safe from tigers," or, "It's good for a snake-year person to be born in the winter." More often, people will comment on their own, generally unfavorable, fate. Yongsu's Mother attributes her hard life and diverse misfortunes to the inauspicious hour of her birth.

> I was born at seven in the morning on the eighth day of the third lunar month. I should have been born in the evening, and so my fate is wretched [*p'alchaga sanapta*]. They told me I should marry late, but even that didn't help because my husband died anyway.[3]

Similarly, my neighbor, Hangil's Mother, lamented,

> I never much liked my husband. When I got married I didn't know my husband had been married before. I think my brother and his wife knew when they arranged the match, but they didn't tell me. The fortunetellers all said I had a wretched fate, said so every time I had my fortune told. They said I'd have to marry someone much older or someone who had been married before.

People with bad fates, the *mansin* say, should perform frequent exorcisms to keep ghosts, restless ancestors, and noxious influences at bay. A wretched fate implies not only personal hardship and grief, but defenselessness before the supernatural. Household gods, angry at the paucity of offerings in the Kim household, struck the wife and drove her into a fit of madness. It was her wretched personal horoscope, in Yongsu's Mother's opinion, that accounted for both the Kim woman's difficulties in life and her vulnerability at the perilous touch of gods and ancestors. She was caught in a cycle of poverty, materially poor and therefore unable to perform rituals to secure supernatural abundance in the form of the continuing good graces of her household gods. "It was her own bad fate. Neither her brothers nor her brothers-in-law had her rotten luck. She had no good fortune, so she didn't have any money, so she couldn't give rice cake to the supernatural Official in her home. Then, when she went to her natal home with two bags of rice, the angry [and jealous] supernatural Official grabbed her and the ancestor grabbed her."

Individual eight-character fate can be overwhelmingly good or bad, but it is not immutable. One's personal prognosis changes in relation to each year's horoscopic properties and is colored by each changing day, month, and hour. Mr. Pyŏn was susceptible to malevolent forces by virtue of an unlucky horoscope year. Because he had a death fate, Yongsu's Mother rubbed the white chicken against his sore chest and cast it away as a scapegoat.

Since personal horoscope shifts from year to year, some members of a family will be more vulnerable to supernatural attack in a particular year than others. The victim is not necessarily the direct object of supernatural wrath. Rather, angry gods, ancestors, or ghosts seize the most susceptible member of a household to register their displeasure with the larger group. Munae's Mother came to Yongsu's Mother with an inflamed leg. She had been to both a small out-patient clinic and an acupuncturist. The acupuncturist's needles left a series of nasty bruises along her calf. After limping about the village for two weeks with no sign of improvement, she went to Yongsu's Mother. Yongsu's Mother divined the presence of a "restless ancestor [*chosang malmyŏng*] who died young." Munae's Mother disclosed a family secret—her father-in-law had had two wives in succession. The second wife, now a widow, denied the first wife her ancestor rites in an attempt to obliterate her memory. The dead first wife had no direct grievance with her daughter-in-law. Although the entire household was technically accountable for the ritual lapse, her main quarrel was with the living second wife. Nevertheless, because the daughter-in-law's year fate was bad, she was a ready target. The first wife touched the daughter-in-law's leg and interfered with the healing process to protest her own unjust treatment.

The *mansin*'s conceptualization of the interplay between personal horoscope and vulnerability to supernatural malevolence recalls our current knowledge of disease contagion. Members of a given population receive equal exposure to infection. Some are predisposed to it, others escape unscathed. The *mansin* and her clients use fate to explain vulnerability, but the total prognosis is not a dead-ended fatalism. Mr. Pyŏn's year fate, compounded by age, weakness, and his serious medical condition, made it all but impossible to save him. Yet, there was a margin of struggle left. The *mansin* exorcised the patient and urged the family toward more and better medical care and a more elaborate healing ritual.

Personal fate, then, predisposes certain individuals to affliction—a particular husband rather than his wife, a particular daughter-in-law rather than her mother-in-law. But the arena of affliction is the total household. Individual illness bespeaks more things amiss under the roof. Restless ancestors, ghosts, and noxious influences barge in through weakened defenses. How, when, and why do they enter?

Of Wood Imps and Earth Imps: Moving in the Right Direction

When Yongsu's Mother performed Mr. Pyŏn's exorcism, she went about the newly built gate and shed, fumigating the house of wood imps and earth imps stirred up when the Pyŏns moved earth for construction and brought wood and wooden objects into the house on unlucky days. Here again, abstract cosmological principles act in concert with the machinations of supernatural entities.

The Chinese-derived almanac describes a complex system for regulating human activities in accord with the flow of days and seasons. One should avoid certain potentially dangerous activities on certain days. Building a house, repairing a house, moving, cutting trees, or starting a journey can have ill-fated consequences (see also Dix 1980). Ominous forces *(son)* block each direction for two days in a ten-day cycle. Many villagers who could never read an almanac know by heart the simple formula for avoiding ominous forces.

> On the first and second [of a lunar month] they're in the east
> On the third and fourth, the south
> On the fifth and sixth, the west
> On the seventh and eighth, the north
> On the ninth and tenth, none at all

The cycle begins again in the east on the eleventh and twenty-first days of the lunar month. To start a journey, cut firewood on the mountain and bring it home, to bring furniture into or move it around inside the house, to move earth, build or repair a house, or take a journey is to risk tangling with the ominous forces of a blocked direction.

It is safest to plan potentially dangerous activities for the auspicious ninth and tenth, nineteenth and twentieth, and twenty-ninth and thirtieth days. My village landlord and his cronies determined auspicious days for me when I moved into and out of Enduring Pine Village. Village women told me to wait for an "unblocked" day to arrange my furniture in my new room in Seoul when I left the village. Housewives heed unblocked directions when they perform simple exorcisms, and when a woman runs away from the house with a full gourd dipper after a *kut* or exorcism, she carries the scraps and millet in an unblocked direction and there casts them out.

When someone in the family violates directional principles by performing a dangerous act on an inauspicious day or in violation of directional principles, they stir up imps *(tongbŏp)*—wood imps *(nanggu moksin, moksin tongbŏp)* and earth imps *(chisin tongbŏp)*.[4] Unleashed in the house, these malevolent imps instigate or perpetuate illness. Wood and wooden objects brought into the house are a common source of trouble. A woman told me, "My mother-in-law was sick last year so we did an exorcism. She had a headache and ached in her arms and legs. The *mansin* said it was because of some wood they brought in and stored under the porch." A Cho man suffered from a nagging congested chest. During the Cho family *kut,* the *mansin's* visions revealed wood imps clinging to the Cho man's chest. On the final morning of the *kut,* a *mansin* burned moxa and red pepper around the base of the newly constructed toilet shed and along the woodpile to drive out the troublesome imps. Yongsu's Mother's newly married daughter reported that her husband had severe stomach pains. Yongsu's Mother suspected that her son-in-law had incurred a wood imp when the couple rearranged a cabinet and dish chest in their rented home on a blocked day.

A *tongbŏp*-induced affliction—an infestation of wood imps or earth imps—is attributed to abstract cosmological principles on two counts. First, directional principles were violated when someone performed a potentially dangerous act or brought a potentially dangerous object into the house on an inauspicious day. Second, a family member—not necessarily the person who performed the ill-fated action—fell victim to the imps because of an inauspicious horoscope.

Villagers usually choose a day free of malevolent forces when they make a major change of residence, initiate construction, or lay in a winter's supply of firewood. They are less likely to think of the calendar when they move furniture or bring wooden or stone objects into the house. Yongsu's Mother did not ask her daughter for the precise day she moved the cabinet and dish set. She assumed that her daughter, like most people, performed these simple acts heedless of the calendar. The husband was sick, the couple had moved furniture, there were wood imps loose in the house.

The *mansin* exorcises offending wood imps and earth imps from her patient when she sends off ghosts and other noxious influences. But the *mansin*'s work is not complete until she burns moxa to fumigate the whole house and catches the imps in a bubbling caldron. Otherwise, infection persists in the body of the house and someone else may fall victim to the troublesome imps. As a precaution against further infestation, the *mansin* pastes charms on the vulnerable spots. Through all of these activities, she secures the house boundaries.[5]

Malevolent Forces from beyond the Wall

Restless Ancestors and Ghosts

The dead—restless ancestors *(chosang malmyŏng)* and ghosts *(yŏng-san, chapkwi)*—are a common source of affliction. There are the acknowledged dead, that is, known ancestors and the ghosts of one's own family. There are also anonymous ghosts, those whose ceaseless craving draws them to households where they are unknown. While ancestors *(chosang)* have produced male issue and are thus entitled to receive libations and feast food *(chesa)* from sons and grandsons, *yŏngsan*, or ghosts, died unmarried, without issue, often violently or suddenly when far away from home. A *mansin*'s chant acknowledges "ghosts of the drowned, ghosts who were shot, ghosts who died of carbon monoxide poisoning, maiden ghosts, bachelor ghosts," and many more. Because they are not entitled to *chesa* food, ghosts are perpetually hungry. Whenever feast food is served, they gather about the house gate, but they are most likely to hover about their own families. Because they died unsatisfied, they wander angry and frustrated, venting their anguish on the living.

Ancestors, far more fortunate than ghosts, were married and had children when they died, often at a ripe old age and in the bosom of their families. Yet even these properly deceased ancestors carry unrequited resentments *(han)*. When they appear in the person of the *man-sin,* they cry for all they have missed in life. A man who toiled to provide for his family vents his frustration at dying before he could enjoy the fruits of his labor. A first wife who knew poverty in her married life is bitter when she sees her husband's present wife living comfortably. Grandparents rejoice at the birth of a grandchild but regret dying before they could hold the baby in life. An old woman went to her grave craving a fancy rice cake and carries this hunger through eternity. By Korean social expectations, these are all legitimate desires that have been thwarted by fate.

There are also instances where emotional attachments draw the dead to the living. Although these ancestors have no malevolent intent, their presence has negative consequences. A mother pities her married daughter's poverty and touches her, driving the daughter temporarily insane. A grandmother fondly strokes her infant grandchild, causing the baby to sicken. A father-in-law reaches out in gratitude to the young man who married his hunchback daughter, but the grateful touch of the dead makes the young man lame.

When the family's spiritual defenses are weak, when the household gods drop their guard, any of these ancestors may grow restless and consequently dangerous. The *mansin* say that "the hand of the dead is a hand of thorns" *(chugŭn sonŭn kasisonida);* it cannot touch living flesh without inflicting injury.

Mr. Pyŏn, in his vulnerable seventieth year, was victimized by his family's numerous restless ancestors and ghosts. His first wife drowned along with one of the children. His mother died craving a fancy rice cake and so carries an eternal appetite for this food. One son was shot during the war and another died in a traffic accident, both as childless bachelors. Indeed, it would be hard to find such a complete collection of restless ancestors and ghosts in a single household. According to Yongsu's Mother, a family with these ominous shades lurking about should do frequent exorcisms because any illness is potentially dangerous. They should also do periodic *kut* to placate their hovering ancestors and ghosts and to secure the gods' protection.

While ancestors linger close to home, ghosts range wide in their mischief. When they are not looming in the shadows of their own gateway, they trail after the nameless legion of wandering ghosts that roam the byways. Perpetually hungry, they are drawn to any household where feast food is being prepared. They attach themselves to the feasting family and guests. Participants who return home from a birthday feast, wedding feast, or death anniversary with a digestive complaint, or who contract one soon after, may have been followed home by wandering ghosts. Ghosts are attracted by the gift food that guests bring home from a death anniversary or a *kut,* or by the *chesa* sweets the family distributes to neighbor households. Someone, usually the housewife, tosses out a lump of rice cake or a piece of candy to lure away any ghosts or noxious influences who may have followed the food. Only then do family members safely imbibe the potentially dangerous treats.

Out of worldly craving, ghosts and restless ancestors sometimes enter the house by clutching onto newly purchased clothing. The *mansin* attributed one baby's illness to ghosts clinging to his new shirt. The Clear Spring Mansin's son suffered from ghosts attached to a skirt the *mansin* had received as a gift. Envious dead siblings ride into the house on a sister's brightly colored marriage quilt.

The world outside the house gate is filled with ghosts. Those who travel about in the world acquire, over time, an entourage of baleful shades. Sick with a nagging cold, I fell asleep at a *kut.* Yongsu's Mother told me that I seemed to have a "cold" aura; my condition was ghostly *(kwijŏk).* Ghosts hovered about me, so I should sponsor an exorcism. The *mansin* explained the source of my affliction: I had gone around with the *mansin* to *kut* and eaten feast food in many houses. I often traveled back and forth to Seoul, dining out in strange places. In the course of these wanderings, I had acquired enough ghostly hangers-on to merit a ritual purging.

Many women in Enduring Pine Village reported ghostly afflictions. Representative is the statement of a woman whose son had become ill after a party.

> Last year my son was sick; he had a fever. I went to the *mansin* with a sack of rice, a measure of millet, and about three hundred won worth of fruit. I set a five-hundred-won bill and a thousand-won bill on the altar. The *mansin* said my son was sick because he went to a house that was having a baby's hundred-day party. My son ate rice cake and something went wrong.

Another woman went to the *mansin* for an exorcism on behalf of her grandson.

> Three months ago my grandson was sick. He just felt bad. I don't
> know what it was, a cold or something. The *mansin* said ghosts were
> hovering about.[6] Which ghosts? How can you tell which ghosts?

Other women know very well which ghosts and ancestors are giving
them grief.

> I did an exorcism because of some ghost [*kwisin*]. Which one? Oh,
> well, [embarrassed giggles] you see, my husband's finger was sore. His
> dead first wife grabbed ahold of it, so it didn't heal.

Ghosts, familial or anonymous, and restless ancestors bring illness
with their touch, but they act in concert with other malevolent forces.
Let me describe these other baleful entities as they were described to
me by the women and *mansin* I interviewed. This list, while extensive,
is probably incomplete. These are not mutually exclusive diagnoses
but rather the combined elements of complex afflictions.

Red Disaster

Red disaster *(hongaek)* is a malevolent cloud, an accretion of misfortune that engulfs people and intensifies illness or calamity.[7] Red disaster is contagious, contracted from the scene of another's misfortune. If
one has a bad fate and goes to visit the sick *(munbyŏng)* or attends a
funeral, one risks infection by red disaster. The scene of a past accident is particularly perilous for bus and taxi drivers. The accumulated
red disaster of the previous calamity reaches out and provokes another
accident. Yangja's Father is a bus driver. Yongsu's Mother divined a
horde of red disaster at a bridge on Yangja's Father's bus route. There
had been other accidents in that spot. She told Yangja's Father to cast a
handful of millet out the bus window when he passed this ominous
place to drive the red disaster from his path.

When a *mansin* gives her clients a New Year divination, she divines
which family members will be particularly vulnerable to red disaster
throughout the year. She warns that family members with bad fates
must avoid visiting the sick or going to funerals. Certain children
should neither swim nor climb mountains in certain months. At the
start of the year, the *mansin* exorcises "red disaster of the road" *(kŏri
hongaek)* from children who must ride the bus to school.

Like one's own ghostly following, one's personal store of red disaster builds up as one goes about in the world outside the house even if one does not collide directly with an ominous cloud of red disaster. Yongsu's Mother suggested that I bring coarse millet for an exorcism when I made a New Year offering (Hongsu Megi) at her shrine. "You've gone here and there, you've gone to America and come back again. You went to Japan. You go to Seoul all the time. So you've picked up red disaster. Besides, next year is unlucky for you. We should drive out all the bad red disaster now and make you clean."

Red disaster and ghosts, like diverse bacteria, are everywhere, although ghosts are most likely to accumulate around feast food while red disaster festers at the scene of an illness, accident, or death. Like ghosts and other noxious influences, red disaster afflicts those whose year fate predisposes them to contagion or those who encounter a massive or cumulative dose. The house, subject to periodic ritual purging, is "cleaner" and consequently safer than the squalid world outside the gate.

Death Humors

The term *sangmun*, which I gloss "death humors," indicates a "house in mourning." Death humors attack those who have contact with death or with rites for the dead. Following polluted persons or objects, they enter a house where offended gods have dropped their guard. Digestive complaints after a relative or neighbor's *chesa* feast are the most common and obvious work of death humors. According to Yongsu's Mother, "If you go to a *chesa* house and eat *chesa* rice, then you can get a death humor. You may get a stomachache." But death humors can also be fatal. My landlady recounts the greatest tragedy of her life, the death of her middle-school-age son who died within a few days of eating *chesa* food.

> I went to help at the *chesa* of our kinsmen. All the old men who were there to perform the ancestor rite thought Minsu was so cute, they gave him a lot of sweets to take home. That night he already had a headache and was chilled. He'd kept the sweets wrapped up beside his pillow. I snatched them and cast them out. He said, "Why are you doing that? They told me to keep those sweets and eat them later on." I said, "You can get more tomorrow."

The next day, he had a bad headache and couldn't go to school. His father took him to the doctor, who said it was a cold and gave him a shot, but he wasn't any better the next day. His father took him on his back to the one who doctors with needles.[8] That one took one look at Minsu and said, "A death humor has entered him. Go right away and do an exorcism. Hold a mock funeral."

We called the *mansin* and she did an exorcism. My son's father kept setting down five-hundred-won bills and saying, "I'll give you whatever you want, just save my son."

The next day, Minsu said, "I have to go to school," and dusted off his cap and book bag. I went to the kitchen to fix breakfast. I heard something and ran back to the inner room with a premonition. Minsu was already dead. He had crawled from the hot spot all the way across the room. He had seen the Death Messenger come to snatch him away and had tried to escape from the inner room. That's why he had wanted to go to school.

Mansin and their clients attribute a variety of major and minor complaints to death humors. Women told me:

> I had a headache that wouldn't stop. The neighbors told me to go to the *mansin*. She did an exorcism and threw millet. That was all. I got better. I don't know if the exorcism had anything to do with it or not. The *mansin* said a death humor was causing the trouble.

or:

> My eldest daughter was sick and weak last year. The *mansin* said it was because of a death humor. The *mansin* did an exorcism and my daughter took medicine.

Like ghosts, death humors attach themselves to the unwary and follow their victims home. If death humors gain access to the house, they can seize their victims inside. The Paek household incurred a heinous pollution when kinsmen carried an infant's corpse inside. Since corpses are carried out, and the dead leave the living, the intrusion of a corpse into the house was an inappropriate and, consequently, an extremely dangerous act. Angry household gods allowed death humors to enter with the corpse. Before any mishap befell the Paeks, they called in a *mansin* to exorcise death humors from their rooms. Nevertheless, still at large within the walls, the death humors invaded a room the Paeks rented to a factory worker. The youthful factory worker, Mr. Yi, had a bad fate. He awoke in the middle of the night in a fit, trembling and foaming at the mouth. The New Village Factory where he worked helped pay for his healing *kut.*

One of the Clear Spring Mansin's clients came to her shrine to make New Year offerings while still polluted from a funeral. Incensed, the gods in the Clear Spring Mansin's shrine let the death humors following the polluted client move about in the Clear Spring Mansin's house. Her son had a sore leg that would not heal. Moreover, he could not get his security clearance to work in Saudi Arabia. The Clear Spring Mansin had Yongsu's Mother perform an exorcism.

Persons who have incurred a death pollution outside the home must exercise caution before their own gods. The Rice Shop Auntie went to a funeral and was still in a state of death pollution when she prepared rice cake offerings for her household gods. Offended, the gods refused the cake and let death humors from the funeral move about in the house. The woman quarreled with her mother-in-law. Her husband drank, threw things, feuded with the neighbors, and jammed his fist through a glass window. Here, death humors were responsible not for illness per se, but for an acute malaise of social relations.

Invisible Arrows

The Chinese character for the term *sal* is glossed "evil spirit, baleful influence." The term is homophonous with the character for "death." A pure Korean term, *sal* without Chinese characters means "arrow." All of these possible definitions figure in the popular conceptualization of *sal.*[9] Like death humors, invisible arrows (my gloss for the Korean term) cause a variety of complaints, social as well as physical. According to the aged Brass Mirror Mansin, "Parent and child do not get along with each other, husband and wife fight, things like that."

Arrows strike when mother and child are sequestered in the birth room and someone violates a birth taboo. Pollution occurs when a menstruating woman or the infant's older sibling enters the birth room, or when the child is smeared with blood at birth. While the event of birth is, itself, minimally polluting, the household makes an effort to protect mother and child in the birth room from external pollution and danger. Ghosts and ancestors are an immediate threat to the infant, but arrows incurred at birth may not manifest themselves until late adolescence or early adulthood. One of the Brass Mirror Mansin's clients had a grandson who was rebellious at home and neglected his studies. From delinquent companions, he was learning the art of petty thievery. The *mansin* "removed the arrows" in a special exorcism *(salp'uri).* Two of Yongsu's Mother's clients had trouble finding suitable mates for their sons. None of the prospective matches the parents arranged worked out until the *mansin* removed the arrows. With the logic of ritual analogy, a child's disrupted passage into the family—emerging bloody from the birth canal or intruded upon in the womblike birth room—provides, in retrospect, the source of a difficult transition to full adult status.

Far more dangerous than these slow-detonating arrows are the swift arrows that strike at funerals and subsequent funeral rites. One woman remembered, "Eighteen years ago, my father went to a house where they were having a funeral feast. He drank wine and ate pork and was killed by an arrow. I don't miss him or even want to think about it because he disappointed the children when he took a concubine."

A young man had been married for only a month when he went to his father-in-law's funeral. He fell ill there and had to be carried home. He died soon after, and the family attributed his death to a funeral arrow. Hangil's Mother told me that her father-in-law died when he was struck by an arrow at a funeral. After his death his body was covered with a blue-green bruise. One of Yongsu's Mother's grandnephews was struck as he helped carry his cousin's funeral bier.

> Four people carried the corpse, including the dead boy's cousin. As they walked along, the cousin felt someone grab his arm. He felt something numbing come from his shoulder down his arm and he couldn't walk. He had to ask them to stop the procession.
>
> The mother knew that it must be an arrow because he'd been struck at a funeral, but the mother-in-law wouldn't listen to her daughter-in-law. She kept saying, "If we go to a *mansin*, she'll just tell us to do a *kut* or something." They were using Western medicine but it didn't work at all.
>
> At the last minute my husband's nephew, the boy's father, asked me to come over. It was already too late. The boy's arm was paralyzed and his stomach swollen way out. I said, "Why did you wait so long to call me? I came here to help but I don't think I can save him. I'll do something to comfort the parents and the child, but don't even say that I've been here." That was in October. In December, they sent the death announcement.

Yongsu's Mother uses this incident to emphatically illustrate a point. "That's why funerals are dangerous. People get sick and they have no idea why they're sick. They may think it's just a fever, but they die. It's very difficult to cure. Those who have been shot turn all green and blue. Even after they're dead, they're green and blue all over."

Arrows spring from the ritual danger of transitional situations. More serious and irrevocable transitions yield more noxious arrows.[10] Birth intrudes a tentative new life into the household but does not occasion a significant rearrangement of adult social relationships. Birth is a quiet, in-house event, with mother and child sequestered in the birth room. The family acknowledges the child's social existence with a modest celebration one hundred days after the birth. Birth arrows are relatively benign and they afflict only the growing child. Major transitions occasion feasts where arrows strike within a broad social field. Anyone at a wedding, sixty-first birthday feast, or funeral —if their fate is bad—can be hit by an arrow. Weddings and sixty-first birthdays are major passage rites for both individual and family. A woman leaves one household and village to enter another household and village. A parent completes a full cycle of life and becomes an elder. Death is the most irrevocable transition of all, and the transition that engenders the most danger. An adult leaves not just the household and village—like a bride—but the entire social universe. The corpse goes to the mountain and away from the world of men and women.

The Ideology of Illness in a Korean Village

It is an unhappy consequence of a short ethnographic account that bits of information culled from many months of observation and interview appear clumped together in one condensed dose. Since the whole of this chapter is given over to the supernatural, it would seem that waking lives in Enduring Pine Village are riddled with anxiety over death humors, invisible arrows, and ghosts. A close focus miserably distorts the field of action. The supernatural appear when a shaman diagnoses a client's tribulations in a divination session, when women share tales of past tragedies on an idle winter afternoon, or when an anthropologist asks a housewife probing questions (questions like, "When was the last time you did an exorcism? Why did you do an exorcism then?"). For the most part, wood imps, ghosts, and noxious influences lurk in the shadows until affliction propels a woman to the *mansin*'s house and the *mansin* sights their mischief in her divination.

The *mansin*'s visions account for otherwise inexplicable ill luck, but villagers seek this explanation with discretion. It has a price: "If we go to a *mansin,* she'll just tell us to do a *kut* or something." Some of the cases cited above hint at the tension behind a household's decision to consult a *mansin* or sponsor a ritual. In my discussion of *mansin* and medicine, I suggested that similar tensions underlie most major decisions in the health-seeking process. The authority of *mansin* and gods is sometimes mustered to sanction major or continuing medical expenses. Villagers can accept the possibility of supernatural machinations while rejecting a particular *mansin*'s diagnosis as inappropriate or too expensive. Things may work themselves out without more involved care and more serious expenditure. The supernatural can cause considerable mischief, but they may not lurk behind this *particular* affliction at all.

The ideology of affliction described in these pages reflects Korean peasant experience. In affliction the household is the most immediate unit under siege; the physical house is an appropriate metaphor. Individual illness threatens the larger body with medical and ritual expenses, labor loss, anxiety, and death. Illness, business reverses, thefts, and intrafamilial quarrels are household afflictions. Any or, more often, a combination of these sorry states can occasion a major *kut,* like the Chŏns' *kut,* staged and choreographed about the house. Exorcisms, like the one performed for Mr. Pyŏn, focus more exclusively on individual affliction, but always with an eye to the safety of the total house. The woman who performs the exorcism lures ghosts and noxious influences outside the gate and away from the dwelling. In Mr. Pyŏn's exorcism, Yongsu's Mother chased wood imps and earth imps from the very house walls. This ideology of affliction is not without elements of ambiguity, as evidenced by the fact that an exorcism for the Paeks in the inner house *(anjip)* failed to protect their renter in a detached room from death humors at large within the walls.

Individual fate, set in juxtaposition to the regular cycling of years, months, days, and hours, explains individual affliction—why one person is struck ill rather than a sibling or a spouse. *Mansin* and clients use cosmology, personal year fate, to link individual affliction with the supernatural state or the household. When pollution or divine wrath weakens the household's defenses against danger from without, horoscopically vulnerable individuals succumb within.

Like the Trojan horse, goods carried into the house transport malevolent supernatural entities. Ghosts grab hold of newly purchased clothing and ride into the house. Wood imps enter with firewood or wooden furniture. Death humors trail after polluted persons and run amok inside. Leaving the protection of one's own house walls, one is vulnerable to hordes of ghosts and red disasters at feasts, in the homes of the sick, or simply by going about in the world.

The house wall is the last line of defense but, by the very fact that it is strategic, it is the point of greatest danger. Changes in the physical structure of the house pose ritual danger to the family. Repairing the house walls, adding a storeroom, fixing the roof, or rearranging furniture, the family risks an infestation of wood imps or earth imps. Equally dangerous is moving an entire household and its possessions to another dwelling. Cosmology here promises order and, in order, safety. Potential danger can be avoided if one gears significant actions and journeys to the cycling of auspicious days.

Construction and relocation disrupt the physical body of the house, while weddings, sixty-first birthdays, and funerals disrupt the social fabric of the household. For the feasts that mark these transitions, the household suspends normal activity, spends wealth, and throws the house open to a broad array of kin and neighbors. Because it is a liminal state, a time of betwixt and between and a departure from normal activity, the feast carries a hint of danger for all participants. Through the open gate ghosts and noxious influences pillage where they may. But again, cosmology offers a possible dodge. Families buffer themselves against some of the dangers of transition by setting feasts on auspicious days.[11] The horoscopes of prospective spouses are scrutinized as part of the marriage negotiations, and I have heard diviners comment on the horoscopic compatibility of children still in the womb and their prospective parents. Persons with inauspicious horoscopes can avoid weddings and funerals in other households.[12] With a shaman's New Year divination, a housewife can protect vulnerable members of her household by performing appropriate rituals at the first full moon.

To live in harmony with the cosmos is a luxury. Villagers therefore use cosmological principles but hedge their bets. They are not irrevocably doomed by the shifting properties of each day, month, hour, and year, only more vulnerable. Where vulnerability inheres in the household, women bear the burden of protection. Honoring, placating, and cajoling the household gods and ancestors, shaman and housewife secure the house as a defensive bastion, and it is this process that the next two chapters explore.

A woman tries to prevent the Death Messenger from snatching the ancestor's food. *Photograph by author*

A tearful ancestor appears in *kut*. The *mansin* clutches "travel money" in her hand. *Photograph by Homer Williams*

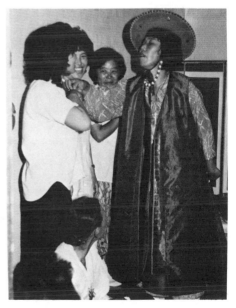

The supernatural Official teases the daughters-in-law. *Photograph by Homer Williams*

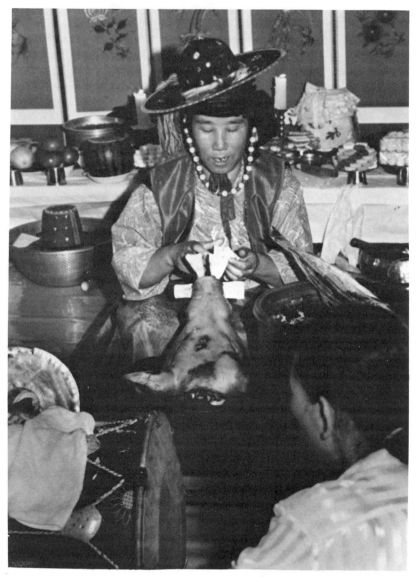

The supernatural Official sticks thousand-won bills into every orifice of the pig's head offering. *Photograph by Homer Williams*

SIX

The Care and Feeding of
Household Gods and Kindred Spirits

It is true we find no "god-shelves" in the house, but the
gods are there just the same, and if you enter the house you
will find that for a small mud hut the average Korean house
has an over-supply of supernatural occupants.

Rev. George Heber Jones
The Spirit Worship of the Koreans

The Mountain God of the Yi Family arrives.
The Generals descend.
We bid you, honored ones, open wide your eyes.
We have prepared for you, many offerings.
We bid you feast, and save our lady Yi

Kyönggi shaman chant

To enter the ritual realm of the Korean woman, you must first step
inside her home. Even inside, the spirits of the place may yet remain
hidden. The Korean home lacks the florid iconography of a Chinese
household altar or the intricately lacquered *butsudan* or *kamidana* of
Japanese household worship. Shaman shrines, like Buddhist temples,
depict the pantheon in boldly colored paintings or prints, the former
now much prized and dearly purchased by aficionados of Korean folk
art. But inside the Korean home the eye could easily miss the packet of
pine needles stuck on the roof beam for the House Lord or the earthen
jar of rice grains for the Birth Grandmother. These simple placings
early earned for Korean folk religion the imprecise and now archaic
epithets of animism, or fetishism.[1] Some families honor particularly
powerful house gods by demarcating their presence with jars of grain
or nests of paper, but place is more significant than placing.

Korean household gods hide inside the structure of the house itself.
The House Lord (Sŏngju) is in the roof beam above the porch, the
Birth Grandmother (Samsin Halmŏni) in the inner room, the House
Site Official (T'ŏju Taegam) behind the house, the Mountain God
(Ponhyang Sansin) and Seven Stars (Ch'ilsŏng) on the storage jars
beside the house, the Kitchen God (Chowang), the Toilet Maiden

(Pyŏnso Kakssi), the Foundation God (Chisin), and the Door Guard (Sumun) in the threshold of the Great Gate. The lesser Five Direction Forces (Obang T'ŏjŏn) abide in every room, storeroom, and stock pen within the walls, and in at least one city home, in the dog house.

In addition to the basic gods of house and house site, some additional gods receive special consideration in certain families. One household owes its prosperity to a Talking Female Official (Marhanŭn Yŏ Taegam). They keep an earthen storage jar of fresh grain on the porch as a placing for the Female Official, and when they offer rice cake to their household gods, they give her a full steamer of cake. Some gods emerge from the particularities of individual dwellings or their immediate environs. Where a shaman has divined their active presence, these gods demand special attention. A merchant family with a shop at the front of the house honors the supernatural Shop Official (Kage Taegam, Sangŏp Taegam). The *mansin* determines that a Massacring Official's (Salyuk Taegam) road intersects the house site. A Goblin Official (Tokkaebi Taegam) lurks in a thicket beside some houses.

There are gods who are especially strong in certain households by virtue of the family's particular traditions and history. We have seen how the Chŏns honor a powerful and demanding Great Spirit Grandmother because a shaman ancestress fills this slot in their pantheon. Chŏn wives have also prayed to the Seven Stars for the birth of sons, and honor this god with periodic offerings. Women honor the house gods at home, but they also leave the house for the temple, *mansin*'s shrine or sacred mountain. Ties to sacred places and obligations to particular deities inform the household tradition a woman either learns from her mother-in-law of unearths through a *mansin*'s divination. Let us first consider the gods inside the house.

Rice Cake for the Gods

The gods of house and house site receive special offerings called *kosa*.[2] The rites of *kosa* appear deceptively simple. A woman sets a cup of water beside a burning candle on the lid of an earthen storage jar; she leaves a tray of rice cake under the roof beam and bobs a stiff bow. The casual observer might easily equate these modest, quiet acts with perfunctory superstition, like the contemporary American's sheepish toss of salt over the shoulder or the reflex "knock on wood." Korean folklorists provide ample discussion on the subtleties of regional variation in household pantheons, but one finds little mention of Korean house gods in Western-language studies of Korea. (Jones' [1902] description of spirit worship, J. Lee's [1975] essay on shamanism and the Korean home, and Guillemoz' [1983] recent ethnography being lone exceptions.) Nevertheless, housewives honoring household gods provide the basic building blocks of shaman ritual much as filial sons honoring family ancestors provide the basic building blocks of male ritual.

In *kosa* the housewife demarcates the gods' presence when she offers divine tribute throughout the house, bowls of wine and heaping plates of rice cake. She sets the largest piles, sometimes whole steamers, of red bean rice cake under the main beam for the House Lord and at the chimney behind the house for the House Site Official. As a tasteful accompaniment to their wine, she gives them each a dried fish. Grilled meat would be offered in a more elaborate *kosa,* or more ostentatious yet, an entire cooked pig's head. In contrast to these virile gods of great appetite, the Birth Grandmother, guardian of conception, childbirth, and young children, nibbles white rice cake, pure water, vegeterian relish, nuts, and candy in the inner room.

The housewife rubs her hands in prayerful supplication, executes a stiff bow from the waist, and quickly petitions the gods: "Please make us rich. Please make this house peaceful. Please make the children turn out well." It is a matter of seconds. The woman leaves the offerings set out for perhaps half an hour, usually in the quiet of the night. Then she cuts up the rice cake and distributes it to family and neighbors.

Kosa food is family sacrament. The male household head's spoon and rice bowl, filled with uncooked grain, sit on the House Lord's offering tray. Later, the house head will eat rice cooked from this grain. He and his wife will share the House Lord's wine. A child's bowl and spoon rest on the Birth Grandmother's tray. Children eat rice made from the grain in this bowl, and drink water from the Birth Grandmother's and the Seven Stars' offerings.

In Enduring Pine Village a rice cake *kosa (ttŏk kosa)* in the tenth lunar month marks the end of the harvest. The housewife uses some of the new grain for the gods' cake. Some households in Enduring Pine Village discontinued the tenth-month *kosa* when they stopped farming and sold their land, but some made ritual accommodations to a changed life-style. When my landlord's family sold their land, they stopped performing the tenth-month *kosa*. However, whenever my landlord brings home the quarterly government stipend he receives as an instructor of traditional dance, his wife offers a small wine *kosa* *(sul kosa);* she sets up cups of rice wine under the roof beam and throughout the house. She considers this *kosa* equivalent, in principle, to the offerings she used to make after the harvest.

A significant financial transaction merits a small wine *kosa*. One woman set out wine when the family sold their cow to pay the child's school fees. Substantial amounts of grain, money, or goods brought into the house make the gods, in the shaman's words, "open wide their eyes" *(nunŭl ttŭida)*. Thus, while some villagers explain the *kosa* as an act of thanksgiving for a bountiful harvest or a turn of luck, it is also a preventive measure against misfortune precipitated by the slighted, angry gods.

A woman might make a small wine *kosa* when she has had a bad dream *(sikkŭroŭn kkumjari,* lit. "noisy dream") interpreted as a sign of divine displeasure. A few women make wine offerings on the first and fifteenth of every month. On the seventh day of the lunar month, when the grain is ripening and the outcome of the harvest certain, some women offer a *kosa* to the Seven Stars, special protectors of children. A woman makes flour pancakes *(milttŏk)* and offers them with rice wine to the Seven Stars atop the storage jars and to all of the other gods throughout the house.[3] Shamans also prescribe *kosa* when they divine that neglected household gods are the source of a family's immediate problems and providing the situation is not serious enough to merit a more elaborate ritual *(kut)*. A *kosa* might also be recommended if the family cannot afford the more elaborate ritual, or if city neighbors will object to the noise of the shaman's drum.

The *mansin*'s *kosa* is midway between a housewife's quiet *kosa* and a flamboyant *kut*. The gods speak, giving the family divinations and advice, but without the costumes, drum music, dancing, extensive drama, and mime play of a *kut*. It is a relatively cheap way to learn the will of the gods and restore the household to their good graces. One woman told me that she often hires a *mansin* for the tenth-month *kosa* because she enjoys hearing the gods' optimistic predictions.

Yangja's Mother hired Yongsu's Mother to do a *kosa* after a bad dream. Yangja's Father, a taxi driver, had been incarcerated on a manslaughter charge after his second major traffic accident. He found work as a bus driver shortly after his release from prison but the family was anxious lest, in the high-risk business of driving, he suffer yet another accident. In the *kosa* the household gods promised improved fortunes for all of Yangja's household. Yangja's parents would eventually be able to buy their own house, the supernatural Official promised. For the present, the god advised, they should exercise financial caution, but move from their cramped rented room to more auspicious quarters across the street. Yangja's Father's Body-governing Official warned him of a dangerous spot near a bridge on his bus route where there had been accidents in the past. An accretion of red disaster made this place increasingly perilous. Yangja's Father should cast out a handful of millet to drive off the red disaster when he passes this spot in his bus.

The gods are in and of the house and every house has them. The *kosa*-holding group is a distinct residential unit gathered under one roof and within one set of walls. This group includes co-resident married children with their spouses and children and co-resident parents-in-law retired from active household management. An unmarried son or daughter living away from home for work or military service receives blessings bestowed in *kosa* since this child may yet legitimately reside at home. Unmarried sons have not yet established a separate household under a separate roof, and unmarried daughters have not yet joined another family. Non-kin boarders or farm laborers are also part of the household. The housewife sets rice cake in their rooms and they reap supernatural benefits as if they were children of the house. When a married son, even the primary heir, lives apart from his parents, his own wife gives *kosa* to their household gods. A house is sufficient precondition for the existence of a household pantheon under the House Lord's sway. According to Yongsu's Mother, "Every house has a roof beam, so every house has a House Lord. There is a House Lord in the beggar's hovel and a House Lord in the tile-roofed house." I once mentioned to Yongsu's Mother that American houses lack House Lords. Usually receptive to cross-cultural comparisons, she told me flatly that this was impossible.

The House Lord[4] is the house tutelary. The House Lord is also the male household head's supernatural counterpart; the head's rice bowl, filled with grain, is part of the House Lord's offering. The *mansin* say, "Where there is a man of the house [*taeju*], there is a House Lord [Sŏngju]." They describe the House Lord as "king," and when he appears in *kut,* they dress him in the red robe and high-crowned hat of a magistrate or king. The House Lord reigns from the main roof beam above the porch, where the house head gives *chesa* to the family's ancestors.

Pollutions accrued from births and deaths cause the House Lord to flee the house. A *mansin* is called in periodically to help the family call back and "receive the House Lord" *(Sŏngju padŭngŏt).*[5] The House Lord who flees birth and death and who must periodically be restored to the house suggests cycles of household succession, of fathers who become ancestors and sons who become house heads. Although the male household head is said to "receive" the House Lord, women perform the summoning on his behalf. A few men have the capacity to receive the House Lord on a shaking branch, just as a few men have a compulsion to dance *mugam* at *kut,* but no house head should summon his own House Lord.

According to the *mansin,* a family should conduct the House Lord back into the home once every three years, in an auspicious year by the household head's horoscope. Only a few houses in Enduring Pine Village conscientiously receive the House Lord this often. Receiving the House Lord is a dramatic event. I witnessed several receptions during *kut.* Each case conformed, more or less, to the following description. A woman squats on the floor, holding a pine branch upright in a tub of rice grain. She need not be a member of the family, a neighbor with a known capacity for receiving the House Lord can hold the branch. A *mansin* kneels beside the woman, shaking a bell rattle and singing an invocation to the House Lord. After some minutes the pine needles flutter ever so slightly. The *mansin* now actively coaxes the House Lord into the home. The branch wobbles back and forth in the woman's hands, seemingly on its own strength. The woman rises jerkily to her feet, as if pulled up by the will of the branch. While the drummer plays a steady, rapid rhythm, the branch pulls the woman about the house, off the porch, into the courtyard, and often far out into the fields and alleyways beyond the gate. Another woman runs beside her carrying wine and rice cake to treat the House Lord. Eventually the woman returns to the porch, the branch still shaking in her hands. She stretches up and taps the roof beam, securing the House Lord once again in the home. Later the *mansin* will wrap some pine needles from the branch, rice grains, and a few coins in white paper and paste them to the beam as a placing for the god.

The village tutelary (Sŏnang, Todang) is the collective equivalent of

Sŏngju in the household. When a village sponsors a *kut* to honor the Tutelary God and purge the community of baleful forces, the *kut* follows the form of a household *kut* with the community's Tutelary God substituted for the House Lord. Women represent each village household before their combined gods, and ancestors from any village house can be summoned up to speak through the *mansin*. Like the House Lord, the village Tutelary God descends into the community on a shaking branch, a branch cut from the village shrine tree. I saw one summoning in a village where the male god was paired with a consort. An elderly couple held branches for the male and female village Sŏnang. The wife's spirit proved the more vigorous and led her down the road well in advance of her husband.

As the House Lord presides over the cycles of household succession, the House Site Official patrols the temporal household, the land *(changso)* within the house walls. The House Site Official controls the prosperity and good fortune of the family dwelling on the site. One woman told me that her household sponsors periodic *kut* because the site is said to be strong. The House Site Official would seem a personification of abstract geomantic principles, but for a crucial difference. The geomancy of the house site or grave is either inherently good or inherently bad, with the fortunes of the family showing the consequences. One House Site Official is neither better nor worse than the Officials of other house sites, although the Official of a particular house site may be stronger, more vigorous *(seda)* than another. This is a mixed blessing. A strong supernatural Official can work to the family's benefit, but only if periodically satisfied with tribute. When wealth enters the family and the Official is not acknowledged, he punishes the offenders. Yongsu's Mother told me of a family that had failed to offer *kosa* when they sold the house. "The House Site Official wanted a drink of wine, so he stirred up trouble. The wife got sick and they had to spend a lot of money on hospital bills." Like the other spirit Officials, the House Site Official appears in the *mansin*'s *kut* wearing a blue vest and broad-brimmed black hat, the costume of the magistrate's avaricious underling. Like the other Officials, he makes known his greedy appetite, ostentatiously hauling away his tribute food on top of his head. A full steamer of rice cake, the legs of a cow, the head of a pig, or even the weighty head of a cow are the offerings the supernatural Officials claim as proper tribute. True to form, the House Site Official drinks heavily, and shamelessly demands cash.

When a family moves, they should announce their intentions to the

House Site Official and bid farewell with libations of wine. Otherwise the House Site Official is unsettled when people and goods move in and out. He follows the former occupants, making trouble for them in their new abode. When Yongsu's Mother moved to Enduring Pine Village she offered wine to the House Site Official in her old house and asked him to stay in place. She claims that the new residents did not treat the god properly, and he followed her despite the farewell libation. He now receives offerings in her new home.

Emigration may pose serious supernatural problems. In the case of at least one family, the wife worshiped the household gods and patronized a *mansin* before the family emigrated to the United States. But when the family left home, they had neither the money nor the inclination to propitiate the household gods and bid them stay in place in Korea. Once in the United States nothing went well. Parents and children were sick and the husband had trouble finding and holding a job. The wife wrote to her sister in Korea and asked her to contact her regular *mansin* to divine the cause of their misfortune. The *mansin* determined that the unpropitiated House Site Official had followed the family to the United States along with several restless ancestors. These supernatural émigrés fluttered about, unsettled and angry, the source of the family's ill luck.

The family sent money to the sister in Korea for a *kut,* held in absentia, to propitiate their restless spirits. This *kut* was tape-recorded and sent to the family so that they might benefit from the gods' counsel spoken through the *mansin's* lips. The family dedicated a costume to their Official, which the *mansin* would store in her shrine, thus settling the god there. The Official would drink, feast, and play whenever the *mansin* wore his costume in *kut.*

The House Site Official must be settled and, so too, the ideal family. The abandoned House Site Official's disoriented frustration reflects some of the ambiguity in contemporary residence patterns. In Enduring Pine Village, families switch dwellings and move back and forth between town and country. Emigration overseas poses new challenges to a ritual system predicated upon a relatively stable and continuous relationship between family, house, site, and gods. With the aid of a ritual specialist, families make shifts and adaptations to contemporary needs; the tape-recorded *kut* is a timely innovation.

The House Site Official has jurisdiction over all of the residents who live within the house walls. When a family of boarders in the rented room of a larger dwelling offers *kosa* or *kut* to their own pantheon, they make an offering to their own House Site Official and to their landlord's Official as well, since the boarder occupies a subdistrict within his jurisdiction. Honoring the gods in a rented room is tricky business, since other gods dwelling under the same roof will not be propitiated. Some women even claimed, "You don't do *kosa* in a rented room," but other women, like Yangja's Mother, set out rice cake in rented rooms. Even *kut* are held in rented rooms, but are especially difficult when several separate families and their own pantheons live together in a single house. The sound of the drum makes all of the gods "open wide their eyes" *(nunŭl ttŭida)*. I recall a series of *kut* held in a three-family dwelling in the burgeoning new satellite town of Tranquil Spring. The landlord's family rented rooms to two other families. One renting family vended food, wine, and sundries in a shop on the street side of the house. Because business was bad and the daughter-in-law ill, the inexperienced *mansin*, Okkyŏng's Mother, advised the family to hold a *kut*.

Shortly thereafter, the family's perennially alcoholic landlord began to drink heavily, carouse late into the night, and beat his wife when he returned home. The much-abused landlady held a *kut*. Yongsu's Mother, who returned to the Tranquil Spring house for this second *kut,* said that the renting family should have held their *kut* in Okkyŏng's Mother's own shrine. There, the sound of the drum and the sight of the feasting and playing would not have awakened the gods and ancestors of the landlord's family. From the day of the landlord's *kut,* the family in the second set of rented rooms noticed that much was amiss. The baby had crying fits, the husband had pains in his limbs, and the young wife, burdened by inexplicable dread, could not bring herself to step outside the gate. The *mansin* returned to perform a *kut* for this third set of gods and ancestors stirred up by the *kut* in the landlord's quarters. Boarding families are an awkward exception to the overriding rule that a house implies a single main roof beam, a single roof beam implies a single tutelary House Lord, a male household head, and a female house manager who tends the household gods.

Household Ritual as Women's Ritual

Only one woman in the household, the senior woman, does *kosa*. Wives of first sons living with the husband's parents do *kosa* and other women's rituals when the mother-in-law dies or when she retires as active manager. Other women begin to offer *kosa* when they "set up housekeeping" *(sallim halttae put'ŏ),* establish their own house. The woman who offers *kosa* is mistress of her own home, petitioning her own gods in the interests of herself, her husband, and her household.

We have seen Korean women visiting shaman shrines, sponsoring *kut,* holding simple exorcisms, and importuning the *mansin*'s gods. We have seen some Korean women, professional shamans, divine the future, summon the gods, and cast out malevolent spirits. It should not surprise us that the Korean housewife invokes and petitions the house gods, that she is vested with priestly authority within the home. The ethnography of Chinese and Japanese household religion, however, would lead us to other nuances of interpretation. In Japan, women prepare and serve offerings to the ancestors and house gods when they prepare and serve the family's food. They feed the spirits much as they feed everyone else, no special priestly role is implied (Morioka 1968; Smith 1974, 118–120). In China, women similarly see to the routine feeding of the ancestors, but men worship the kitchen god as an attribute of male authority in the household (Freedman 1979b, 283). I will discuss significant contrasts between the family structure and the structure of family religion in these three societies in my conclusion, but some particular features of Korean women's *kosa* bear mention here. Although the House Lord is identified with the male house head, a woman petitions this god on her own, not her husband's, authority. The offering she makes to the gods consists of special food, distinct from the meals she serves her family.

China anthropologists have cued us to the social significance of different types of offering food (A. Wolf 1974, esp. 176–178). One serves a feast to certain categories of the supernatural, to the ancestors who are family. In Korea women cook the ancestors' food, but men make the formal offering. Women feed the recent dead during the mourning period when ancestral souls linger among the living family. Rice and soup are offered to the ancestors as a meal shared among living and dead kin (see chap. 7). With the official-like gods, one would not presume common dining. The gods' offering food at *kut* and *kosa* is either a wine-tray treat or tribute to be carried away. In *kut,* supernatural Officials hoist steamers of rice cake and chunks of meat to their heads; they carry cows' heads and pigs' carcasses on their backs, cackling gleefully. In *kosa,* a housewife offers cups of wine, steamed rice cake, dried fish, grilled meat, and sometimes even steamed cow's legs or a steamed pig's head, but—and this is crucial—no steamed rice.

"Pabŭl anmokŭmyŏn siksaga andoenda," Koreans say, "If you don't eat rice, it's no meal." Korean women describe the food they set out in *kosa* as *anju,* snack food to accompany wine. The steamed pig's head is very special *anju.* When the shaman in Enduring Pine Village offered a pig's head in her shrine, the old men in her neighborhood all paid a less than subtle social call, seeking the sweet meat of the pig's head with a round of wine.

In *kosa* a woman petitions the gods with a treat of wine and delicacies as her husband might try to win the good graces of a minor local functionary. A god is a fallible official, plump and greedy and amenable to bribes and flattery. A comic opera type, a costumed shaman mirthfully portrays the House Site Official as a conceited creature of insatiable appetite. When a woman offers *kosa* to such a being, she is not simply "feeding the gods along with everybody else." Petitioning the gods inside the home, she parallels her husband's strategies to win the good graces of the powerful outside the home. The form and content of the rite suggest accepted masculine behavior, not domestic catering.

It could still be argued that a woman performs *kosa* as her husband's representative before the household gods, demonstrating his authority as household head rather than her authority as housewife. Husbands do benefit from *kosa* since the gods protect the household's interests and those interests depend, in large part, on the husband's health and success. But women represent households not husbands, for in other contexts Korean men offer *kosa* themselves. When a company opens an office, when musicians occupy a new studio, or when a restaurant relocates, the group offers *kosa* led by the director or manager. I once saw men set up *kosa* offerings in the foyer of the Garden Tower Apartments, a high-rise office building in Seoul, where a cement company had just opened an office on one of the upper floors. The man in business dress who was arranging the pig's head told me that the *kosa* would benefit both his company and everyone else in the building. I suspect, but could not then confirm, that the offering in the foyer was for the House Site Official of the Garden Tower Apartments. Perhaps the most elaborate *kosa* of the decade was held in 1978 to commemorate the opening of the Sejong Cultural Center, a luxurious theater complex in downtown Seoul.

At the Tano Festival at Kangnŭng, on Korea's East Coast, shamans entertain the county Tutelary God (Sŏnang). Each morning, before the shamans begin their *kut,* the assorted local functionaries that constitute the festival committee don the costumes of an antique magistrate's court and make their offering to the Tutelary God. Although the ritual form resembles a Confucian sacrifice *(che),* the committee called these offerings *kosa.* Public space is men's space, and here men petition the gods themselves—in offices, in public buildings, or as the official representatives of a community. The house is women's space and women represent the household before the household gods.

In some Korean communities men do petition one or another house tutelary. In some villages in Kangwŏn Province men care for the House Lord (Sŏngju) and women tend the Stove God (Chowang), but both gods are honored in household rituals called Chisinje. Folklorists note that in this region there are two kinds of House Lord, one in the roof beam and one on the hearth, male and female respectively (MCBCPP "Kangwŏn," 156–159). In villages in North Ch'ungch'ŏn Province the household's senior couple makes offerings to the house gods and earth gods on an auspicious day. If the husband or wife has died, the surviving partner makes these offerings alone (MCBCPP "Ch'ungbuk," 85). In some communities on Cheju Island men make offerings to the Earth God (T'osinje) while women honor the gods inside the house *(anje),* an arrangement compatible with Korean perceptions of husband and wife as "outside" and "inside" persons (MCBCPP "Cheju," 85). In at least one east coast village, the sex of the officiant does not seem to be important (Guillemoz 1983). No doubt other examples of men honoring house gods exist. While these examples belie the tidy dichotomy of domestic ritual in Enduring Pine Village, they suggest the complementarity of male and female roles in the house god's cult, not the exclusion or subordination of women.

Women's Gods and Traditions

The housewife's *kosa* is a prayer for the continuing prosperity of the household as a unit of production and consumption, and she officiates as female house manager. Other gods and other ritual procedures reflect the aspirations and experiences of women as mothers and grandmothers. These "womanly" observances are a part, but not the whole of Korean women's religious experience.

The Birth Grandmother[6] resides in the inner room, the most sequestered part of the house. The inner room is women's space, and it is here that conception, gestation, and birth take place. Infants are nurtured in the inner room and young children sleep here under the Birth Grandmother's protection. An infertile woman "receives the Birth Grandmother" *(Samsin padŭngŏt)* as the male household head "receives the House Lord." To induce conception in an infertile or sonless woman, the *mansin* coaxes the Birth Grandmother into a gourd dipper filled with rice grain. The dipper shakes in the hands of the woman who would become pregnant. The woman must carefully carry the dipper of grain into the inner room and set it down, conduct the fertile seed into the metaphoric womb of the house (Kendall 1977c).

With childbirth the inner room becomes a separate sacred space sheltering mother and baby from potentially dangerous forces outside. In the ideal situation, seldom honored in busy country homes, mother and baby remain sequestered in the birth room for three weeks after the birth. The family guards the ritual cleanliness of the birth room and, by extension, the entire house, lest pollution offend the Birth Grandmother. Those who assist at the birth must be ritually clean, neither menstruating nor from a house in mourning. Only members of the household enter the birth room during the postpartum period. Only a few houses in Enduring Pine Village hang the traditional hemp rope festooned with pine needles and peppers or lumps of charcoal to warn outsiders of a recent birth, but villagers still honor the proscription. For fear of offending the Birth Grandmother, only those free from pollution *(pujŏng ŏmnŭn saram)* dare enter the house.

Some women return to their natal homes to be delivered by their own mothers, and though clinic deliveries are growing in popularity, most villagers expect the mother-in-law to assist at the birth and deliver the child. "Your mother-in-law delivers you, who else would deliver you? She's the senior member of the household, so you can trust her. It's painful; she does the massage. You can't go out so she does the cooking. She keeps everything clean and protects you so you won't catch cold wind [*ch'an param*]. Your mother-in-law is the best one to do all that."

The family may ask other experienced neighbor women to help. They are described as grandmothers or neighborhood grandmothers *(tongnae halmŏni),* older women who have had considerable experience both giving birth and attending deliveries. In some villages an old and experienced midwife may even be called a Birth Grandmother (Dorothea Sich, personal communication). On Cheju Island old women who pray for children's health are Birth Grandmothers (Soonyoung Yoon, personal communication). Ideally, the mother-in-law does the housework while mother and baby are sequestered in the birth room, for if the mother should emerge too soon, she may catch cold wind and later suffer from arthritis, body weakness, and a general susceptibility to cold.[7] With the mother-in-law/grandmother thus intimately involved in the birth process, the birth spirit also assumes the guise of a white-haired grandmother *(hayan halmŏni)*. An experienced older woman guards the physical and ritual safety of mother and baby during the birth and postpartum.

There is an appropriate blending of old woman and bodhisattva in the shaman's portrayal of the Birth Grandmother, the Buddhist Sage (Grandmother), and the Seven Stars. In *kut,* all of these divinities wear white robes and peaked cowls, the costume worn in Buddhist ritual dances. The Korean term *posal,* "bodhisattva," has many applications. Women who maintain Buddhist temples as the wives or widows of monks, as nuns, and as lay caretakers are called *posal.* A type of inspirational diviner who chants with a round drum and recites sutra-like invocations is also a *posal.* A woman who maintains a private temple and leads an ascetic existence is a *posal.* By broadest extension, the grandmother who observes fasts and rigorously worships at temples, shaman shrines, or mountains for the sake of her children and grandchildren approaches the status of *posal.*

The mother-in-law/grandmother is not an entirely benevolent figure, nor is the Birth Grandmother an eternally benevolent presence. The mother-in-law can be a harsh and petulant taskmaster; the Birth Grandmother becomes angry when her commands are ignored and when she does not receive her proper due in offerings. When an infant sickens or dies soon after birth, the *mansin* often divines that the anger of the Birth Grandmother is the cause. A *mansin* attributed an eight-day-old infant's persistent diarrhea and crying to the family's greed and carelessness. After the birth they brought meat and chicken into the house. The whole family had feasted without making a special offering to the Birth Grandmother, who was ultimately responsible for the safe delivery. Angry at this neglect, the Birth Grandmother did not protect the child from its own grandmother's ghost. The dead woman, pleased with the birth of her grandchild, reached out to stroke the baby. This touch of the dead, even though well-intentioned, caused the infant to sicken.

Greeting the Birth Grandmother with elaborate offerings before or shortly after birth insures her good offices (Samsin Me). At the very least, for three days after the birth the mother-in-law sets rice and kelp soup beside the mother's pillow. She prays to the Birth Grandmother to "make the milk flow." The mother consumes the offering food to foster a copious lactation.

The Birth Grandmother, like any statused elder, is affronted by neglect and cajoled with feasts and flattery. Birth Grandmother and living mother-in-law together preserve mother and child and, ultimately, the continuity of the house. Rites of the Birth Grandmother and her offerings in *kosa* and *kut* acknowledge that the heirs of the house are of woman born and by woman delivered. New life is fragile and requires a "grandmother's" practical and ritual knowledge through the cooperation across generations of potentially antagonistic in-marrying women.

In some households women make special offerings to the Seven Stars (Ch'ilsŏng). The Seven Stars protect children, especially children under the age of seven. A child with a sprinkling of seven freckles or moles is called "child of the Seven Stars" and receives their special attention. Mothers also pray to the Seven Stars for grown sons' safety, occupational success, or academic progress. One woman could afford only simple offerings.

> For the last thirteen years, I've offered a bowl of water on the seventh day of every month. I set a bowl of water on the storage jars [for the Seven Stars] and a bowl of water in the inner room [for the Birth Grandmother]. I started doing this when my son went to Vietnam. My mother-in-law showed me what to do. She used to make offerings to the Seven Stars, but now we're poor, so we just offer river water. I do this for my children.

Like the Birth Grandmother, the Seven Stars influence conception. Where the *mansin* divines that a woman is infertile because "the Seven Stars don't open their eyes," the woman prays to the Seven Stars on a mountain. A woman in Righteous Town told my assistant, "I couldn't get pregnant. Everyone said I should go to the mountain. I went with a *mansin* and a friend. I took rice grain, kelp [for soup], and fruit, and prayed beside a mountain spring."

When the Seven Stars answer a woman's prayers and she gives birth to a son, the Seven Stars are honored in her house. I had already gone to three *kut* with Yongsu's Mother when I first saw a *mansin* in white

Buddhist robes invoke the Seven Stars on the storage jars beside the house. I asked what was happening and why I had not seen the Seven Stars at the other *kut*. Yongsu's Mother told me, "They've done it this way in this house from long ago." At the time, her answer appeared to be a frustrating ethnographic dead end. Months later, when I had some feeling for the significance of household traditions in religious practice, she explained. Where women have prayed to the Seven Stars for the birth and health of sons, they honor this god on the seventh day of the seventh lunar month. They offer rice wine and flour pancakes throughout the house, and some women make special offerings at the *mansin*'s shrine. In houses where they are honored the Seven Stars descend and possess the *mansin* in *kut*.

Women's mountain pilgrimages *(sanŭl ssŭda)* are another way to honor the Seven Stars. Some women go to the mountains to worship them at the same time that they worship the Mountain God. Mountain worship illuminates the interconnection between household ritual traditions and a woman's power-charged relationships with particular gods. Women told me, "You pray on the mountain so your children will all grow up well and get established in life. You pray that they will have long lives and attain high position." Yongsu's paternal grandmother made mountain pilgrimages throughout her married life. Yongsu's Mother explained,

> My husband told me that when he was a boy, he would go up the mountain with his mother, carrying the firewood on his back for her. She washed the rice and cooked it on the mountain. She prayed, "Please make my children grow up well."
>
> In my husband's family, there were six brothers and two sisters besides one child who died. My mother-in-law raised all these children. She sent her daughters to their husbands' homes and saw all of her sons take wives before she died. But look at them now! The daughters-in-law haven't used the mountain, and now they're all widows or widowers in the Yun family. When I married into that family [as a second wife], my mother-in-law was already dead. My sisters-in-law should have told me about using the mountain, they should have showed me what to do. Now my sons are growing up without a father.

By using the mountain, the woman assumes a serious responsibility. If she breaks her obligation, her household is vulnerable to disaster. Divining, Yongsu's Mother would often ask a new client, "Didn't someone in your husband's family use the mountain? Ask them when you go home if you don't know." Then she instructs her client in the business of making a mountain pilgrimage.

Using the mountain is a secret, quiet, private act fraught with potential danger. A woman carefully prepares herself for the journey. Yongsu's Mother instructed me,

> For three days you must eat no fish or meat and have no contact with mourners. You must be very clean, no menstruation. You take a bath before you go and wash your hair. You wash the rice grains absolutely clean, picking out every last small stone.

Between her home and the sacred spot on the mountain where she will pray, the woman passes through dangerous transitional space. An untoward event will undo all her efforts. Yongsu's Mother cautioned,

> On the way up the mountain, if you see a snake or dead frog or insect, you have to come back down again. If someone comes up and says, "So-and-so has just died," you can't go up the mountain. You have to be very quiet going up and down. You shouldn't talk, but once you're there, it's all right. And you can't say things like, "My feet hurt, let's rest." When you come back, you can't respond to greetings. If someone asks you where you have been, you can't say anything. That's why it is best to go up very early in the morning or at ten or eleven at night when no one is around.

Mountain worship requires scrupulous ritual purity and a secret, quiet detachment from the social world of greetings and conversation as one passes from mundane to sacred space and back again. "Look at the ground, Tallae. Don't greet anyone, whatever they say!" Yongsu's Mother hissed when we reached the edge of the village after worshiping at the tutelary shrine shortly after dawn. With a tub of food and ritual equipment on her head, she cast her eyes down, flung her arms behind her back, and bolted across the final stretch of road into her own door. She hit the brass bells in the shrine and bowed, then ripped the kerchief off my head and shoved me to the floor in a bow. She announced to the gods of her shrine, "Tallae has gone and used the mountain." Now we could talk again.

A false move, an improper word, and things will turn out worse than if the pilgrimage had not been attempted in the first place. The

Clear Spring Mansin and a few of her clients were going to use the mountain together. One woman began to menstruate that morning. She went to the arranged meeting place and told the women why she could not go with them. Her husband, a taxi driver, was killed in a collision the very next day. "Stupid woman," said Yongsu's Mother, "they were going to use the mountain and she came and talked about things like that. She should have just said, 'I'm sorry, but I can't go with you today!' "

Yongsu's Mother attributed family quarrels and her heavy heart to excessive chattering with her own sister when they went up the mountain together. She planned to pray at the stone Buddha of a hillside temple in Seoul to undo her ill luck, but a death in the neighborhood, throwing everyone into a state of ritual pollution, upset her immediate plans. After a long period of illness and few clients, she used the mountain behind the village on New Year's Day and returned light-hearted.

Mountains are pure and powerful, elevated and separate space. When women honor Mountain Gods in household *kosa* and *kut,* they place offerings on storage jars beside the house, elevated high off the ground and away from the overhanging roof. Koreans consider the storage platform, where the family keeps huge quantities of essential condiments, the cleanest place within the walls, the proper analogue to a mountain.

Women return from the mountain and give birth to sons. Men carry corpses away "to the mountain," the euphemism for a hillside grave. The Mountain God holds the family's dead in place, keeps them from lurking about in the world below. He receives a libation at the graveside. Between them, the Seven Stars and the Mountain God oversee birth and death, entrance and exit from life in the villages and towns below the mountain.

The Mountain God of the Native Place (Ponhyang Sansin) is associated, however broadly, with the terrestrial location of one's husband's family. When her household moves away, a woman uses the most significant mountain near her new home but continues to acknowledge the original Mountain God in *kosa* and *kut.* When Yongsu's Mother did *kosa* at Yangja's house, she invoked the Mountain God of Chiri Mountain, the most famous mountain in Yangja's Father's native province. Yongsu's Mother goes by bus and taxi to the foot of a stately peak in the next province. Her mother-in-law worshiped here and her husband's kin live nearby. The Mountain God of their Native Place reigns here, but Yongsu's Mother also visits the village shrines on a hillside near her present home.

Mountain worship is analogous to the diffusion of extended kin groups. Branches diffused over time and space hark back to the original lineage seat and site (read mountain) of the founders' graves. Branches establish their own geographical identity and their own mountain graves but they hark back to the source in genealogies and, where possible, members return to the ancestral mountain for high-level graveside lineage rites. Sacred mountains are not, to my knowledge, gravesites. Death pollution seems antithetical to the purity of sacred mountains, but the geomantic power of a gravesite, the source of an extended kin group's blessings, is analogous to the power of sacred mountains where women's prayers channel sons and blessings to their families.

Powerful Gods and Family Traditions

Yongsu's Grandmother did menial work in a Buddhist temple. Her first son was born while a monk tapped his wooden clapper and chanted in the next room. Throughout her life Yongsu's Grandmother denied neighbor women's suggestions that she honor the Buddhist Sage. In her dreams she offered white rice cake, but on waking she ignored the implications. Her eldest son died in the Korean War. Another son died of measles. When her only surviving son crippled his hand in an accident at work, Yongsu's Grandmother started worshiping the Buddhist Sage and the Seven Stars lest further misfortune befall her last son. The Buddhist Sage was vengeful for having been denied for so long, and Yongsu's Grandmother has suffered. Her husband left her for a secondary wife, sons died, and now, in old age, a shrewish daughter-in-law makes her life miserable.

In the world of shaman and housewife, present misfortune is linked to past history. Powerful gods and lost traditions emerge from a *mansin*'s divination and a kinswoman's confirmation. Restoring the family's connection to sacred places and acknowledging spiritually powerful beings brings healing.

Chinsuk's Grandmother gave birth only to daughters until she prayed on the mountain. Then Chinsuk's Father was born. Chinsuk's

Father fled south during the war. Chinsuk's Mother, his second wife, lived with her husband in Righteous Town. It never occured to Chinsuk's Mother that she should pray on the mountain. Chinsuk's Mother came to Yongsu's Mother for a divination when her household seemed to be falling apart. Her husband, nervous and distracted, was obsessed with a woman some thirty years his junior. The stepson neglected his studies and stole petty cash. The young reprobate belligerently demanded his own way with glaring eyes and threatened blows. On Yongsu's Mother's advice, Chinsuk's Mother held a *kut* and prayed to the Seven Stars on a mountain near her home.

Like Chinsuk's Mother, the Waterfall Valley Auntie had married a refugee and knew little about her husband's family. When she first came to Yongsu's Mother for divination, Yongsu's Mother had a vision of a woman in a white robe and peaked cowl. She asked the Waterfall Valley Auntie, "Was there someone long ago who was the same sort of person I am?" The Waterfall Valley Auntie explained that her husband fled the North when he was still young, so she did not know. Yongsu's Mother told her to ask at home. The husband's elder sister in Seoul confirmed that the mother had been a *posal,* a Buddhist-style diviner, long ago in North Korea.

Like a *mansin,* a *posal* receives her calling through divine possession. A *posal* recites what are supposed to be sutras and does not dance like a *mansin.* She divines and performs simple rituals. The Willow Market Auntie's mother-in-law was a famous *posal.* Yongsu's Mother said of her, "She lived in a little house on the mountain; she felt compelled to live there from the time she became a *posal.* When she saw someone approaching from a distance, she could tell if it was a menstruating woman or someone from a house of mourning. She would shriek out, calling them 'filthy bastards.' She would dream about her clients and know exactly what was on their minds when they came to see her."

Dead *mansin* and *posal,* by virtue of their powers, influence the fortunes of their descendants' households. Both the Willow Market Auntie and the Waterfall Valley Auntie honor the Buddhist Sage, the divine manifestation of *posal* women. They have dedicated white robes and cowls to the Buddhist Sage, costumes embroidered with their husbands' names and stored at Yongsu's Mother's shrine.

In households where the women long patronized a particular *mansin,* she appears as the Great Spirit Grandmother in their *kut.* The transformation is appropriate. In life she invoked the family's ancestors. As the Great Spirit Grandmother she still leads their ancestors back into the home. She remains the family's link with the netherworld. At an Yi family *kut,* their old *mansin* appeared in the Great Spirit Grandmother's sequence, greeting Yi sisters-in-law and neighbor women who had been her clients with joyful nods and smiles of reunion.

Sometimes these meetings are not so amicable. When the *mansin* who initiated and trained the Chatterbox Mansin appeared as the Great Spirit Grandmother at a *kut* for one of Chatterbox's kinswomen, Chatterbox and her spirit mother quarreled over past grievances. The dead *mansin* lambasted the Chatterbox Mansin for breaking trust and going out on her own. The Chatterbox Mansin yelled back, blaming her spirit mother for the rupture. She criticized the dead *mansin*'s stinginess when Chatterbox Mansin's father died.

Other gods emerge from other household traditions. A Cho ancestor established a shrine to Mirŭk Buddha (Maitreya) and generations of Chos maintained the shrine over the years. Cho women prayed there. When a Cho household held a *kut,* Mirŭk appeared with the Buddhist Sage.

Like a *mansin* or *posal,* an illustrious male ancestor can become a pantheon deity. Sometimes a *mansin*'s divination reveals "someone who carried a sword in the palace," a military official. This ancestor, however distant, influences the household as a strong pantheon General. The family dedicates a broad-sleeved robe and high-crowned hat to the General or a black robe with red sleeves to the Spirit Warrior. This practice suggests lineage rites honoring illustrious forebears, but only in murky approximation. Either the client remembers an officeholding ancestor in the recent or genealogically distant past, or the *mansin* suggests, "You're of the Munhwa Yus [a far-flung surname group]. Many of the Yus served in the palace." All Korean surname groups claim office holders in their genealogies. In the *mansin*'s rites, demonstrated genealogical proximity is not at issue.

The Great King of the Pae family stands above this tenuous, ad hoc appeal to illustrious forebears. The Paes, a local branch of a recognized *yangban* lineage with a scrupulously maintained genealogy, claim close connection to the main line. Two Pae ancestors held high office as advisors to the king in the early years of the Yi dynasty. A secondary son of one of these officials founded the Willow Market branch of the Pae lineage.

Two high officials appear as Great Kings in the pantheons of Pae families. The Pae local lineage maintains a shrine for its Great King and his wife. In the shrine Pae women store two boxes of robes: broad-sleeved red robes and high-crowned hats for the king, yellow blouses and red skirts for his "princess" wife. Before weddings or sixty-first birthdays, Pae women present handkerchiefs as tribute to the royal pair. The shrine holds bundles of these gauzy strips of cloth. Every five years or so, the local lineage sponsors a *kut* for the Great King's pleasure, so that he will continue to foster harmony and prevent dissension among lineage members. When a Pae household holds a *kut* women fetch costumes from the shrine for the *mansin*. The Great King and his wife appear just before the family's close ancestors arrive. The pair sometimes appears when Pae women make offerings at the *mansin*'s shrine.

Other pantheon deities exemplify neither social nor religious attainments. The Child Messengers (Tongja Pyŏlsang) and the Princess (Hogu) lived short, inglorious lives, dying as children or young maidens, often of smallpox or measles. Those who died without issue cannot remain with the family as ancestors. As ghosts they are banished from the house to roam the world as hungry beggars. By force of mischief a few of these otherwise insignificant beings win a place in the family pantheon and receive gifts of bright clothing, pocket money, and treats to pacify their caprice.

Two of the Wine House Auntie's siblings, a boy and a girl, died in childhood. With a child's love of bright colors, they followed the rainbow-striped marriage quilt their sister brought to her husband's house. Thereafter, the Wine House Auntie's married life was filled with hardship and strife. Yongsu's Mother told her to buy two little suits of Korean clothing, sold in the market for boys' and girls' first-birthday celebrations *(tol)*.[8] The Wine House Auntie put a small bill in the embroidered pouch attached to each suit of clothing. Yongsu's Mother performed *kosa,* and the Wine House Auntie dedicated the clothing. The Child Messengers appeared, whining for candy and complaining that the Wine House Auntie had forgotten to buy the little boy a festive cap.

Child Messengers appear in *kut* with the Special Messenger. The *mansin* ties their little outfits to the Special Messenger's belt and manifests them with a high, childish voice. Demanding sugar candy and small change, Child Messengers cry a lot "because they are children."[9]

The Princess is a maiden who died before she married or just after her marriage. Like the Child Messengers, she follows a sister or close friend when the living woman marries. Envy draws her to the bride, who wears an antique palace woman's small crown and rainbow-sleeved jacket or, in modern-style weddings, a white veil. In the bride's new home the Princess stands between husband and wife so they see each other in an unfavorable light. She stirs up strife between them. As the Princess says in *kut,* "I go flutter, flutter, flutter in the inner room." Like the Official, the Princess "opens wide her eyes" and makes trouble out of jealousy when the family brings luxury goods into the house. She is particularly stirred by pretty clothing. Women dedicate a yellow blouse and red skirt to an active Princess, but preventive measures are more effective. On the eve of the wedding some families offer noodles and rice cake, wedding fare, at the *mansin*'s shrine to give the ancestors the first taste of feast food, as is their due. The rite, *yŏt'am,* also holds potentially rambunctious children and maidens in place and prevents them from working mischief in the bride's home.

The more powerful pantheon gods are settled, transformed from wrathful adversaries to benevolent patrons, when a woman dedicates an appropriate robe. The robe is embroidered with the client's name and stored in the *mansin*'s shrine. After a woman dedicates a robe at the shrine, her petulant god is amused whenever the *mansin* wears the costume and dances in *kut.* But when a woman dedicates a robe, her ritual responsibilities accelerate. The robe implies an active deity. An active deity grows impatient for a *kut* every several years, and requires that, in the interim, the woman make regular offerings at the *mansin*'s shrine.

When the robe grows old and worn, the god demands a new one. Recall the Great Spirit Grandmother of the Chŏn family who complained that her own costume compared unfavorably with Grandmother Chŏn's rumpled skirt. At a *kut* in a Pae household, the Buddhist Sage grabbed the housewife by the ears and shook her, expressing rage that the robe the woman had dedicated years before was now riddled with moth holes. The Pae woman bought a length of white fabric for the new robe and dedicated it at the *mansin*'s shrine three days after her *kut.*[10]

Dancing in the *Mansin*'s Robes

Mansin distinguish the Body-governing God from both a pantheon god, who "descends" *(naerida)* into the costumed *mansin* in *kut,* and the ancestor or ghost, who possesses by "striking" (mach'ida) a victim. The Body-governing God "ascends" (orǔda) and compels an ordinary woman to dance. When a woman dances in the mansin's robe (mugam) during an interlude in kut, her Body-governing God (Mom-ju) ascends. A woman wears the mansin's costume appropriate to her own Body-governing God. If a woman has dedicated a robe to a strong pantheon god, she wears this robe for mugam. The woman places money on the drum, dons the appropriate costume, and bows with her head to the floor. She dances, gracefully at first, then leaps into a sequence of rapid jumps to the quickened drum beats. When the woman has danced to exhaustion, her Body-governing God is satisfied and the woman acquires fortune (chaesu) for herself and her family.

Everyone has a Body-governing Official and can wear the Official's blue vest to dance mugam. Some Officials are passive and the women have no inclination to dance when they hear the drum. Some women, like Yangja's Mother and the Rice Shop Auntie, have strong, greedy Officials. The women feel driven to dance mugam whenever they go to kut.

Strong pantheon gods descending upon the mansin during kut reappear as strong Body-governing Gods ascending in women during mugam. A Body-governing Great Spirit Grandmother and a Body-governing Seven Stars appeared when women danced at the Chŏn kut. Spirit Warriors, Mountain Gods, and Buddhist Sages ascend as Body-governing Gods in families where they reign as particularly strong pantheon deities.

Some women have more than one Body-governing God. The daughter-in-law of the Chŏn family had both a Body-governing Seven Stars and a Body-governing Great Spirit. Chinsuk's Mother wears the monk's white robe over the Official's blue vest when she starts to dance. While dancing, she casts the white robe off, and the mansin says, "The Seven Stars played and now the Body-governing Official is playing."

Like the posal or mansin who becomes a household god after death, a woman who rigorously worshiped the Seven Stars while alive acquires the supernatural force to ascend when the women of her household dance mugam. The An women in Tranquil Spring have a strong Body-governing Seven Stars because the deceased grandmother prayed on mountains throughout her life. When the junior line held a kut, a married daughter of the senior line danced mugam in the Seven

Stars' robe. Although the *mugam* dancer is usually silent, this woman began to shout and curse. Speaking for the grandmother, she shrieked that the junior An household had not provided her special rice cake. She struggled when the woman tried to restrain her. Foul expletives poured from her lips to the consternation of Okkyŏng's Mother who, seeing me furiously scribbling notes, begged, "Tallae, don't tell them such bad things about Korea in America." Calmer, the possessed woman held the daughter-in-law of the junior line by the shoulders and murmured over and over, "You're the most unfortunate one, the most pathetic one."

At a *kut* for the neighboring Kim family the next year, the An mother-in-law danced in the white robe and was possessed by her Body-governing Seven Stars, the same ancestral grandmother who had possessed her kinswoman, but was now in a more benevolent mood. Trailing her sleeves through the air, gracefully dancing, her face lit with an ethereal smile, she gently smoothed Mr. Kim's hair. Yongsu's Mother said, "The Seven Stars are really strong in the An family."

Women, then, color the household pantheon with their own traditions, transmitted from mother-in-law to daughter-in-law, down through generations of in-marrying women. As we have seen, some family members transmute themselves into the pantheon. Ancestors assume godly positions through social or ritual attainments; men who were officials and women who were *mansin* and *posal* become gods in descendants' households. Their power for good and ill exceeds and outlasts the power of a mere ancestor. Particularly troublesome children and maiden ghosts wheedle, through their rambunctious behavior, the status of minor gods. A woman who scrupulously worshiped the Seven Stars ascends as a Body-governing God.

Extensions of Godly Power

Kosa is a ritual of the household, and the gods of *kosa* belong to the house—to the structure, the site, and the inner room. Powerful pantheon gods emerge from larger family traditions, and, as such, their influence extends beyond individual households. More than household gods, they are kindred spirits. The senior and junior house of the Song family combined resources to assuage the wrath of the Great Spirit Grandmother, their *mansin* ancestress. Because the Great Spirit

Grandmother was impatient for a *kut,* a son of the senior line drowned and a son of the junior line suffered a prolonged illness. Finally persuaded, the Song family held a *kut* (see chap. 7). By broadest extension of family, the Great King and his wife appear whenever any household in the Pae local lineage holds *kut.* The perimeters of ritual responsibility are open to negotiation and debate, mediated by the shamans' perceptions of divine will and family politics. When the Body-governing Seven Stars lambasted the Ans for neglecting a special offering, the *mansin* loudly declared that the offering to the Seven Stars was the senior house's sole responsibility. The *mansin* saved their client's face before neighbors and kin. Okkyŏng's Mother whispered to me that if the Ans had been willing to spend more money, the *mansin* would certainly have arranged a special offering for the Seven Stars.

The Willow Market Auntie's dilemma betrayed both an ambiguous ritual responsibility and an uncomfortable domestic situation. The Willow Market Auntie had married a Kim man whose mother was a famous *posal.* She makes offerings at the *mansin*'s shrine in honor of the Buddhist Sage, and when she dances *mugam,* the *posal* ancestor ascends. When the Kim husband died the Willow Market Auntie married an Yi man. Her sons by the Kim man are now grown and married. When the Willow Market Auntie made offerings at the shrine on Seven Star Day, the Buddhist Sage complained. As the Buddhist Sage of the Kim family, she could not eat offerings made by a woman from the Yi family. Yongsu's Mother told me later that the eldest Kim son's wife should honor the powerful Buddhist Sage, but both the eldest son and his wife consider shrine worship superstitious and begrudge the expense, so the Willow Market Auntie continues to honor the Buddhist Sage on behalf of her sons by the Kim man. Yongsu's Mother attributes poverty and frequent accidents in the Kim family to the senior daughter-in-law's ritual lapse. The second son bowed to the Buddhist Sage in the shrine before reporting for military duty; Yongsu's Mother predicts that his prospects are bright.

The prime perpetuators of these traditions are women, and godly influence transcends the boundaries of the patrilineal house *(chip).* Child Messengers and the Princess follow an out-marrying sister and assume an inauspicious presence in her new home. Other gods follow women to their husbands' homes, where they work for the family's benefit or detriment depending on the treatment they receive. A Monk

Buddhist Sage followed a Pae woman when she married, but she neither made offerings at a *mansin*'s shrine nor held *kut* until after the untimely deaths of two of her children. A woman in Righteous Town, ashamed of her shaman stepfather, spirited her mother away from him as soon as she had established her own business. After the stepfather's death, he possessed the woman and compelled her to be initiated as a *mansin*. The stepfather became the Great Spirit in her pantheon. A young matron in Willow Market dances *mugam* for the ascent of a Body-governing Buddhist Sage Great Spirit, her own mother, who had avoided the *mansin* calling and had died as a consequence.

As a final demonstration of the varied directions of supernatural influence, consider the complex relationships between women and gods in the Chŏn family *kut* (see fig. 1). Grandfather Chŏn's mother prayed to the Seven Stars for his birth and auspicious rearing. Both the daughter who married out of the Chŏn family and the daughter-in-law who married into the Chŏn family had a Body-governing Seven Stars rise up when they danced *mugam*. Grandmother Chŏn, who, like her daughter-in-law, married into the Chŏn family, danced the ascent of a Body-governing Great Spirit, the *mansin* ancestress from her own natal home. Her sister, married into yet another family, also manifested the Body-governing Great Spirit. As a result of Grandmother Chŏn's marriage, a strong Great Spirit entered the Chŏn pantheon. The daughter-in-law was possessed by both a Body-governing Seven Stars and a Body-governing Great Spirit. She inherits responsibility for the Great Spirit Grandmother as well as the Chŏn women's obligation to the Seven Stars.

Gods make their claims on living families through the *mansin*'s visions. My single-case diagram establishes no rules of absolute transmission, only possibilities. In the midst of the Chŏn daughter-in-law's dance, the Chatterbox Mansin perceived a Body-governing Great Spirit and flung the yellow robe over the dancing woman's shoulders. Grandfather Chŏn's sister danced in the Official's blue vest, not in the Seven Stars' white robe.

Women protect their ritual families by learning from mother-in-law and *mansin* the care and feeding of powerful gods. But a woman's concerns sometimes go beyond her ritual family, back to her own natal home and to the households of married daughters. Her gods are kindred spirits extending their influence out across families in all possible directions. In the Korean woman's ritual realm, neither gods nor

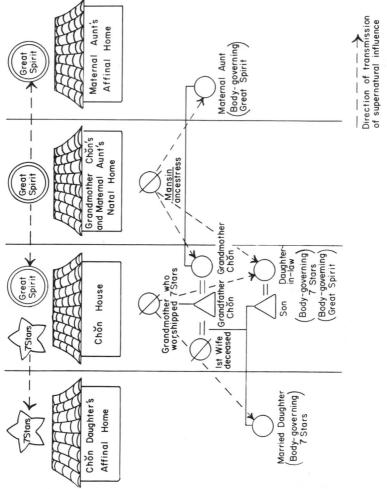

Fig. 1. Women and their gods in the Chŏn family *kut*

ancestors nor ghosts stop short at the boundaries of male-defined kin ✓
groups.

Kindred Spirits Rising

Special and particularly powerful gods in different household pantheons imply both the uniqueness of each family's history and the shaman's powers of discernment. When a woman acknowledges potent
gods, she also establishes a *tan'gol* relationship with a *mansin*, who
holds the gods' robes in her shrine and summons the gods on ritual
occasions. Shamans claim the power not only to envision these special
gods and sense their moods, but to call them down periodically to
address the family's present situation.

Inside the shrine at the New Year or on the seventh day of the
seventh lunar month, the *tan'gol* sets out her offerings. She has
abstained from meat and fish, "bloody food," for three days and is not
menstruating. She has bathed and washed her hair; she has put on
clean clothing. Now she draws her hands together high above her
head and bows, pressing her face to the floor. The *mansin* hits her
cymbals and begins to chant, like a monk chanting in a Buddhist temple while the worshiper performs a series of prostrations.

But now the *mansin*'s body jerks. The gods descend and speak
through her lips. Strong household gods impose a vivid presence. The
Rice Shop Auntie's Official demands wine and chides her for rudeness
to her mother-in-law. Yangja's family also has a supernatural Official
of great appetite. The god denounces the simple meat offering Yangja's
Mother has brought to the shrine. "Where are the spareribs? Where's
the pig's head?" Appeased with wine, the Official once again promises
to drive noxious influences from Yangja's Father's bus route. The
Waterfall Valley Auntie's Buddhist Sage Grandmother commiserates.
There are "winds and storms in the house." The eldest son drinks and
the stepfather quarrels with the children. The god asks for a *kut*.

The Wine House Auntie's Child Messengers scold her for forgetting
their candy. Still clutching her cymbals, Yongsu's Mother, possessed by
the Child Messengers, snatches money from the altar and bolts to the
roadside store. Giggling like a naughty child, she runs back, gripping a
cellophane package of sweets. A Pae woman runs to this same store
for a kettle of wine to treat the Great King.

A few ancestors and ghosts appear at the end of a shrine rite. If it is a busy day, an impatient and exhausted *mansin* speeds them on their way unless they bring special messages to the living. The Kim woman's son has crushed his foot in an accident, and the recently deceased Grandfather comforts the sobbing woman. The *mansin* expels a long list of restless ghosts from the Kim family. The *mansin* sends the *tan'gol* back to the inner room to eat some of the rice the *tan'gol* had brought to cook at the *mansin*'s house and placed on the altar. Yongsu's Mother gossips over lunch with her favorite *tan'gol*. The *tan'gol* takes some fruit and candy home, leaving the *mansin*'s house without a salutation.

A *mansin*'s own flower-greeting or leaf-greeting *kut,* held at the shrine in the spring or autumn, dramatizes the cooperative relation-ship of the *mansin*'s own descended gods, the source of her power to do *kut,* and the gods of her *tan'gol,* who receive *kut* and *kosa* in client households. A *mansin*'s flower-greeting *kut* is, first and foremost, for the *mansin*'s own family gods and ancestors and reflects the peculiari-ties of her own pantheon and history. At Yongsu's Mother's shrine, Yongsu's Father "plays as a Spirit Warrior" after he has appeared as an ordinary ancestor. Yongsu's Mother quarrels with the ancestral shade of her husband's first wife, a perpetual source of problems. Two sib-lings who died in childhood of measles and smallpox appear as Child Messengers. Yongsu's Mother balances herself, somewhat awkwardly, on her long iron blades for the pleasure of her Knife-riding Great Spirit and General. When the Great Spirit appears, Yongsu's Grandmother's Body-governing Buddhist Sage Great Spirit also rises up. The old woman puts on the god's robe, takes a monk's wooden bell from the shrine, and chants, rocking forward in a bow as she kneels on the floor.

The gods from *tan'gol* houses also feast and play. When Yongsu's Mother manifests the Official, she puts on several layers of blue vests, all those dedicated by the *tan'gol* who have active Officials. There are vests from Yangja's Mother, the Rice Shop Auntie, and the anthropol-ogist. When she manifests the Buddhist Sage, Yongsu's Mother wears a white robe from the Willow Market Auntie and one from the Water-fall Valley Auntie. The Wine House Auntie's Child Messengers appear when their little costumes are tied to the Special Messenger's belt.

Yongsu's Mother brings out all the lengths of cloth women left at the shrine when they dedicated sons or grandsons to the Seven Stars.

During the *kut* the Seven Stars whirl the piles of cloth through the air to bestow additional blessings on the male children. Yongsu's Mother pelts Yangja's father with coarse millet to exorcise the noxious influences responsible for his traffic accident. As the Spirit Warrior, she flourishes her sword and cuts away ghosts clinging to the chest of another client. Yangja's Mother and the Rice Shop Auntie dance *mugam* to appease their active Body-governing Officials. A Han woman's General accepts her gift of a battle fork and broadsword. Chinsuk's Mother dances her Body-governing Seven Stars in *mugam*. Women from the Pae family wear the Great King's robe and high-crowned hat to dance.

SEVEN

The Care and Feeding of Ancestors

The father's sister is a restless ancestor.
The mother's sister is a restless ancestor.
Kyŏnggi shaman chant

A division of labor bisects the ritual life of the Korean home. Women worship the gods of the house, men, the ancestors. The two spheres merge in affliction. When angry, affronted gods let the dead move among the living, the women propitiate restless ancestors and ghosts. When a family, like the Chŏn family, holds a *kut* to entertain the gods, the ancestors also appear and receive feast food from a special tray.

In *kut* the ancestor is a vocal, weepy presence filled with appetite, longing, or anger. The ancestor inspires tears of grief or compassion in the eyes of a sibling, child, or spouse, but the women also bicker with the dead: "Why did you die young then?" "We did everything we could for you [so why complain?]." "We bought you medicine when you were sick." "Take your travel money and go." "Go away to a good place." By contrast, the ancestor of male rites maintains a silent, awesome presence while the men solemnly offer libations and carefully prostrate themselves.

The Male Rite

Family ancestor worship receives considerable attention in Korean ethnography; a short description will therefore suffice here. My observations come from the several rituals, or *chesa,* I saw in my landlord's home and in the homes of his kinsmen.

Men are born, live, and die among their close consanguineous kin. A first son inherits the household headship and eventually becomes an ancestor in his natal *chip,* the big house *(k'ŭnjip).* A secondary son establishes a related minor house *(chagŭnjip)* and, after death, becomes that new *chip*'s founding ancestor. The eternally ambiguous *chip* implies, in appropriate context, the separate "household" of a single son or the ritual "family" of several sons' households.

A "big house" with an unbroken tradition honors ancestors up to the fourth ascending generation *(sadaebongsa).* Branching descendants gather at the big house for *chesa,* an occasion for brothers, nephews, and cousins to offer libations to parents and grandparents. A secondary son offers wine and prostrates himself before the ancestors in his eldest brother's house, the house where he grew up. His own household will not hold their own *chesa* until he, or his wife before him, becomes an ancestor.

Senior uncles come to the house when junior kin offer ancestor rites, and are honored guests at the midnight feast immediately after the *chesa.* Although these elders offer advice on ritual procedure and add the final touches to the offering tray, as genealogical seniors, they neither offer wine nor prostrate themselves before genealogically junior ancestors. Sisters and daughters often return for a death-day anniversary, just as they would return for a living parent's birthday celebration. These daughters of the *chip* help in the kitchen and join in the feasting, but they do not offer wine in the rite itself.[1] Neither will they become ancestors in their natal *chip.* Marriage severs them. As mothers of sons, they will one day receive their ancestral due in their husband's house.

Two concepts of agnatic kin emerge from the assortment of relatives gathered together at a death-day anniversary. The men who offer wine dramatize the principle of patrilineal primogeniture within the *chip* and the hierarchical relationship between primary and secondary *chip:* the senior son holds *chesa* in his home, while younger sons and grandsons offer wine in the home of a senior son or grandson. But a more generalized group of agnatic kin, including the *chip*'s out-married women, come from a distance to gather together for an evening of preparation and conviviality and for the rich feast of offering food after the rite.

Men hold *chesa* at midnight before a death anniversary and in the early mornings of lunar New Year's Day and Ch'usŏk, which is celebrated at the start of the harvest (lunar 8.15). Villagers contrast the death anniversary's solemn atmosphere with the lighter mood of holiday rites. Death anniversaries occasion a feast with food as elaborate as the family can afford. On holidays ancestors and family receive special holiday fare.

Ancestor worship is a male prerogative, and once plates of offering food are passed up onto the porch, they are in the men's hands. Women perform the essential task of preparing *chesa* food. Every household kitchen has its own traditions, which the eldest daughter-in-law learns from her mother-in-law. When kinswomen from other households help prepare *chesa* food, they defer to the polite instructions of a woman who may be their junior in both age and generation. Women say that the first son's bride must be immaculate and conscientious, since she will inherit the responsibility of preparing *chesa* food. Women teased me that, being left-handed, I must never marry a firstborn son, since any offerings I prepared would be unacceptable to the ancestors of my husband's *chip*.

The form of *chesa* is the form of a meal.[2] All of the food on the ancestors' tray is ready for consumption. Apples and pears have their topmost skin peeled; there are peeled and sliced chestnuts, or substitute sugar candies in the shape of sliced chestnuts that the family buys for thrift and ease in preparation. The women bring rice and soup steaming to the porch. The men, in turn, fill cups of wine and set them on the *chesa* tray. The master of ceremonies raps a pair of chopsticks against an empty bowl, sets the rice bowl lid ajar, and dips a few grains of rice into the soup with a spoon. Finally, he replaces the soup with a bowl of rice water to signify the meal's end. The men punctuate each step in this sequence with head-to-floor bows. They turn their backs away from the offering tray, bowing slightly from the waist, so that the ancestor may eat in peace.

Families in Enduring Pine Village do not maintain wooden tablets as permanent spirit placings *(sinwi)* for the ancestors. Instead, a skilled calligrapher prepares a temporary placing of thin rice paper with the ancestor's name and the honorary title "student" in carefully rendered Chinese characters.[3] Immediately after the formal rite one of the men burns the spirit placing and the prepared congratulatory address. He tosses the ashes out beside the storage jars, the cleanest place in the home. In *kosa,* women set the Mountain God's offerings here and at the end of men's *chesa,* the dead return to mountain graves. Do the castaway ashes symbolize the return? I did not know enough to ask.

As soon as the men finish the *chesa* women take the offerings to the kitchen where they pile trays high with food to feast the men. Women and children eat last, either in a separate room or at trays the men have vacated. The etiquette of dining, like all Korean etiquette, honors hierarchial principles: first the ancestors by generational seniority, then the men by age, then the women and children. An ancestor receives the first tray of food as guest of honor at a death anniversary feast. The ancestors, by generational seniority, receive the first portions of special holiday treats—rice cake soup on New Year's morning and filled rice cake dumplings at Ch'usŏk. Family solidarity and continuity are expressed through communal feasting.[4]

When a household head performs ancestor worship, he demonstrates ritual propriety before a broader group of kin and community. Older men impress upon younger men the momentousness of ancestor worship and the importance of correct procedure. Sloppiness and negligence in the performance of *chesa* is the mark of an inferior person. Men learn ritual form as they grow up. They watch rites in the home, and fathers take sons to *chesa* in the homes of agnatic kin. Whereas men patiently coach a boy through his libation and bows, softly chuckling at his awkwardness and hesitation, a young man receives a swift, gruff reprimand for a slight slip. By now, he should know better.

Korean social philosophers have argued that ancestor worship is no literal invocation of the ancestor's shade, but merely a metaphoric display acknowledging one's eternal obligation to parents and grandparents (Pyun 1926; Clark [1932] 1961, 114–116). The residents of Enduring Pine Village, however, use *chesa* to express concern for the needs and desires of remembered dead. My landlord told me, "I gave my father an extra cup of wine because he used to like wine so much." A widow explained why she had prepared an abundance of offering food. "Before my husband died, he always felt hungry. His illness made him feel that way. He kept asking for food, but was never satisfied, so I fixed a lot for him this time."

Sentiment and a sense of literal evocation are yet more pronounced in shaman rites where the ancestor claims a dramatic presence in the person of the possessed *mansin*. The dead confront the living. There is anger, there are reproaches, there is grief and repentance, but always, there is reconciliation. The ancestral sequence in *kut* transforms these dread and dangerous spectres into familial allies. For example, in the scheme of ancestors and ghosts, a dead first wife is expected to work at cross purposes to her husband's present wife. First wives were partly to blame for Yongsu's Father's death and for the death of Mr. Pyŏn. A dead first wife desires her former spouse and tries to carry him away with her. Resentful of her husband's remarriage, she stirs up trouble in the house and unsettles the children. When the dead first wife appeared in Chinsuk's Mother's *kut,* she flung open the doors of all the cabinets, grabbed at the neat piles of quilts and mattresses, and glared at Chinsuk's Mother. But after this predictable venting of envy, she accepted wine and "travel money" and became Chinsuk's Mother's backer. Chinsuk's Mother had been unable to discipline her wayward stepchild, a Korean stepmother's common complaint. The boy's own mother, speaking through the *mansin,* berated him for his rebellious behavior, then stroked Chinsuk's Mother's arms and thanked her for caring for the children.

When they appear in *kut,* dead mothers often attempt to reform errant sons. The Im woman in Tranquil Spring had a husband who was a perennial alcoholic. One winter he again took to the bottle. Staggering home late at night, he would beat his wife and loudly abuse her. The Im woman held a *kut* and her husband's parents appeared in the ancestors' sequence. The husband's mother bent over him, hands on his shoulders, and sobbed, "Oh my son, you must not drink so much. It makes your head ache." The husband listened, head bowed. The ancestor turned next to her daughter-in-law and, bending over her, wept in sympathy. "You've had nothing but hardship since you came to this house." A Kim woman was similarly comforted by an ancestral mother-in-law who lamented the bitter life that had pushed the Kim woman into a fit of madness. The ancestor begged her son, the Kim woman's husband, "By whatever means possible, however you can, please save her. Then get her something fancy to wear."

In the Ancestors' Opinion

Shaman rituals assume and reinforce the morality of ancestor rites. The possessed *mansin* articulates a slighted ancestor's just grievance. When Munae's Mother asked Yongsu's Mother to divine the cause of her badly inflamed leg, Yongsu's Mother attributed her trouble to the father-in-law's deceased first wife, aggrieved because the second wife refused to prepare offerings for her predecessor's death anniversary. The *mansin* held an exorcism for Munae's Mother, and was possessed by the first wife. The hungry shade demanded her due. At Chinsuk's Mother's *kut* her husband's dead first wife also demanded a death anniversary feast. The women told her, "You died in the North; we don't even know your death day. We give you food on holidays." They eventually reconciled this ancestor to her unjust fate.

The *mansin,* when she gives voice to the dead, permits adjustments in the care and feeding of ancestors when life does not follow ideal form. Fathers die without sons; kin are separated, killed, or disappear during war and social upheaval. These ruptures imply a moral breach in the ritual continuity of generations and expose the family to super-natural danger. A *mansin* confirms the deaths of relatives lost in the North or separated during the war. Through a cathartic ritual confrontation and by subsequent offerings, family members alleviate grief and guilt as they draw lost kin back into the home for periodic family feasting.

Ancestors, speaking through the *mansin,* sanction necessary or desirable compromises with ritual form. One woman told me,

> My husband is a second son. His elder brother went to Japan before the war and the family hadn't heard anything from him for years. My husband and I took care of the *chesa* for my husband's mother. Six years after our marriage, a letter came from my husband's long-lost brother in Japan. He was willing to perform the mother's *chesa.* We consulted a spirit medium [*kwisin chŏmjaengi*] who told us that my mother-in-law wanted to stay in Korea; she didn't want to go to Japan. So we continue to make offerings for her here.

A Yang woman was the only daughter of a sonless man. She gave her father death-day offerings in her own husband's house until a *mansin* warned her that her parents-in-law, also deceased, were vexed by the extrafamilial ancestor's presence. The *mansin* told the Yang woman to place her father's tablet in a Buddhist temple and make his death anniversary offerings there. When the Yang woman went to a *kut* at a friend's home, a *mansin* warned her that her father was hungry for *chesa.* The Yang woman grew agitated at this. Despite her best intentions, she was not always able to go to the temple on her father's death anniversary. She claimed that she could not depend on her mother to make the offerings. The *mansin* told her to set her father's death-day offerings on the storage jars beside the house. "That's just as good as going to a temple."[5]

The *mansin* interject a necessary element of flexibility into the tight structure of ancestor worship. While men serve the ancestors in accord with ritual manuals and orthodox custom, the women argue with the ancestors, bargain with them, and eventually effect their reconciliation into the bosom of the family.

The limited number of clearly demarcated ancestors honored in *chesa* contrasts with a far broader spectrum of ancestors appearing in the *mansin*'s divinations, exorcisms, and *kut*. Women do not question the patrilineal principles demarcating an exclusive group of ancestors for worship in *chesa*. But when they consult a *mansin,* the women accept that all manner of ancestors who would never qualify for positions of honor at the household *chesa* tray influence the fortunes of the family. Ancestors and ghosts from a woman's natal home affect the health, wealth, and well-being of members of her affinal *chip,* and a married daughter wanders back to her natal household after death. When and why do these ethereal entities arise? Does their presence imply another view of significant kin, one predicated on a woman's life experience as she passes from her natal to her affinal home?

The Unquiet Dead

The *mansin* assumes that when the household gods drop their protective guard, the ancestors and ghosts stir *(paltong hada).* When the dead move among the living, it bodes no good.

What manner of being are these restless dead? Students of Korean religion disagree on the Korean conceptualization of the soul. Certain of Biernatzki's informants provided an elaborate three-soul scheme *(samhon)*: one in the ancestor tablet, one in the grave, and one in hell or paradise (Biernatzki 1967, 139). Clark (1961, 113) and Gifford (1892, 171) concur, and deGroot ([1982–1910] 1967) encountered the three-part soul in China. Janelli and Janelli (1982, 59–60) claim the three-part soul has little to do with conscious popular belief in the village they studied. Informants invoked the three-part soul only when pressed to explain the anomaly of a soul in three locations at once.

By the three-soul scheme, the soul in the grave passively transmits the beneficent geomantic properties of the gravesite to descendants. One soul returns to the house with the ancestor's tablet or photograph that the mourners carry in the funeral procession and bring back from the grave. This soul remains with its placing on the porch of the house and receives rice offerings twice daily until the Great Send-off (Tae-sang) on the second death anniversary. The Great Send-off marks the end of the mourning period, when the living family severs the dead from their midst. Hereafter the soul will only return for holiday and death anniversary feasts. A third soul stands trial before the King of Hell (Yŏmna Taewang), who metes sundry tortures to transgressors and sends the righteous dead to the Lotus Paradise (Kŭngnak).[6]

By this scheme the second soul is the ancestor proper, brought into the home with a soul placing and honored with periodic *chesa*. But the *mansin* and her clients speak of and deal with the ancestor in the family, in the grave, and in hell as much the same being. When the dead suffer discomfort in any context, they reach out with thorny hand and meddle in the affairs of the living.

The ancestor of *kut* does seem most akin to the ancestor of *chesa*, returning periodically to feast with the family. When the women prepare offerings for the ancestors in *kut*, they approximate the arrangement of food on the *chesa* tray, observing the most basic principles—red (apples) in the east and white (pears) in the west. In violation of *chesa* form, they set bowls of cooked rice and cups of wine for several ancestors on the offering tray all at once and without ceremony. In *kut* the ancestors lack paper placings since they appear in the *mansin*'s person.

While the *mansin* voices the ancestor's wrath at neglected offerings, she also attributes family misfortune to the ancestor's physical discomfort in the grave. The corpse's condition, determined through a *mansin*'s divination, is a legitimate source of ancestral grievance.

Mrs. Im's son fled after a taxi accident and stayed away in hiding for several years. A *mansin* told Mrs. Im that her husband's body had shifted in the grave, allowing dirt to enter the coffin. Ancestral discomfort wrought the son's misfortune and the long separation of parent and child. The *mansin* urged Mrs. Im to call her son home, consult a geomancer *(chigwan)*, and relocate the grave. Another woman fretted over a prodigal nephew who periodically borrowed money against nonexistent job prospects. The *mansin* divined that common ancestors—the woman's parents-in-law, the nephew's grandparents—lay twisted in their graves. The erring nephew's father, now deceased, had planted bamboo beside the tomb, and bamboo roots had forced their way into the coffins, disturbing the corpses. Again, the *mansin* told her client to consult a geomancer.

The *mansin*'s divination is analogous to a geomancer's skill. An adroit geomancer perceives the condition of a buried corpse by merely gazing at the grave site from a distance (H. Yoon 1976, 5–6); the *mansin* sees the corpse in her visions. But the *mansin* does not claim geomantic expertise. She reveals a problem, then sends her client to an expert, "one who reads books." Only the professional geomancer, versed in the esoteric principles of the lay of the land, knows how to reorient the buried corpse.

The *mansin*, the geomancer, and their respective clients assume that the corpse's condition in the grave affects the descendants' fates. A grave site's positive qualities wither when water, dirt, or roots enter the coffin and disturb the corpse (ibid., 75). The *mansin* considers the ancestor's physical comfort while the geomancer uses correctly placed bones as the passive transmitters of a site's beneficent properties.

The *mansin* and her clients also aid the soul's progress through the Courts of Hell to the Lotus Paradise. The Courts of Hell, also vividly conceptualized in Chinese popular religion (Eberhard 1967; Yang 1961, 2, 88), probably entered the Korean religious imagination with Buddhism. In Korean Buddhist temples the Ten Kings of the Ten Courts of Hell have a separate shrine. The walls bear garish paintings of tortures awaiting the condemned soul. Erring souls are manacled, chained, strapped to wooden cangues, flayed with knives, sawn in two, or cast adrift in vats of boiling oil. Bishop, the intrepid gentle-woman traveler of the last century, called the hell paintings "horrible beyond conception, and [they] show a diabolical genius . . ." (Bishop 1897, 136).

By Buddhist doctrine the soul suffers in hell for forty-nine days after death. Some Korean families hold a memorial service at a temple on the forty-ninth day. Monks chant prayers to ease the soul's passage out of hell and into paradise. According to an early observer, some families hire a shaman for the forty-ninth day. The King of Hell, speaking through the possessed shaman, guarantees the soul's release. The soul appears and expresses gratitude (Korean Mudang and Pansu 1903, 205–206).

Some families hire a *mansin* to guide the dead soul from hell months or even several years after death. When a *mansin* divines that unquiet dead cause current misfortune, she advises a *kut* with a special segment at the end *(chinogi)* where the family sends their dead along the road to the Lotus Paradise. One dead soul departs, or an assortment of ancestors from several related households are sent off in sequence in genealogical order. Children who died without issue go only after proper ancestors have "opened the road."

A family sends off its dead when it has honored all of the spirits within the house walls and the *kut* moves outside the gate, usually on the morning of the second day. The *kut* for the dead is a highly theatrical event, meriting more extensive treatment than I am able to give it here.[7]

The women set up a fresh offering tray for the ancestors outside the gate with a smaller tray of rice, fruit, and candy for the Death Messenger (Saja), who snatches the dead away to the Court of Hell. Immediately after a death, the family sets out a tray of Death Messenger's rice, and the Death Messenger's arrival in *kut* re-creates the event of death.

A *mansin* disappears around the side of the house. She ties a cap of rough hemp cloth onto her head with coarse rope and winds more rope around her waist. She thrusts a dried fish, wrapped in a length of hemp, into her belt to signify the dead soul. The *mansin* reappears as the Death Messenger, leaning on a wooden staff. The hempen head covering, coarse rope belt, and wooden staff all approximate traditional mourners' apparel. Face twisted into a grotesque leer, the Death Messenger rushes at the house gate, but the women crowd the doorway and repulse his assault. They defend the home against this dread force of death. The Death Messenger squats before the small tray and appears to gobble up vast quantities of food in a theatrically disgusting show of gluttony. The *mansin* crams food into her mouth, smearing some on her face in the process. She spews forth the overflow into a dipper she holds under her chin. The Death Messenger tries to snatch additional fruit and sweets from the tray prepared for the dead, dodging irate women who guard the food intended for their own kin. The Death Messenger demands money, threatening to strike the fish the *mansin* carries to represent the captured soul. Women provide small bills, imploring the Death Messenger to treat the dead soul well. The Death Messenger disappears around the side of the house, and the *mansin* removes her costume.

A *mansin*, dressed in the rainbow-sleeved costume of a princess or a bride, sings the long ballad of Princess Pari, the seventh daughter of a sonless king and queen. The royal parents cast out this last unwelcome girl child, but Princess Pari, raised in obscurity and coached in magic, braves the perils of the underworld to find a magic herb and restore her parents to life. A filial daughter,[8] Princess Pari inverts the ideal of the filial son. Men give sustenance to their parents through *chesa* after death; women lead the dead through the dangers of hell and restore them to life in the Lotus Paradise. The *mansin* say that they sing the ballad of Princess Pari's journey to teach the dead the path through the netherworld. After the song, the *mansin* circumambulates the offering table, pacing the netherworld to guide the soul.

The *mansin* now asks a fee to get the dead past the Thornwood Gate (Kasi Mun) of hell.[9] Finally, relatives and neighbors hold out long strips of cloth, stretched taut in their hands to make the road out of hell. They put cash contributions on top of the cloth to help "open the road" and drape nylon clothes for the dead over the length of cloth. A *mansin*, fish/soul bound to her waist, rushes at the cloth road. She jabs it with a knife and thrusts her body along the length of the fabric. The soul advances. She rips her way through a length of coarse hemp, the road out of hell. She rips through a length of finer cotton, the road into the Lotus Paradise.

When death is recent, the *mansin* uses several yards of cloth to illustrate a difficult, reluctant separation. Several times the *mansin* stops her journey along the cloth. Speaking for the dead soul, she declares her unwillingness to continue. The dead soul demands one last look at a favorite relative, bolts back inside the house, seizes kin or friends by the shoulders, and weeps. The women urge the unwilling soul, "Go on, go on. You're going to a good place." As in the ancestors' sequence of *kut*, kin and friends must acknowledge the necessity of separation and urge the dead to depart.

Once the soul is sent off, the family holds a *chesa*, or more appropriately, a mock *chesa*. The male household head may, but does not necessarily, perform this rite. An available junior son or nephew or even a wife or daughter-in-law can, with the *mansin*'s coaching, offer cups of wine, rap a pair of chopsticks against a bowl, and bow, the essential gestures of *chesa*. There is no congratulatory address, no spirit placing for the ancestor, and there are no extended prostrations by a group of junior male kin. Women and *mansin* merely approximate *chesa* form as a fitting way to honor the dead. Immediately after the mock *chesa,* the dead appear one final time in the *mansin*'s person. With sobbing expressions of gratitude, they promise to help their living kin.

Mansin borrow both the terminology and intent of Buddhist ritual, but the dead soul of shaman rites articulates another view of death and afterlife. In both Buddhist doctrine and in my *mansin* informants' idealized explanations, punishment in the Court of Hell makes just retribution for life's transgressions. Justice may be seasoned with mercy only when sincere prayer inspires a bodhisattva's intercession on behalf of dead kin (Clark 1961, 54). The *mansin*'s rite offers another view of legal process. Scholars of Chinese folk religion acknowledge the parallel between the temporal and the supernatural bureaucracy—the Court of Hell corresponds to an earthly yamen (Yang 1961, 156–158; A. Wolf 1974, 133–145). Where Koreans adopted Chinese-style bureaucratic institutions, certain reinforcing religious assumptions followed.

Shaman rites add a cynical twist. The dead fall into the clutches of the Death Messenger who, like the extortionate yamen runner of old, demands treats and cash favors to insure the good treatment of his charge. In dynastic times, "wretched underlings" sent by the magistrate snatched the accused away and demanded remuneration of their journey (Hahm 1967, 67). According to Moose, a bribe from relatives or friends softened the blows a prisoner received in the yamen (Moose 1911, 186), as women in *kut* stay the Death Messenger's hand with cash. The prisoner of old depended on the mercy of relatives and friends for food, warmth, and eventual release from torment (Hulbert [1906] 1970, 64, 182–184). Likewise, the family gives the dead soul food, clothing, and travel money. They bribe the soul out of hell with a fee at the Thornwood Gate and pave the road to paradise with cash. Without the help of kin, both the accused in prison and the soul in hell might starve, suffer ceaseless torment, and become malevolent ghosts.

The *mansin*'s ritual is more than a morality play of retribution and reward. Although the *mansin* dramatizes the soul's progress out of hell and into the Lotus Paradise, the actions of the *mansin,* kin, and neighbors also portray the separation of the dead from the house and the living family. The family invites the ancestors back into the home for periodic feasting, but when the dead are too much with the living, misfortune results. The family must send off the dead, albeit to a "good place," outside the gate and away from the house.[10] Ritual necessity contradicts familial ideology and emotional attachment. But when the send-off is, at once, the soul's release from hell's tribulations, severance becomes a palatably virtuous and mutually beneficial act. And the dead return, at the proper time and place, for *chesa* and *kut*.

Ancestors and Ghosts in *Kut*

Before the *mansin* perform the ancestors' sequence in *kut*, they determine the deceased relatives of the house up to four ascendant generations *(sadaebongsa)* and deceased male relatives and their wives within four degrees of relationship—the senior and junior households *(chip)* of one's own, one's father's, and one's grandfather's generation. Superficially these core ancestors resemble the patrilineal ancestors of ancestor worship, but there are important differences. Ancestors of the main house *(k'ŭnjip)* and husband's and father's younger brothers appear in *kut*. A younger brother would not do *chesa* in his own home for ancestors who receive *chesa* at the main house. Neither would his household normally offer *chesa* to his younger brothers or to his father's younger brothers.

The appearance of these kindred ancestors in *kut* does not reflect the hierarchical relationship between households so much as the inclusive solidarity of related houses. The living members of related households appear when a member house celebrates *chesa*, weddings, funerals, and birthdays. In like manner, the ancestors of related households gather to feast and play at a *kut*.

Otherworldly influences pass freely between major and minor houses. Related households cosponsor *kut* where the *mansin* divines a common source of supernatural malaise. Two Song households sponsored a lavish *kut*. The eldest son in the junior line had agonizing headaches. The *mansin* determined that a *kut* for the Songs' powerful Great Spirit Grandmother was overdue. Last year the second son of the main line, a bachelor, had drowned. Now the ancestors and ghosts of the Song family, the drowned bachelor foremost among them, gathered about the eldest son of the junior line, causing his illness. If the Songs had done a *kut* earlier, the *mansin* maintained, both the drowning and the illness could have been avoided. Although the senior Song household—headed by a widow—was considerably poorer than the minor house, the senior house contributed cash and grain to send their wretched bachelor ghost to paradise.

In *kut* the *mansin* must invoke certain categories of ancestor, relatives within four generations. She claims that other ancestors and ghosts appear, unbidden, before her eyes. Sobbing, she gives them voice. Dead children are *yŏngsan,* ghosts, not *chosang,* ancestors, but they nevertheless were born into the house. Sons, daughters, nieces, and nephews appear in the ancestors' sequence inside the house, although as *yŏngsan* they belong outside the gate. They do not partake of the offerings prepared inside for the ancestors. Instead, the family feeds its kindred *yŏngsan* outside the gate with the other wandering *yŏngsan.*

The ambiguous treatment of dead children in *kut* suggests the ambiguous position of dead children in the family. Dead children are not ancestors in that, with no descendants of their own, they neither establish nor continue a household line. But because they are children of the house, affective ties draw them inside. Dead children of the house claim prerogatives denied the other *yŏngsan* who crowd around the gate like beggars at a feast, impatient for their allotment of scraps and coarse grain.

More surprising is the appearance of the husband's deceased sisters, both married and unmarried, sometimes accompanied by their husbands. Patrilineal familial ideology holds that a married sister ceases membership in the household on her wedding day. Yet she returns. In similar fashion deceased married daughters are drawn back to their natal homes by the ancestors' sequence. For the *mansin,* this appearance is quite logical. "When a married daughter is alive, she goes back to visit her natal home. After death, it's the same thing." Now, however, death taints the daughter and she brings illness or misfortune to her natal home. A family must send a dead daughter to the Lotus Paradise and urge her to stop visiting her own kin. Death accentuates tensions implicit in a married daughter's relationship to her natal household. In life the daughter's visits home inspire contradictory emotions. Her own kin, especially her mother, are happy to see her. But the daughter is also a robber woman *(todungnyŏ),* so called because she carried family wealth away when she married and now continues to inveigle family resources for her own husband and children.

Married daughters and husband's sisters are children of the house *(chip).* Legally and ritually they join another family and household

when they marry, but they retain ties with their natal homes throughout their lives. Married daughters visit their natal homes on at least
their parents' birthdays or death anniversaries, if distance and propriety do not permit more frequent visiting. Many women deliver their
first child in their natal homes or attended by their own mothers. It is
not unusual for a married daughter to turn to her own kin in time of
adversity. If father and siblings begrudge her aid, a mother will slip the
daughter rice or cash on the sly. When a mother or a brother's wife
holds a *kut,* the married daughters of the house, both living and dead,
often return for the feasting and play.

An old woman's sorry tale reveals a married daughter's recourse to
her natal home, and her enduring attachment beyond death. The
woman consulted Yongsu's Mother because her husband had a lingering cold. During the divination Yongsu's Mother detected the presence
of a restless ancestor, "someone who went back to her natal home and
died young." The old woman immediately acknowledged that this
would be her own daughter. After marriage the daughter went to her
husband's home in Seoul. During the war, while her husband was
away, the daughter lived in a bomb shelter with her husband's family.
When her first confinement approached, the daughter asked permis-
sion to return to her natal home. Carrying her possessions in a heavy
bundle, she walked all the way to her parents' village, a day-long journey. When she reached her parents, she was in pain. Her mother
thought that she was weak from wartime hardship and the journey.
The mother purchased restorative tonics, but the family lacked funds
to continue the treatment. The daughter's labor was long and difficult.
Her parents sent for a midwife. In desperation the mother went to a
mansin for an exorcism *(p'udakkŏri),* but to no avail. The daughter
delivered her child and died. Yongsu's Mother was satisfied that the
unfortunate daughter was the restless ancestor of her divination.

Daughters marry out but, living or dead, they are not strangers.
Conversely, ancestral and ghostly influences from the wife's natal
home pass through the walls of the husband's *chip* (see app. 3). A
woman's own parents and, less frequently, her grandparents, appear
in the ancestors' sequence of a *kut.* A woman's dead siblings, both
married and unmarried, frequently appear. The *mansin* attributes a
woman's marital misfortunes to the ghostly influence of unmarried or
childless siblings. A married sister who died pregnant or in childbirth
(haesan'gi) is particularly threatening because she would have a great

sense of unfulfillment. Dead children, *tongja,* follow the brightly colored marriage quilt and, with the capriciousness of youth, stir up turmoil in their married sister's new home. *Yŏt'am,* offerings made to the ancestors and ghosts of the bride's family on the wedding eve, keep these rambunctious ghosts in place so that daughters will be ritually clean, purified of negative supernatural influences when they marry. This rite could be interpreted as part of the ritual process severing the bride from her natal *chip* during her wedding, but *yŏt'am,* as an optional rite, carries the implication that when precautions are not taken, family ghosts and ancestors will follow the bride. Many women find their dead siblings sighted in the *mansin's* divinations, years after marriage, as the source of domestic strife.

The groom's family may also offer *yŏt'am,* and some families offer *yŏt'am* before a sixty-first birthday feast. *Yŏt'am* is performed in the *mansin's* shrine where some of the feast food and spirit clothing or a gauzy handkerchief are offered to the family dead, who appear, weeping, and possess the *mansin.* Most women claim that they offer *yŏt'am* out of ritual propriety: the ancestors, as senior members of the *chip,* should be invited to partake of the feast food before anyone else. The *mansin* shares this view but stresses that, without *yŏt'am,* dead siblings will follow the bride and disrupt the marriage. In the course of *yŏt'am* the *mansin* manifest dead children of the *chip* along with the ancestors.

If ghosts and ancestors from the wife's natal home are everywhere a negative influence, their appearance in shaman ritual might merely reinforce male-centered values decreeing that married women must be severed from their own kin. By this interpretation, enduring ties are ritually dangerous because they contradict familial ideology. It is my impression, however, that ancestral and ghostly influences from the wife's side are no more negative than ancestral and ghostly influences from the husband's side. Indeed, grooms' families also offer *yŏt'am* to their own ancestors and ghosts. Close contact with the unquiet dead is dangerous, a principle that applies to husband's and wife's kin alike. Ritual separates the dead from the living, and the dead of either side, when properly propitiated, exert a positive influence on their kin. Hence, the *mansin* divines that a dead mother follows and helps her married daughter, and a dead sister assists a favorite sibling to succeed in school.

The influence of the wife's dead kin may even exceed that of her husband's. A young housewife experienced a cathartic burst of grief when she confronted her own dead kin in a *kut*. After the ancestors' sequence she spoke of the loss, all in the space of a few years, of her mother, father, brother, and sister-in-law. Her eyes brimmed over when she claimed to have heard her own dead kin call her by her child-hood name as they reached out to touch her in the ancestors' sequence. The *mansin* remarked afterward that the wife's ancestors were a far stronger presence in that house than the husband's ancestors.

A mother's death is particularly grievous. While the mother lives, the married daughter is always welcome at home. A stepmother or brother's wife might not be so generous. Elsewhere I have described a "Mrs. Kim," who received considerable support from her own kin throughout her impoverished and grief-ridden married life. The final death rites for the woman's mother triggered a temporary fit of insanity, partially attributed to possession by the pitying mother who expressed enduring concern for her daughter from beyond the grave (Kendall 1977a).

While women and *mansin* acknowledge the influence of a woman's own kin, the concept of ancestor in *kut* is not pronouncedly matrila-teral or even strictly bilateral. Both in gross numbers of manifestations and in the range and variety of kinship categories represented, ances-tral and ghostly manifestations are skewed in favor of male-linked kin (see app. 3). Usually only the immediate members of the wife's natal household—parents, grandparents, and siblings—appear.[11] Woman-linked ancestors do not stretch back far over time since a woman becomes an ancestor in her husband's home. A mother's natal kin are minor figures in a daughter's conceptualization of her own kin. In their daily lives women have most frequent contact with their affinal kin. The patrilateral bias in *kut* reflects this social reality but does not totally eclipse a woman's attachment to her own kin.

Kut and the Living

While dramatically acknowledging a woman's affective ties to her own dead kin, a *kut* also reaffirms bonds between a woman and her living kin. Like natal ancestors, living mothers, sisters, brothers, and brothers' wives gather when a woman holds a *kut* in her husband's home (see also Shigematsu 1980). A woman's own kin occasionally

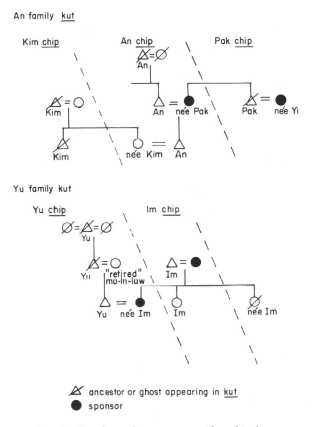

An family kut

Kim chip   An chip   Pak chip

Yu family kut

Yu chip   Im chip

⚠ ancestor or ghost appearing in kut
● sponsor

Fig. 2. Ties through women manifested in *kut*

contribute to the *kut* fee if their ancestors or ghosts go along the road to the Lotus Paradise with the husband's ancestors. Living and dead participants in the following two *kut* emerge from a chain of households linked by out-marrying women. These ties, as manifested in *kut*, are diagramed in figure 2.

The An family held a *kut* on the initiative of the mother-in-law, née Pak.[12] The Ans held this *kut* because the family store was losing money, the son's present employment held no prospects for advancement, and the daughter-in-law, née Kim, was perennially weak and tired easily. Restorative medicines had not helped her.

The Pak woman's sister-in-law, née Yi, jointly sponsored this *kut*.

Her husband, the Pak woman's brother, had died in a factory fire, leaving the widow with three small children. A wife and married daughter from the An big house, the primary *chip*, came to the *kut* but did not contribute as cosponsors. As ancestors, An family parents and the Pak woman's own brother went along the road to the Lotus Paradise. The *mansin* also placated an unfulfilled ghost from the daughter-in-law's family, a brother who had died in his youth of an unspecified illness. The Kim daughter-in-law's father appeared in the ancestors' sequence. Significant ancestors and ghosts in this *kut* thus represent three separate *chip* linked through women: Pak, An, and Kim.

The Yu family held a *kut* because Mr. Yu and his wife, née Im, had both been ill off and on for several months. The wife's own mother helped sponsor the *kut*, bringing an unmarried daughter with her to the Yu house.

Yu family ancestors—the father, grandfather, and grandfather's two wives—were sent to the Lotus Paradise. The Im woman's elder sister, who had married but died of a miscarriage, went along the road with a set of spirit clothes. Technically this dead woman was two households removed from her sister's husband's home, yet mother and sister collaborated in sending off her soul.

Women, Ghosts, and Ancestors

Ties through women receive dramatic ritual validation when the ancestors descend into the possessed *mansin*. As Werbner (1964) noted in another cultural context, the out-marrying woman is an axle between two kin groups; woman-centered rituals accentuate this tie. In Korea the married woman mediates between the living and dead of two *chip*.

Some would consider the appearance of the woman's natal ancestors and gods in shaman ritual a survival from an earlier, more matriarchal stage of Korean society (Akiba 1957, 105). Conversely, others might argue that the social and supernatural presence of the wife's kin reflects a watering down of traditional patriarchal ideology. Indeed, Koreans did marry uxorilocally a few centuries ago, and any community study contains ample evidence for the breakdown of traditional patterns. But even allowing for systematic variation over time and space, a system of belief in ghosts and ancestors that includes out-marrying women and wife's kin can be explained, quite simply, on its own terms. Marriages establish affinal ties. Women are intimately involved with the kin of two related households.

Contradictory ideas of ancestor reflect complementary principles of social organization. The ancestors of men's *chesa* and women's *kut* reflect two contrasting but essential notions of family. The patrilineal family concentrates resources and loyalties within itself. Wives who marry in and sister and daughters who marry out puncture the family with radial spokes connecting diffuse bilateral kin. While women make the most frequent appeals to their own kin, men turn to their affines for a variety of services. One turns to the wife's kin for material aid or labor at funerals, weddings, and other significant occasions (M. Lee 1960, 210). They are potential creditors (Clark Sorensen, personal communication) and backers in applying for government loans and in property disputes with the husband's kin (S. Han 1977, 107, 91–92). They extend the family's marriage network, providing information and potential candidates (ibid., 60; Osgood 1951, 12). They exchange gifts and visits and provide a convenient home away from home (S. Han 1977; Brandt 1971, 15).

Both husband's kin and wife's kin are a store of potential aid, but they are also a potential drain on one's own resources. Relationships with the kindred,[13] like dealings with the dead, are ambivalent and potentially dangerous. Kindred and dead alike must be dealt with gingerly. Both must be brought together periodically in acknowledgment of a bond. They must be given their due and implored for assistance, and, when necessary, they must be distanced.[14]

EIGHT

Women's Rites

She neglects to worship ancestors, serving Buddha
She gives away all the clothes of her family to the shaman
      witches and the blind for their exorcising,
Behold, her children look like a bald kite.
                Song of a Mediocre Woman

Public powerlessness and private strength, this contradiction permeates a Korean woman's entire life. She follows a few steps behind her husband on village lanes, but once inside the house she uses a sharp tongue and managerial acumen to good effect. In *kut* she transmutes this contradiction into high drama and comedy. She acknowledges the powerful with flattery and an occasional treat, but she shouts back even at the gods when they presume too much.

The system of ritual and belief described in these pages implies a housewife, usually the senior woman of a household, who deals with the supernatural on behalf of the house, and a professional shaman who can, when the need arises, invoke and become possessed by the gods, ghosts, and ancestors of client households. Women hold this corner of religious life in an overtly Confucian society where, as my male informants would often remind me, "Man is respected and woman lowly [*Namjon yŏbi*]," where men hold public power and prerogatives. Confucian wisdom and scholarly expectations anticipate an interpretation of women's rituals as a peripheral religious subculture wherein female specialists minister to the particular needs of women. By this interpretation, Korean women's rituals are an expression of women's powerlessness, not a flourishing of the positive powers women wield on behalf of husbands and children.

A careful, selective editing of material contained in the foregoing pages could suggest that the religious activities of Korean women and shamans provide cathartic compensation and limited redress for Korean women's otherwise miserable state, and that this is their singular function. By this interpretation, Korean women and their rituals are of only incidental interest to students of Korean society and religion. Some rituals do suggest a woman's preoccupation with the conception and rearing of healthy children, her first source of security in her husband's home and her last source of security in old age. A *mansin* lures the Birth Grandmother into a gourd dipper which the woman who would become pregnant carries to her own inner room. When an infant is sickly, the *mansin* placates the Birth Grandmother in the shrine and exorcises afflicting ghosts. Children with short life fates are given to the Seven Stars' protection, and a *mansin* writes the child's name and address upon a white cloth "Seven Star bridge" and stores it in the shrine. *Mansin* lead clients to mountain shrines, where they pray for the birth, health, and success of children, or women make the mountain pilgrimage alone and in secret. At home they make their own offerings to the Birth Grandmother and the Seven Stars. Early in the new year women visit the shrine to learn which of their children or grandchildren will need ritual attention under the first full moon.

The giddy atmosphere of a *kut* and the housewife's own euphoric *mugam* dancing might again suggest that Korean women seek ecstatic catharsis and that this is why they sponsor *kut*. Women do expect to enjoy themselves at a *kut*. The Chŏn women, their female kin, and the neighbor women drank, sang, joked, and danced up their spirits in the bright robes of officials, monks, and kings. But recall also that Grandfather Chŏn was robed and urged to dance and that the *kut* was expressly, although not exclusively, held for his benefit. A narrow focus on women's rituals as women's safety valve misses their broader social import. Women's rituals neither constitute a separate female cult nor are they subversive of men and men's objectives. The *mansin* ministers to a downtrodden Mrs. Kim, to Munae's Mother victimized by the family secret, to Chinsuk's Mother with her many anxieties, and to the Rice Shop Auntie with her fractious spouse. But wives also summon the *mansin* for ailing Grandfather Chŏn and Mr. Pyŏn, for young Mr. Yi, who was possessed by death humors, or for accident-prone Yangja's Father.

The *kut* is a woman's party, but total exclusivity is neither necessary nor desirable. The male house head must greet his gods and ancestors, and each spirit delivers a divination to each member of the family. The afflicted are exorcised. Men, as well as women, collide with the ritual action of a *kut,* as direct as a pelting of millet or a tongue-lashing from the ancestors and gods. Some men must be shoved into the center of the porch. Most men vacillate between their own party and a sideline view of the dancing shamans. A few men are enthusiasts. Vain of their skill or compelled by their own Body-governing Gods, they dance on the porch to the thump of the *mansin*'s drum. In the words of the Chatterbox Mansin, "A *kut* is for women's pleasure. The women are treated with wine and food and they play. But when men hear the hourglass drum, they play too."

The view that Korean "women's rituals" are the rituals most appropriately performed by women is a gross tautology. It is also an accurate description. The senior housewife honors the gods of the entire household. With other village women, she greets, pleads, and bargains with the gods of the entire community when shamans perform a village *kut.* Some women make secret mountain pilgrimages to greet the Seven Stars and the Mountain God. Some women perform simple exorcisms, flourishing a kitchen knife and casting out handfuls of millet when they suspect that ghostly interference is compounding a sudden or persistent illness in the house. "Parents have to be half shamans [*pan mudang*] to raise up their children," my landlady told me when she deemed her daughter's cough and fever worthy of aspirin and an exorcism.

Korean shamanism is a professional elaboration upon Korean household religion. Shaman and housewife perform analogous tasks and deal with the same spirits. A *mansin* claims the capacity to trance, to envision and become possessed by the gods and ancestors of all her client households and to muster the power of supernatural generals and warriors against ghosts and noxious influences. In a *mansin*'s *kut* the gods and ancestors weep, lament, and console the living, and the house gods claim their due in tribute. The family, friends, and neighbors confront the gods, are exorcised of malevolent influences, and receive a variety of blessings and prognostications. *Mansin* also perform a number of smaller, less dramatic rituals to provide women with a periodic prognosis on each member of the household, to speak for the gods and ancestors, and to cast away malevolent influences. As we have seen, women monitor the supernatural state of their households through divination sessions at the *mansin*'s house. As they learn the appetites or particularly powerful gods and restless ancestors, many women also establish a formal relationship *(tan'gol)* with a particular shaman and her shrine. They dedicate costumes and equipment for their own strong gods, sell their children to the protective Seven Stars, bring candles, grain, and delicacies to the shrine at the New Year and on lunar 7.7, and drink and dance at the *mansin*'s own flower-greeting *kut*. Refugee wives and first-generation townswomen rediscover lost traditions through the *mansin*'s visions and a kinswoman's confirmation. In modern Korea the unfolding of a *tan'gol* relationship sometimes includes the religious education a woman once learned from her mother-in-law, kinswomen, and neighbors.

Between them Korean men and women perform the rituals of household and family. Where the early ethnographers saw separate religions, subcultures, or historical strata in the ritual activities of Korean men and women, I find a working complementarity. Recall the young man who received a divination in a *mansin*'s shrine and dedicated his own brass bell because his Christian wife would not perform these actions on his behalf. This compromise was possible, but awkward, and provoked giggles. Again, in defiance of all propriety, Yongsu's Mother read the invocation at her husband's *chesa* because her two adolescent sons, overwhelmed with embarrassment, refused to perform. A good mimic, she struck the proper cadence and declaimed in a pompous baratone, much to the amusement of the neighbor women who had been invited to share the *chesa* feast.[1] That neither the man in the *mansin*'s shrine nor the woman reciting the *chesa* invocation behaved in a manner appropriate to their sex was both awkward and amusing. Their willingness to compromise suggests that both accepted the religious premises that underlie these activities.

Men's rituals are a product of Korea's literate and respected Confucian tradition. The moral axiom of filial piety and its dramatization in the rite of ancestor worship sanctify hierarchical relationships among patrilineal kin. The expression "moral axiom" comes from Fortes, who suggests that where kinship is a significant principle of extrafamilial social organization, the moral axioms of a society are implicit in its kinship relations (Fortes 1957, 346). The Confucian world has elaborated upon Fortes's hypothesis. Filial piety, a son's obligation to his father, is the foundation of Confucian social philosophy, self-consciously expressed in meticulously codified rituals that sanctify hierarchical relationships among patrilineal kin. These are the rituals of *family.* More than proper, the ties that bind kinsmen are essential. In village Korea agnatic kin are a common source of labor exchange, mutual aid, advice, and consent (Brandt 1971, 136–142; Dix 1979, 76).

The moral axioms contained in women's rituals are not the articulate stuff of social philosophy. Nevertheless, these rituals of the *household* demarcate and sanctify another aspect of Korean experience and world view. My exploration of Korean women's rituals began and ended with the house. The physical house is the primary metaphor for women's rituals. The household is the irreducible unit of the Korean peasant's social, political, economic, and religious life. It is the *household* that sends a representative to village and hamlet meetings, registers its births and deaths, pays taxes, contributes to village feasts and funerals, makes offerings to the village tutelary gods, honors its own gods, and falls under the onus of birth and death pollutions. Dangers are abroad in the outside world, and the household gods, when properly propitiated, defend the family against a battery of ghosts, restless ancestors, and noxious influences from without. *Kosa* offerings indicate the house gods' presence throughout the house site. In *kut* the gods stand up large as life when the *mansin* summon them outside the gate, on the porch, in the inner room, beside the storage jars, and behind the house. During an exorcism and after a *kut,* noxious influences are lured out of the gate and carried away into distant fields. When women and shamans hold a *kut* for the community, it is as though the entire village were a single house with one resident tutelary and a full complement of household gods and ancestors.

It is from the perspective of *household,* not *family,* that women deal with the ancestors of their own and their husband's house. The ancestors come to shaman ceremonies as visitors, visiting kin for whom one may have strong yet mixed feelings. Potentially benevolent and wise persons, kin are occasionally spiteful and demanding, and because they claim the prerogatives of kinship, they cannot be ignored. It is women, as shamans and kin, who lead the dead through the perils of the underworld into paradise, and safely away from the house.[2]

Many of the gods, ancestors, ghosts, and living kinswomen who appear at women's rituals travel along paths of relationship established by marriage. As ancestors and ghosts, married daughters return to their natal homes, and dead mothers follow living daughters. Dead women exercise a prerogative living women claim—occasional visits to their natal kin or to their own married daughters and appeals for succor from them. A married woman derives emotional sustenance from her own kin, and mothers greet their married daughters with warmth. Sometimes a woman delivers her own daughter's child, sometimes she brings a troubled daughter to the *mansin,* sometimes she slips the daughter food from her own larder to feed a hungry family. The daughter's longing for her own kin and the mother's affection for her married daughter find a voice when ghosts and ancestors speak in shaman rituals. Traditions of the daughter's natal home follow her in the claims of kindred spirits.

Women's kin rarely appear in Korean ethnography, but they do serve certain mundane needs and are a recourse in crisis when aid from the husband's kin is either unavailable or inappropriate. Yangja's family got rice from Yangja's Mother's kin when Yangja's Father was in jail. When Mr. Yi was struck by death humors, his mother-in-law sought out a shaman's cure. While they are unacknowledged in male rituals, kin linked through in-marrying and out-marrying women are yet an active presence in Korean social life, and gods, ghosts, and ancestors from women's natal homes assume an active presence in living women's rituals. Sometimes a *kut* musters women across the boundaries of patrilineal kinship to deal with their common restless spirits.

In Enduring Pine Village men's and women's ritual division of labor reflects men's and women's contrasting social experiences. Men grew up among the brothers and cousins with whom they will offer *chesa* to parents and grandparents of living memory. Women leave the household and neighborhoods where they grew up. In early adulthood they assume authority over independent households and honor the gods of these physically discrete houses. Married women have passed between two kin groups, as have many of the gods and ancestors who make their presence known in women's rituals. Women are the most appropriate officiants at rituals of the household and the most likely placators of bilateral gods and ancestors. Men's and women's rituals dramatize different, but not necessarily contradictory, components of Korean social organization. Korean men live in households and on household budgets. Korean women spend nearly all of their adult lives among the husband's agnatic kin. Korean men exploit their associations with wife's and mother's kin and daughter's or sister's husband's kin. Korean women's rituals combine with men's *chesa* to encompass a full range of social relationships, consisting of autonomous households, agnatic families, and a more diffuse bilateral kindred. Women's rituals are neither simple nor primitive nor separate. While the moral axioms they dramatize are not consciously articulated in written texts and aphorisms, they are essential.

The Korean ritual division of labor is tidy and predictable, consistent with the social experiences of men and women. Yet in China, where women also marry patrilocally, we find quite another arrangement. In Taiwanese households Chinese men, not Chinese women, worship the house tutelary, and the most powerful shamans are men. A comparison of men's and women's, layperson's and shaman's roles in these two so similar societies reveals the full import of Korean women's activities. Japan offers yet another variation. Let us now consider how other East Asian societies use sex roles and ritual to state and restate the complementary notions of household and family.

East Asian Comparisons: Family and Household

In all of the household religions of East Asia, we find some semblance of a household pantheon coexisting with an ancestor cult. Chinese and Japanese ethnography conveys a familiar pattern of gods dispersed through a dwelling, and we find, amid other acknowledged deities, traces of reigning household tutelary gods, fertility and childbirth goddesses in inner sactums, and site guardians outside the house but somewhere within the compound.[3] Whatever the surmisable common origin, diffusion, or convergence of these beliefs, the way men and women divide ritual tasks in each of these three societies conveys very different conceptions of family and household, male and female.

In Japanese households the two cults blend. The gods' offerings, special tiny rice cakes, can be distinguished from the mini meals the ancestors receive, but Japanese households do not emphasize a dichotomization of cults. Women prepare and serve the gods' and ancestors' offerings along with the family food, but men might occasionally make these offerings when they have the time and inclination to do so. Men are expected to officiate at major offerings, but venerable widows often claim dominant roles in the household ancestors' cult (Morioka 1968; Smith 1974, 118–120). The Japanese do not seize upon a ready sex dichotomy to distinguish the household cult from family ritual. They have no need, because the ancestors belong to a household that is likely to be but is not necessarily a biological family

(Nakane 1967, 1–40). According to Plath, "So far as intramural household rites are concerned, the ancestors are ancestral to the entire household as a collectivity. They relate to all the members and only the members." To use Plath's phrase, "the family of God is the family" (Plath 1964, 303). By extension, the household gods are sufficient to the family, the ancestors are sufficient to the household.

The sex-typing of Japanese religious specialists betrays a similar flexibility. In her comprehensive account of Japanese shaman practices, Blacker (1975) notes that historical shamans and blind mediums are women and village oracles, associated with folk Buddhist traditions, tend to be men, but even the ethnography that she presents suggests a more motley picture. Female mediums *(miko),* more common in the past, were associated with Shinto shrines or were semi-itinerants who served a small range of villages. Sometimes the female *miko* was paired with a male Shugendo priest who synthesized Shinto and Buddhist practices (Hori 1968, 182–183, 200–212; Fairchild 1962). Blacker observed a community ritual where, in the absence of a local male medium, a professional female *miko* was hired to summon the tutelary *kami* (Blacker 1975, 256–263). Mountain *kami* possess both male and female pilgrims with no apparent discrimination (ibid., 279–297; Fairchild 1962, 95).

Chinese ethnography reveals a very different arrangement of men's and women's ritual roles, another notion of men and women in families. In the following discussion I will lean heavily upon accounts and analyses of Chinese religion in Hong Kong and Taiwan communities. Although this is a shamefully limited perspective on China, contemporary understandings of Chinese religion, ritual, and social structure nevertheless hang on three decades of fieldwork by scholars restricted to these two geographic regions.

In China individual households and the broader family present a clash of interests and strategies, a conflict between *sons* who would keep the father's family intact and *brothers* greedy and impatient to stake independent households. Although brothers may be the actual initiators of family division, the Chinese themselves blame brothers' wives (Cohen 1976, 193–226). According to Freedman, the Chinese consider women "by nature quarrelsome, jealous, petty-minded and preoccupied with the interests of their own husbands and children at the expense of the wider family" (Freedman 1979a, 260; M. Wolf 1972). By this logic, Freedman argues, we should expect women to worship the Kitchen God, the household tutelary deity, while men worship the family's ancestors. Indeed, then, we should find a "Korean" situation. But in China we find almost the opposite. Women tend the ancestors, at least in their daily routine care, and men worship the Kitchen God. Freedman suggests that this arrangement adds a supernatural counterweight to women's divisive proclivities. Women fall under the family ancestors' authority; men represent the household before a supernatural authority associated with "domestic discipline" (Freedman 1979b, 283). According to Feuchtwang, only the male household head may presume to address heaven via the Kitchen God (Feuchtwang 1974, 118). Note that the Chinese male household head's actions, petitioning a supernatural authority as the household's representative, parallel the Korean wife's prayers and offerings to her household tutelary.

Notice also that on Taiwan several households, several Kitchen Gods, and several separate cooking budgets coexist under the fiction of a single roof. In Enduring Pine Village the house tutelary resides in the roof beam and demarcates a separate household baldly inhabiting its own house. Where the Korean Stove God receives special tribute, the god is associated with women in complement to a roof beam tutelary associated with men, and women make the Stove God's offerings. In Korea no single roof covers the tension between household and family. There are frankly great houses *(k'ŭnjip)* and minor houses *(chagŭnjip)*. The eldest son inherits the great house and the lion's share of the family's wealth. Secondary sons' claims are best settled when they marry, and they build their minor houses on or, when Koreans married in their teens, within a few years of marriage.[4] If younger brothers smart under this arrangement, the fault lies in the order of birth, not in their wives' supposed scheming. Korean wives, I suggest, do not share their Chinese sisters' profound reputation for intrafamilial destructiveness. If wives are less threatening, then Koreans need not follow the Chinese dodge on an obvious ritual dichotomy. Here, instead, men worship the ancestors for the *family,* and women petition the *household* gods.

The sex-typing of professional shamans in Korea and Taiwan also reflects contrasting perceptions of women and contrasting ascriptions of positive and negative feminine powers. As in Korea, the Taiwanese shaman is one among a variety of divination specialists. Possessed by powerful gods, the *tang-ki* exorcise and heal. Possessed by ghosts and ancestors, they negotiate reconciliations between the living and the dead. Here, too, shamans deal with problems that arise in households and communities. In Taiwanese communities men's and women's roles in household religion are complemented by the different services male and female *tang-ki* provide. According to Jordan, "There seems to be a tendency . . . for female *tang-ki* to be associated often with purely local divinities who answer individual petitions at private altars in the medium's home, whereas male *tang-ki* seem usually to operate by visiting the family of the petitioner or guiding village affairs in the village temple. The distinction is not hard and fast and exceptions occur in both directions" (Jordan 1972, 69n.). The gods who possess the predominently male *tang-ki* are the powerful deities of local cults who give divinations and defend the family and village against malevolent ghostly incursions. Most of the female *tang-ki* seem to be the mediums of "little maids" or "little gods," local or undistinguished ghosts who demand acclaim by seizing their own *tang-ki* (ibid., 54–85, 166). Many of these *tang-ki* are kin to their possessing goddesses (ibid., 166). Similarly, in the Hong Kong New Territories the Cantonese *mann saeg phox* is assisted by her own dead children (Potter 1974, 226–228). Not only are the little gods' *tang-ki* primarily women, they serve a female clientele. "The term little god . . . ," Jordan explains, "is used to refer to divinized spirits of local people, whose oracles are consulted primarily by women for information on the rearing of children and other of the family's affairs that are entirely or largely under the government of women" (Jordan 1972, 141n.). Among their tasks they divine the source of ghostly affliction and arrange "ghost weddings" for souls who die unwed and thus eternally unsatisfied (ibid., 140–141, 169–170).

But if women bring their womanish concerns to the little god *tang-ki* or to other female specialists, they seem to consult male *tang-ki* when the problem merits more powerful supernatural intercession. Conception is most immediately women's concern, and Wolf reports, "In every *tang-ki*'s session . . . there is always a worried looking middle-aged lady who has come to ask what to do about a daughter-in-law who is not showing signs of pregnancy." In the northern Taiwan community where Wolf worked, a male *tang-ki* was reputed to be particularly good at solving problems of infertility "in pigs and brides" (M. Wolf 1972, 149–150). A female healer, a *sian-si:-ma,* calls back the wandering souls of startled children, and mothers sometimes perform soul-calling for their own children (Ahern 1975, 206n.; 1978, 27). In Chaochuang, northern Taiwan, if a mother deems a child's complaint more serious than soul loss, she may bring the child to the high gods' *tang-ki* (Gould-Martin 1976, 107, 122). High gods have more power and high gods tend to possess male *tang-ki*.

Men seem to be the households' most appropriate representatives to the high gods' *tang-ki*. Jordan reports that in Bao-an, his field site in southwestern Taiwan, men assist the male *tang-ki* and Taoist priest *(âng-thâu-á)* in celebrating the cult god's birthday, purifying cult member houses, and defending the community against malevolent ghostly incursions (Jordan 1972, 53–57, 120–128). Similarly, men hold the divinely animated god palanquin *(kiō-á)* in divination sessions and ghostly battles. Jordan remarks, "Women do not perform this task in Bao-an or in any seances that I have seen elsewhere. Other lines of evidence suggest to me that this is probably not because they are prohibited from doing so, but rather because in some sense it is men's work, rather like building cabinets or fixing plumbing in America" (ibid., 64n.). In Korea, of course, divination and the supernatural defense of home and community are the concerns of female shamans and women.

In Taiwan a male Taoist priest intercedes on behalf of souls in the underworld. Although Chinese women converse with souls in seances, the recent dead need a different, more powerful sponsor to see them safely through the perilous nether regions. According to Ahern, "Because the road to the underworld is beset by dangerous monsters and unknown obstacles, the deceased might succumb to some fatal disaster long before arriving unless he receives help" (Ahern 1973, 223). The priest bargains with the earth god and guides the soul, just as Korean women and *mansin* bargain with the Death Messenger (Saja) and lead the dead out of hell.

In short, two categories of Taiwanese *tang-ki* accomplish the work of one Korean *mansin* in Enduring Pine Village. While *tang-ki* divide the ritual tasks, a single *mansin* is possessed both by powerful gods who drive off malevolent supernatural entities, bestow blessings, and issue pronouncements, and by ancestors and ghosts who have urgent business with the living. Another possible generalization is that Chinese women seem to use *tang-ki* to further their predictable "uterine" concerns—fertility, childbirth, and the successful rearing of children— (Wolf 1972) while Chinese men join forces with *tang-ki* and male

Taoist priests to perform other significant ritual tasks that are, in Enduring Pine Village, the ritual domain of women.

Ahern suggests that in the Chinese scheme, pollution beliefs provide a symbolic rationale for women's subordinate ritual status. Menstruation and birth pollution render women ritually unclean, and unclean women deal most directly with unclean spirits, with dead souls and "little low goddesses" who are tainted by association with childbirth. She notes that, "The common relegation of women to the worship of the low, unclean end of the hierarchy is appropriate because women are so frequently unclean themselves. Conversely, the near-monopoly by men of the clean, high end of the hierarchy is appropriate because they are much less often unclean" (Ahern 1975, 206–207). Ahern concludes that pollution beliefs are intimately connected to the Chinese kinship system. Death, birth, and menstruation pollute because they rupture the integrity of bodies and families. Women's greater perceived uncleanliness is a function of women's borderline position in families. "It is because the kinship system is focused on male lines of descent that women are depicted on the boundaries breaking in as strangers. It may be events that are polluting rather than women *per se,* but polluting events are events that intrude new people or remove old ones in a male-oriented kinship system" (ibid., 213).

Korea again poses a contrast. Here, too, women intrude as strangers into a male-oriented system. Here, too, menstruation, birth, and death pollute, and pollution imposes a temporary ban on ritual activity. Women do not worship the household gods or make offerings in the shaman's shrine when they are menstruating or when they have had recent contact with childbirth or funerals. Neither do households sponsor *kut* after a recent birth, when they are in mourning, or when one of the women in menstruating. Menstruation offends the Korean gods, and a particularly good *mansin* will, when possessed, denounce a "dirty woman" for presuming to appear at a *kut* in a state of pollution. But menstrual and birth pollutions are temporary conditions, not an inherent sullying. Ritually clean Korean women worship the high gods and ritually clean female *mansin* are possessed by them.

While pollution beliefs undoubtedly reinforce the ritual dichotomization of the sexes in Taiwan, pollution beliefs, in and of themselves, do not provide an explanation sufficient to account for a contrasting arrangement of ritual roles in Korea. The social assumptions that underlie the pattern of pollution beliefs and ritual roles in the two

societies provide a more satisfying basis of comparison. Ahern rejects
a direct correlation between pollution beliefs and a young woman's
power to disrupt the family, since pollution, unlike fractiousness, does
not serve a woman's own interests. Ahern does suggest that pollution
beliefs impose a "negative sediment" on Chinese women's reproduc-
tive powers, for, "The *power* women have is their capacity to alter a
family's form by adding members to it, dividing it, and disturbing
male authority; the *danger* they pose is their capacity to break up what
men consider the ideal family" (ibid., 200, her emphasis; 212–214). In
Korea the issue is moot. Women do not pull families apart, rather,
couples, except for the heir and his wife, establish their own homes.
Brothers return to the main house and worship the ancestors as family.
Korean families assume and accommodate autonomous households.
Ritually clean women worship the gods of their appropriately discrete
dwellings.

A Korean Reconsideration

Korea today might seem the mirror image of China, with men's and
women's ritual roles rearranged but with the relative significance of
men's and women's rituals preserved intact. Ancestor worship is still
esteemed as an expression of filial piety, while the ritual practices of
women and shamans are disparaged as an embarrassing superstition.
But who levels this judgment? The Chinese literati have scorned Taoist
priests, *tang-ki,* and Buddhist monks no less than the Korean literati
have scorned Buddhist monks and *mansin.* Elite disdain fosters local
defensiveness. People in Bao-an were no more comfortable with Jordan's (1972, 69) initial inquiries about shamans than were the Enduring Pine Villagers who giggled with embarrassment through my early
interviews. Yet Chinese and Koreans hire shamans to deal with gods,
ancestors, and ghosts. The distinctive difference between Korean and
Chinese folk religion is the Korean woman's special prominence in
these activities.

One could argue that Korean women, like Chinese women, are perceived as inherently dirty and inherently inferior. We might also consider women's gods equivalent to the baser little gods or little maids of
Taiwan and not on a par with the powerful high gods that possess Chinese male *tang-ki.* A few of the *mansin*'s gods do, indeed, resemble the

little gods. The Princess and the Child Gods died young, and it is only by harassing the living that these insignificant beings win a place in the family pantheon and gifts of bright clothing, pocket money, and treats to pacify their caprice. They emerge in the *mansin*'s *kut,* but it should be remembered that they make only cameo appearances amid a battery of more powerful gods. *Mansin* claim the full range of spirits that the high and little god *tang-ki* of Taiwan divide among themselves. Powerful gods in the *mansin*'s pantheon heal, revitalize, and defend the house. The General (Changgun) and the Warrior (Sinjang) drive out ghosts and noxious influences with a flourishing of knives and a pelting of millet. The Birth Grandmother (Samsin Halmŏni) inspires conception in a reluctant womb. The gods' greed, a part of the drama and comedy of a full-dress *kut,* is an attribute of the gods' power, power to repel malevolent incursions and power to work good or ill in the house. At a *kut* the gods sing songs of self-praise while they demand yet more tribute, "I'm so wonderful, I just can't say."

The rituals Korean women perform for conception and the successful rearing of children can be interpreted as religious expressions of a mother's desire to buffer her position in a patrilocal kin group. If these were women's only ritual concerns, we might accept standard interpretations of Korean women's ritual as a response to Korean women's wretched and vulnerable state. But Korean women's concerns betray a greater range of authority and responsibility in household and family life than the motherly preoccupations of their Chinese counterparts. Pollution beliefs do not limit women and female shamans to exclusive dealings with the tainted and low-ranking supernatural. Women's rituals revitalize the whole house and all who dwell within. Sometimes women's rituals revitalize the entire community. Women exorcise the sick, tend the house gods, and free the family's restless dead from hell.

Korea merits comparison with one final ethnographic example, Okinawa, where the ritual dichotomization of the sexes is most extreme and probably most complementary. The Okinawan male house head wields all social and political authority as the household's temporal representative. The senior housewife is unambiguously the household ritual authority, representing the household before both gods and ancestors and commanding respect on a par with the male head (Lebra 1966, 176–202 passim). This dichotomization characterized all levels of traditional Okinawan society. At one time hereditary priestesses held ritual authority in concert with male temporal author-

ity. This system persisted until the Japanese annexation in the late
nineteenth century, although Confucian and Buddhist influences had
gradually been eroding the prestige of the priestesses since the seventeenth century (ibid., 117–121). I have introduced the Okinawan
material to suggust that, where women in a geographically proximate
and in may respects similar society held unambiguous ritual authority,
my portrayal of Korean women's ritual is not a bizarre aberration of
East Asian expectations.

Neither in pre-seventeenth-century Okinawa nor in pre-Confucian
Korea did women wield political power outside the domestic sphere.
Their religious authority was thus vulnerable to the zealotry of male
reformers. In Korea today Confucian ideology blends with an infusion
of modernity and colors scholarly attitudes toward both women and
shamans. Even so, the body of ritual described in these pages suggests
the limits of the Confucian transformation. The social historians who
describe residence and inheritance practices in an older Korea would
probably not be surprised to find women performing household rituals, succoring the dead, and occasionally contending with gods and
ancestors from the natal home. Women's rituals are more than the res-
idue of ancient practices; they highlight a distinctive and persistent
feature of Korean family organization: the acknowledged autonomy
of houses and the positive powers of matrons within households and
as links between kin groups.

Conclusion

I have described the ritual practices of shamans and housewives in the
vicinity of Seoul and have suggested that this system provides ritual
commentary on Korean notions of household and kin, notions unac-
counted for in the practice of ancestor worship. Korean shamans first
drew my interest as women ministering to women. I was inspired by a
burgeoning anthropological interest in the little-studied female side of
ethnography. I found Korean women's rituals a complex tapestry of
spirits, practices, and relationships. I have tried to do justice both to
the richness of this tradition and to the zestiness of the women who
perpetuate it. I have intended more than an exotic footnote on Korean
life or a female ethnographer's insular interest in women's culture for
its own sake. Insofar as these practices have been studied as archaic

survivals or as the mechanism for exclusive catharsis of a feminine subculture, scholars have missed a distinctive and vital corner of Korean life. Without the Korean woman and without a careful search behind the Chinese clichés that have heretofore sufficed to define her, Korean society eludes us.

Appendixes
Notes
Glossary
Bibliography
Index

Appendixes

Appendix 1
The Chŏn Family *Kut*

Segment	Gods Manifested	Place	Mansin
First Segment (Haengju Mullim)	Soldier Official (Kunung Taegam)	outside the gate	Chatterbox Mansin
Drum Song to expel pollution *(pujŏng)*	all gods invited in	porch	Chatterbox Mansin
Ancestors' Segment (Chosanggŏri)	distant dead *(sŏpsu)*	porch	Chatterbox Mansin
	Mountain God of Native Place (Ponhyang Sansin)		
	netherworldly guard *(kamang)*		
	Great Spirit Grandmother (Taesin Halmŏni)		
	ancestors *(chosang)*	porch and inner room	
Officials' Segment (Taegamgŏri)	Official (Taegam)	porch, around house site	Yongsu's Mother
	Great Spirit Official (Taesin Taegam)		

Women use the *mugam*

Buddhist Sage's Segment (Pulsagŏri)	Buddhist Sage (Pulsa)	porch	Okkyŏng's Mother
	Seven Stars (Ch'ilsŏng)	storage jars	
	Birth Grandmother (Chesŏk, Samsin Halmŏni)	inner room	

(Continued)

Appendix 1 (continued)

Segment	Gods Manifested	Place	Mansin
	Princess (Hogu)	porch	
	unredeemed souls		
War Gods' Segment (Sangŏri, Sangsangŏri)	General (Changgun)	porch	Chatterbox Mansin
	Special Messenger (Pyŏlsang-sŏng)		
	Warrior (Sinjang)		
	Spirit Warrior Official (Singjang Taegam)		

	Kut stops for the night		
House Lord's Segment (Sŏngjugŏri)	House Lord (Sŏngju)	porch	Town Mansin

	Women use the *mugam* again		
Clown's Segment (Ch'angbugŏri)	Clown (Ch'angbu)	porch	Chatterbox Mansin
House Site Official's Segment (T'ŏjugŏri)	House Site Official (T'ŏju Taegam)	rear of house to front courtyard	Yongsu's Mother
	Grain God (Kŏllip) Foundation God (Chisin)		
	Door Guard (Sumun Taegam)	main gate	
Soldier Official's Segment (Kununggŏri)	Soldier Official (Kunung Taegam)	outside the main gate	Chatterbox Mansin
Final Send-off (Twitchŏn)	ghosts invoked	outside the main gate	Chatterbox Mansin

Note: The segments of the Chŏn family *kut* are standard building blocks, but the sequence varies slightly from *kut* to *kut*. Ch'oe and Chang (1967) list possible variations in the sequence of a *kut*. Their *mansin* informant lives near Enduring Pine Village. T. G. Kim (1978) gives yet another *kut* sequence performed by a *mansin* in Seoul. Yim (1970) diagrams variations by region and type of *kut*.

Appendix 2
Major Concerns Expressed in Divination Sessions

Concern	No. of Clients	
Illness	16	
of husband		6
of self		4
of father-in-law		3
of grown son		2
of baby		2
Husband's or son's career prospects or family enterprise	8	
Adultery suspected or confirmed	8	
own		1
husband's		7
Problems with unruly son, stepson or grandson	7	
son left home, return desired		3
son rebellious		4
Mother-in-law / daughter-in-law relationship	3	
mother-in-law concerned about runaway daughter-in-law		1
runaway daughter-in-law dislikes mother-in-law		1
mother-in-law contemplating co-residence		1
Marriage prospects	6	
of son		1
of daughter		2
of self (one widow, two recent college graduates)		3
"Year's Luck" only	3	

Note: Figures are for forty-four divination sessions. It was impossible to isolate a primary anxiety for seven clients, who had more than one major concern. Two concerns are therefore listed for them.

Appendix 3
Ancestors Appearing in *Kut*

Given the somewhat chaotic circumstances of *kut,* I cannot claim to provide a complete survey of all ancestors and ghosts appearing in each ritual observed. Because of the small size of my sample (twenty-five *kut*), indications of the relative frequency with which various categories of ancestors appear are, at best, tentative. While my sample indicates the breadth of categories of kin appearing in the *kut* I witnessed, additional categories of kin may conceivably appear in other *kut*.

Husband's Kin	No. Appearing	Wife's Kin	No. Appearing
Hufafa's generation		**Wifafa's generation**	
grandfather	8	grandfather	2
grandfather's 1st wife	10	grandmother	2
grandfather's 2d wife	2		
Subtotal	20	Subtotal	4
Hufa's generation		**Wifa's generation**	
father	18	father	6
mother	12	mother	5
father's 1st wife	1	mother's 2d husband	1
mother's 1st husband	1		
adoptive father	1		
adoptive mother	1		
Subtotal	34	Subtotal	12
Husband's generation		**Wife's generation**	
husband	4		
husband's 1st wife	7		
husband's sister	6	wife's sister	5
husband's elder brother	2	wife's brother	4
husband's younger brother	3		
husband's sister's husband	2	wife's brother's wife	1
Subtotal	24	Subtotal	10

(Continued)

Appendix 3 (continued)

Husband's Kin	No. Appearing	Wife's Kin	No. Appearing
Children		**Children**	
son	3		
daughter	3		
nephew	1		
niece	2	niece	1
Subtotal	9	Subtotal	1
Total	87	Total	27

Note: In addition to the above, I also counted appearances by relatives of senior *(k'ŭnjip)* and junior lines *(chagŭnjip)*. Relatives of the senior line of the hu, hufa, or hufafa's generation appeared seven times, and relatives of the junior line of the hu, hufa, or hufafa appeared nine times. Grandparents of the third and fourth ascendant generation and relatives of the third and fourth degree of relationship were frequently mentioned in passing. There was one mention, by my count, of relatives up to the eighth degree of relationship and only one mention of the senior line of the wifa's generation.

Notes

CHAPTER 1

1. The water in the dipper is pollution water *(pujŏngmul)*; ash and water are a traditional soap base. Salt and red pepper are used in exorcism.

2. Chesŏk literally means "Buddha Emperor," but the *mansin* and her clients explicitly equate Chesŏk with Samsin Halmŏni, the birth spirit (see chap. 6), thus my gloss, "Birth Grandmother." In Korea the Seven Stars are enshrined behind Buddhist temples, but the Seven Stars are also known in the Chinese Taoist and folk traditions.

3. Sometimes the Special Messenger is identified as the Smallpox God, but this attribute, like the disease, is happily no longer significant in rural Korea.

4. In other ritual contexts odd numbers are considered auspicious, and the number four extremely unlucky. Here the even number probably suggests a satisfactory completion.

5. Grandmother Chŏn agreed to pay forty thousand won for the *kut*. She delivered the money in a bundle to the Chatterbox Mansin a few days before the *kut*. The Chatterbox Mansin returned most of the money to Grandmother Chŏn before the start of the *kut* and Grandmother Chŏn gave it back gradually in response to the gods' and ancestors' demands throughout the *kut*. The remainder of the money came from the other women—relatives, neighbors, and friends—who bought wine, danced, and received divinations. In 1978, when the Chŏns held their *kut*, five hundred won was the approximate equivalent of one U.S. dollar.

6. Ch'oe and Chang (1967) list major patterns and variations for *kut* in villages near my research site. The Ministry of Culture's (MCBCPP) cumulative

volumes on folk belief contain ample descriptive material on shaman ritual. Both of these works include transcribed texts of shaman songs. T. G. Kim (1971–) has also transcribed texts.

7. Note that these are not absolute blood links. The son and daughter are Grandmother Chŏn's stepchildren.

CHAPTER 2

1. Students of Korean society seem all but obsessed with dichotomies. A number of Koreanists, not necessarily followers of French structuralism, have posed the diverse problems they address as contradictory themes and complementary resolutions. See, for example, Brandt (1971) on village life, Dix (1980) on village religion, Kawashima (1980) on political culture, McBrian (1977) on styles of interaction, and McCann (1983) on *sijo* poetry.

2. In the tradition of E. Evans-Pritchard ([1937] 1976), anthropologists grappling with witchcraft developed the rule of thumb that attributions of supernatural malaise arise from stressful social relationships—co-wives living in a single compound (LeVine 1962), former tenant and former landlord (Yoshida 1967), aging mothers' brothers and their nephew heirs (Nadel 1952), and rival branches in a burgeoning lineage (Marwick 1967).

3. The Seoul Metropolitan Government reports that in 1975 there were 902 shamans practicing in the capital. Since this figure includes only shamans acknowledged in the records of the neighborhood offices, the actual number is probably far higher. According to the Economic Planning Board, there were 6,040 shamans in the entire country in 1963, or roughly one shaman for each 750 households, but again, the count probably falls far below the actual number of practicing shamans. Figures from the 1964 *Korea Statistical Yearbook* and the 1976 *Seoul Statistical Yearbook* are courtesy of Barbara Young. See Harvey (1979, 12) for additional data on the prevalence of shamans.

4. Western-language accounts include significant statements by Brandt (1971, 115–121), Biernatzki (1967), Dix (1977, 1979), R. Janelli (1975a, 1975b), Janelli and Janelli (1982), and K. K. Lee (n.d.).

5. It would be impossible and inappropriate to list extensively the numerous works by Korean and Japanese ethnographers. I will refer to this vast body of scholarly literature throughout the text. See Ch'oe Kil-sŏng's historical overview of significant Korean and Japanese works (Ch'oe 1981, 22–48).

6. The Three Kingdoms are traditionally dated: Paekche 18 B.C.–A.D. 661; Koguryŏ 37 B.C.–A.D. 668; Silla 57 B.C.–A.D. 935.

7. Evelyn McCune (n.d.) raised this possibility in an unpublished paper some thirty years ago. On the strength of subsequent archaeological discoveries, her suggestion merits serious consideration.

CHAPTER 3

1. Unified Silla 668–935; Koryŏ 918–1392; Chosŏn ("Yi dynasty") 1392–1910.

2. In fact, the *ajŏn* functioned within a "system of institutionalized corruption" (Palais 1975, 13). The local staff were not on the government payroll and were expected to sustain themselves through their own mercurial abilities (ibid.). See jaundiced accounts by Hulbert ([1906] 1970, 55) and Griffis (1911, 232).

3. The size of a household's contribution to the two communal rituals is optional, resting on individual inclination and ability. Contributions are posted. Two hundred won was the minimum contribution to the offering for the Mountain God in the fall of 1977. In that year any one of the following would suffice as a wedding or funeral contribution: cash—2,700 won; rice—two measures (600 won per measure); rice wine—two kettles (150 won per kettle).

CHAPTER 4

1. Pyŏngyang-mansin, one of Harvey's informants, reports a similar experience (Harvey 1979, 109).

2. Like the Japanese language, spoken Korean sentence endings are shorter or longer depending on the relative status of the speaker and the addressee. Adults use blunt endings, *panmal,* when addressing children, and children use them when addressing dogs.

3. There are hereditary *mudang* families in the southernmost provinces. Whether by birth or divine will, the point is the same: the female religious practitioner does not voluntarily assume her role.

4. Okkyŏng's Mother moved to Tranquil Spring after I left the field. One of her most enthusiastic clients had found her husband a job there. Many of the residents of Korea's fast-expanding towns are but a few years removed from the countryside. Networks of kinship and friendship still reach into the villages. Tranquil Spring shopkeepers and blue-collar wives called the village ritual specialist to deal with crises. She then settled in their midst.

5. In her Sudong study, Soon-young Yoon found that, "patients might change shamans as often as they did hospitals." One woman, suffering from hypertension, went to eight shamans and four hospitals (S. Yoon 1977b, 124). I discuss the issue of client's choice in more detail in chapter 5.

6. Harvey (1976, 192) reports a similar incident.

7. *Megi* or *me,* contractions of *maji,* mean "rice offered to Buddha." Gari Ledyard (personal communication) suggests that since *maji* can also imply

going out to greet the arrival of a notable; the term implies that women are going out to the *mansin*'s shrine to respectfully greet their own gods.

8. Harvey (1976, 191) also notes that shamans explicitly refuse to see neighbors or relatives.

CHAPTER 5

1. The practice of sending a dying patient home, common in Korea, is not considered callous. Ideally one dies in one's own home, surrounded by grieving kin. Those who die away from home carry resentment beyond the grave. Practicing medicine in Korea, Sich comments frankly on her personal confrontation with Korean values, "They often take the patient home, to let him die in peace. . . . For the family peace and harmony are essential, and the fact that all the family can be united with the ill or dying member. . . . Through the years I have become less and less certain in my conviction that the heroics through which Western medicine submits our terminally ill to save their physical lives is indeed superior" (Sich 1978, 31).

2. See D. Janelli (1977) and Young (1980) for accounts of the theory and practice of horoscope divination.

3. A woman with a strong horoscope is sometimes considered responsible for her husband's death, but she may avoid a "two-marriage fate" by marrying late.

4. Dix's informants refer to *tongt'o*, literally "to move the earth," one of the potentially dangerous activities listed in the almanac. The term is applied to ailments resulting from the machinations of wandering spirits lodged in the family compound (Dix 1980), a concept akin to *tongbŏp* in Enduring Pine Village.

5. Han reports similar beliefs on Kago Island, but here men exorcised a newly constructed fence of an evil spirit after consulting a male geomancer (S. Han 1977, 93).

6. The actual term she used was *kwisin norŭm*, "*kwisin* play." *Kwisin*, literally "ghost/god," is a vague, inclusive term for supernatural beings. Sometimes Yongsu's Mother used it to indicate all of the gods and ancestors of her pantheon. Often women use the term in a narrower sense, to indicate unspecified, unrelated dead, the sense implied here, and hence my translation "ghosts."

7. The term *hongaek*, disaster seen as an ominous red cloud, was probably derived from *hoengaek*, "sudden disaster."

8. Although the reference is to an acupuncturist, from what follows I doubt she meant a doctor trained in Chinese medicine. Women sometimes use common sewing needles to treat children for fright sickness.

9. Yim provides this definition, "*Chudang, sal,* and the like . . . are con-

ceived as a sort of energy or bolt of light. When someone is suddenly taken sick, dies, or is deformed . . . they say it was because of *sal* or a *chudang*" (Yim, 1970, 83).

10. For the anthropologist, arrows evoke Douglas' (1966) and Turner's (1967, 93–111) discussions of transition and danger, based on Van Gennep's ([1909] 1960) early insight.

11. I have heard *mansin* advise clients to schedule a sixty-first birthday celebration in a different, more auspicious month than the actual date of birth. I do not know whether the advice was taken or not. Weddings are a more obvious example of the carefully selected auspicious day.

12. Apparently some parts of a ritual are more dangerous than others. Yongsu's Mother advised one woman that her youngest son should not see the bride enter the wedding hall. Another woman was advised not to run outside and look when the groom's men delivered the bride's chest *(ham)* to her home on the eve of her wedding.

CHAPTER 6

1. Some families house their gods in special placings, the so-called fetishes of missionary accounts. These placings consist of jars of grain, packets of pine needles, or nests of paper. If Jones' (1902) early description of "spirit worship" is at all representative of practices in the Seoul area of his day, spirit placings were far more numerous and elaborate at the turn of the century. Akiba also mentions a plethora of "spirit pots" in houses throughout the peninsula (Akiba 1957, 104ff.). The paucity of placings in contemporary Korean homes need not imply a reduction in the ranks of household gods, nor the gods' abandonment of the house. Place is more significant than placing. Women set down rice cake and wine for the appropriate god in the appropriate part of the house.

2. The rituals I am about to describe are most properly categorized as *ant'aek kosa*, "rites of household tranquility." Although I have seen this term in numerous Korean books, it escaped my notice in the field. My informants distinguished wine *kosa (sul kosa)* and cake *kosa (ttŏk kosa)*, the latter term implying a more elaborate offering. Most often they would simply say *kosa*. I will argue that although there are other contexts for *kosa*, house *kosa* is the basic rite; the others are variations on a theme. Dictionaries gloss *kosa* as "offerings for the household gods."

Passing mention of women's household rituals appears in: Akamatsu and Akiba (1938, 159–160), Biernatzki (1967, 13, 136), C. Han (1949, 210, 212), S. Han (1977, 81–82), Knez (1959, 107, 120), Mills (1960, 24), Osgood (1951, 124–125), and Sich (1978). Find descriptions of the household pantheon in Jones (1902), Chang (1974, 163–175), J. Lee (1975, 1981),

Guillemoz (1983), and the Ministry of Culture and Bureau of Cultural Properties Preservation's (MCBCPP) province by province compendium of folk custom (1969–).

3. The ripening rice is probably analogous to the growing child, much as grain in the gourd dipper symbolized conception. The parallel struck me long after I left the field. I do not know if women and *mansin* would concur with my interpretation.

4. Jones (1902), followed by Akamatsu and Akiba (1938), uses the characters *sŏngjo,* "creator," to indicate Sŏngju. Contemporary Korean folklorists either use the gloss "lord of the castle" or the Korean alphabet to render the name of this god (Yim 1970; Chang 1974; MCBCPP 1969–). "Good ruler," is another possibility. Gari Ledyard (personal communication) suggests "vertical pillar," *"chu,"* as another possible source, suggesting the pine branch used for the House Lord's descent into the home. In religious lore and poetry significant concepts are infused with diverse meanings (see glossary).

5. Also called *Sŏngju tae naerinŭngŏt,* "the House Lord's descent on a branch." The use of a pine or bamboo branch for the descent of a spirit occurs throughout Korea. In northern Kyŏnggi Province a shaking branch also indicates the Village God's descent into the village shrine tree. In a village in rural Kangwŏn Province the descent of a spirit *(kwisin)* on a shaking branch is incorporated into funeral rites (Clark Sorensen, personal communication). See Akiba (1957, 93) for a brief discussion of the symbolic properties and ritual uses of pine and bamboo.

6. In Enduring Pine Village the Samsin was most commonly conceptualized as Samsin Halmŏni, a white-haired grandmother. One of the local shamans recognized a trinity: a Yangban Samsin, a Monk Samsin, and an Ancestor Samsin. One or the other of these birth spirits might appear in conception dreams. This portrayal follows the literal meaning of Samsin, "three spirits," but note also that *sam* has the same pronunciation as the Korean word for "placenta." The *mansin* equate the Samsin with Chesŏk, a figure borrowed from Buddhism. Chesŏk is worshiped in the *mansin*'s shrine and appears in *kut.* As one *mansin* explained, "Samsin Grandmother in the inner room is Chesŏk in the shrine." Chesŏk also oversees the fertility of grain and gives long life. The god is sometimes also a collective representation of the family's ancestors *(choryŏng).* See Chang (1974) for an appreciation of the varied conceptualizations of Samsin.

7. Women seem most likely to receive experienced assistance with delivery and more extensive postpartum care at the birth of their first child. For other accounts of Korean beliefs and practices surrounding conception and childbirth, see Akiba (1957), Chung, Cha, and Lee (1977), Kendall (1977c), Kinsler (1976, 1977), Osgood (1951, 92–93), Sich (1978, 1981), and Sich and Kim (1978). See Pillsbury (1982) for a similar concept of "wind" as it affects the structuring of postpartum care among Chinese women.

8. The *tol* marks the end of the first year of life. After the *tol* the child is considered two years old.

9. A few of Barbara Young's urban inspirational diviners claimed the aid of child gods *(tongja)* and one informant gave her a grisly account of how a would-be diviner secures a dying child's soul to do her bidding (Young 1980). A similar account may be found in Kim Tongni's popular novella, *Ŭlhwa.* Diviners who use children's souls as messengers seem similar to the little gods' mediums in Taiwan and to the Cantonese *mann saeg phox* who is assisted by her own dead children (Potter 1974, 226–228). But the diviners in Young's study do not claim to be *mansin* nor do they provide the *mansin*'s range of services.

10. *Tan'gol* come to the shrine on the third day after a *kut* to make a small offering and receive a final prognosis.

CHAPTER 7

1. But see Janelli and Janelli (1982) for some rare examples of women's participation in *chesa.*

2. The men arrange plates of food on the *chesa* tray following a traditional formula. "Red [apples] in the east and white [pears] in the west; fish in the east and meat in the west; on the right, salt fish; on the left, beef." Even village men who are unable to read and write know this verse of Chinese characters by heart.

The minutia of *chesa* etiquette are contained in household ritual manuals (Kajŏng Pogam) originally written in classical Chinese but now available in inexpensive modern Korean editions. Literacy and experience imply differential access to ritual expertise. A ritual expert among kinsmen makes final adjustments in the arrangement of offering food.

3. Two men in Enduring Pine Village have studied Chinese characters and calligraphy. For a small fee of "cigarette money," they will prepare spirit placings and the written congratulatory address *(ch'ungmun)* chanted to the ancestors after the first libation.

4. In Enduring Pine Village, ghosts, as wandering, homeless beggars, receive coarse grain *(chobap)* and scraps of food. Dead children of the *chip,* that most ambiguous subgrouping of ghosts, receive cooked rice when the shaman propitiates them to exorcise the family of their influence. The Death Messenger also receives rice, a meal that marks both his menial status and the start of a long, difficult journey. These observations were prompted by Wolf's discussion of Chinese gods, ghosts, and ancestors and the sorts of offering food appropriate to each category of supernatural being (A. Wolf 1974).

5. Again, temples are on and of the mountain.

6. Küngnak is most literally translated "(Place of) Extreme Bliss." Since the

residents of Enduring Pine Village envision Kŭngnak as a land of flowering lotus fields, I use the gloss "Lotus Paradise."

7. The *chinogi kut* has intrigued other students of Korean ritual. T. G. Kim (1966) analyzes the ritual form and song texts of this rite for "survivals" of the shaman's archetypal netherworldly journey. Daniel Kiester (1980) compares the *kut* for the dead to the Catholic requiem mass and the theater of the absurd. Lucy Hwang is also researching dramatic aspects of the *chinogi kut*.

8. Yongsu's Mother described Princess Pari to me as a real filial son *(hyoja)*, a stock phrase, then corrected herself to say filial daughter *(hyonyŏ)*. I took her laughter for irony.

9. Although the bribe at the gate was brief and simple in the ceremonies I observed, other *mansin* seize this opportunity for extensive dramatization and high comedy. One of Kim T'ae-gon's informants described an elaborate *chinogi kut* held in Seoul in the 1920s. On this occasion twelve gates were set up in the shrine where the ceremony was held. A shaman stood at each gate demanding certification before allowing the soul to pass the threshold. Kin provided fees, and the shaman would produce a key but declare it too rusty to work; it could be polished for an additional fee. Fees were collected three or four times at each gate before the soul could be led across all twelve thresholds (T. G. Kim 1966, 75–76).

10. Drowning and deaths away from home yield unsettled, dangerous souls. Among Cheju fishermen the shaman's ritual for the dead begins with a progress through the Hell Gates *to* the house, signifying the calling back of one who died away from home. The soul, reconciled to death, is sent back through the gates in the second half of the rite (Beuchelt 1975). The dramatic structure of the Cheju ritual addresses a recurrent tragic motif in seaside villages.

11. I witnessed one *kut* where the senior line of the wife's natal home did appear. The entire senior line had been executed during the war. The wife sent her unfortunate kin to the Lotus Paradise since they lacked direct descendants to perform this task.

12. A Korean wife retains her maiden name.

13. Strictly speaking, the term kindred designates those who are related to ego through bilateral extensions of kinship, but excludes affines. For want of an inclusive Korean term, I will use kindred for a group that loosely approximates a Japanese *shinrui,* an ego-defined group of cognates and affines (Nakane 1967, 27).

14. I owe this insight to Myron Cohen.

CHAPTER 8

1. Limited personal observations and the observations of friends who have also lived with city families suggest that where the descendants are still young

children, the widow arranges the offering food and assumes the most active role in the *chesa*. By precept a childless widow officiates at a husband's *chesa* until an heir is designated.

2. The Janellis found women far more willing than men to attribute affliction to ancestral or ghostly machinations. They attribute women's more negative perceptions of the dead to women's relatively rougher socialization and to conflict-laden experiences with parents-in-law who become women's most immediate ancestors (Janelli and Janelli 1982, 192). Our differences are a matter of emphasis. The Janellis discuss ancestral malevolence in the context of ancestor-related beliefs and practices across sexes. I discuss women's dealings with the ancestors as one attribute of a broader religious role.

3. For China, see Feuchtwang (1974, 107), A. Wolf (1974), M. Wolf (1972, 44, 140), and Wang (1974, esp. 188) et al. For Japan, see Norbeck (1965, 46, 178ff.); Sakurai (1968, 17ff.); Sofue (1965, 150–151).

4. In Korea a separate minor house *(chagǔnjip)* should have the wherewithal to sustain an autonomous household economy: arable land, either owned or tenanted, and a separate house site (C. Han 1949, 83; K. K. Lee 1975, 218). If the main house has surplus resources, secondary sons are endowed with a house site and lands, but even if the main house has nothing to give them, mature secondary sons and their families are expected to leave (C. Han 1949, 83; Sorensen 1981, 313; Janelli and Janelli 982, 104–106). Joint families were never numerically dominant in Korea, nor were they in China. In Korean families, however, brothers' unequal claims on the family estate and the fact that this was never more than a temporary arrangement gave Korean brothers' families less incentive to stay together where population pressure pushed and non-agricultural employment pulled secondary sons' households off the land. The joint household is almost invisible in post-liberation ethnography (see Osgood 1951, 40–41; Brandt 1971; Sorensen 1981, 31).

Glossary

Mansin and other Korean women learn the names of gods and rituals through oral transmission, and shaman chant books are in Korean script. Thus, many terms are ambiguous, with several possible interpretations. I have cited etymologically intriguing cases in chapter notes. For English glosses, functional interpretations are favored over literal translations. For example, I call Hogu "the Princess" because the *mansin* describe her as "just like an old-fashioned princess." Samsin Chesŏk is the "Birth Grandmother" because the god is portrayed as a white-haired old woman and addressed as *halmŏni*, "grandmother." The origins of those few terms from other Asian languages are identified in parentheses following the term. A single Chinese character is equivalent to a single syllabic cluster in *han'gul*.

aegiŏmma	애기엄마	baby mother
aigo, aigo	아이고, 아이고	expression of grief
ajŏn	아전 (衙前)	low-level functionaries at the magistrate's court
amun	아문 (衙門)	magistrate's headquarters
An Mansin	안만신 (案萬神)	Appointed Mansin
âng-thâu-á (Ch-Hokkien)	紅頭仔	Taoist priest
anje	안제 (祭)	offering made inside the house
anjip	안집	innermost quarters

anju	안주 （按酒）	snacks served with alcoholic drinks
ant'aek kosa	안택고사 （安宅告祀）	*kosa* for household tranquility
butsudan (Jp)	仏壇	Buddhist household shrine
cha	자 （子）	son
chaesu	재수 （財數）	luck, fortune
chaesu kut	재수 （財數）굿	*kut* for luck and prosperity
chagŭnjip	자근집	minor house, secondary son's line of descent
ch'an param	찬바람	cold wind, a chilling humor
Ch'angbu	창부 （倡夫）	the Clown (god), acrobat, and songster
Changgun	장군 （將軍）	the General (god)
changso	장소 （場所）	site
chapkwi	잡귀 （雜鬼）	anonymous and diverse ghosts
che	제 （祭）	ritual offering
Cheju (Island, Province)	제주 （濟州）	
chesa	제사 （祭祀）	ritual offering to the ancestors
Chesŏk	제석 （帝釋）	with Samsin, the Birth Grandmother (god)
chigwan	지관 （地官）	geomancer
Ch'ilsŏng	칠성 （七星）	Seven Stars (god)
Ch'ilsŏng Maji	칠성마지 （七星摩旨）	ritual honoring the Seven Stars on lunar 7.7
Ch'ilsŏng/-sŏk nal	칠성 （七星/夕）날	Seven Star day, lunar 7.7
chinogi/-gwi kut	지노기/귀굿	*kut* for the dead

chip	집	house, household, family
Chiri (Mountain)	지리 （智理）	
Chisin	지신 （地神）	Earth God, Foundation God
Chisinje	지신제 （地神祭）	ritual honoring the Earth God
chisin tongbŏp	지신동법 （地神 動法）	earth imp
chobap	조밥	coarse cooked millet
chokpo	족보 （族譜）	genealogy
chŏngsin enoji	정신 （精神） 에노지	spiritual energy
ch'ŏnmin	천민 （賤民）	"mean people," those who followed outcast professions
choryŏng	조령 （祖靈）	ancestral soul or spirit
chosang	조상 （祖上）	ancestor
chosang halmŏni	조상 （祖上） 할머니	ancestral grandmother
chosang malmyŏng	조상 （祖上） 말명	restless ancestor
Chosŏn	조선 （朝鮮）	Korea (term no longer used in R.O.K.)
Chowang	조왕 （竈王）	Kitchen God
chu	주 （柱）	vertical pillar
chudang	주당 （周堂）	malevolent spirit
chugŭn sonŭn kasisonida	죽은손은 가시손이다.	the hand of the dead is a hand of thorns
Ch'ungch'ŏng (Province)	충청 （忠清）	
ch'ungmun	축문 （祝文）	written congratulatory address
Ch'usŏk	추석 （秋夕）	lunar 8.15, holiday
Haengju Mullim	행주물림	opening sequence of a *kut*
haesan'gi/-gwi	해산기 / 귀 （解産鬼）	ghost of a woman who died in childbirth

ham	함　（函）	box of gifts sent to bride
han	한　（恨）	unrequited resentments
harabŏjiŭi pang	할아버지의　방　（房）	grandfather's room, grandfathers' room
hayan halmŏni	하얀　할머니	white (-haired) grand-mother
hoengaek	횡액　（橫厄）	sudden disaster
Hoesimgok	회심곡　（回心曲）	Song of Lament
Hogu	호구　（戶口？）	the Princess (god)
hongaek	홍액　（紅厄？）	red disaster
Hong-/Hoeng-su Megi/Maji	홍／횡수메기／마지　（橫數摩旨）	New Year Rite
hwan'gap	환갑　（還甲）	celebration of sixty years of life, a full cycle
hyanggyo	향교　（鄕校）	Confucian academy
hyoja	효자　（孝子）	filial son
hyodo	효도　（孝道）	filial piety
hyonyŏ	효녀　（孝女）	filial daughter
illyŏn sinsurŭl poda	일년신수　（一年身數）　를　보다	see the year's luck, have one's fortune told
Inch'ŏn (town)	인천　（仁川）	
itako/ichiko (Jp)	市子	diviner
Kage Taegam	가게대감　（大監）	Shop Official (god)
Kajŏng Pogam	가정보감　（家庭宝鑑）	household ritual manual
kamang	가망	netherworldly guard
kami (Jp)	神	spirit, god
kamidana (Jp)	神だな	household shrine for *kami*
Kangnŭng (town)	강릉　（江陵）	
Kangwŏn (Province)	강원　（江原）	

Kasi Mun	가시 문 （門）	Thornwood Gate of Hell
kiō-á (Ch-Hokkien)	車喬…	god palanquin
kisaeng	기생 （妓生）	female entertainer
kiu che	기우제 （祈雨祭）	*kut* for rain
Koguryŏ (kingdom)	고구려 （高句麗）	
Kŏllip	걸립 （乞粒）	Grain God
kŏri hongaek	거리 홍액 （紅厄）	red disaster of the road
Koryŏ (dynasty)	고려 （高麗）	
kosa	고사 （告祀）	ritual offering to the household gods
k'ŭn mudang	큰 무당 （巫堂）	great shaman
Kŭngnak	극락 （極樂）	Lotus Paradise
k'ŭnjip	큰집	big house, major line of descent
Kunung Taegam	군웅대감 （軍雄大監）	Soldier Official (god)
kut	굿	most elaborate shaman ritual
kwana	관아 （官衙）	magistrate's headquarters
kwanch'ŏng kut	관청 （官廳） 굿	*kut* to exorcise and purify public buildings
Kwansaeŭm Pulsa	관세음불사 （觀世音佛師）	Kwanyin Buddhist Sage (god)
kwijŏk	귀적 （鬼的）	ghostly
kwisin	귀신 （鬼神）	ghost/god
kwisin chŏm-jaengi	귀신 （鬼神） 점 （占） 쟁이	spirit medium
kwisin norŭm	귀신 （鬼神） 노름	ghostly play
kye	계 （契）	rotating credit association
Kyŏnggi (Province)	경기 （京畿）	

Kyŏngsang (Province)	경상 （慶尚）	
mach'ida	마치다	to strike or hit
maji	마지 （摩旨）	offering rice in a Buddhist temple (or shaman's shrine)
malmyŏng	말명	restless shade
mann saeg phox (Ch-Cantonese)	問醒婆	shaman
mansin	만신 （萬神）	shaman
Marhanŭn Yŏ Taegam	말하는 여대감 （女大監）	Talking Female Official (god)
me	메	see *maji*
megi	메기	see *maji*
mich'ida	미치다	to be crazy
mich'in	미친	crazy
miko (Jp)	巫女	female medium
milttŏk	밀떡	flour pancake
Mirŭk	미륵 （彌勒）	Maitreya
misin	미신 （迷信）	superstition
misinŭl chal chik-inŭnjip	미신 （迷信）을 잘 지키는 집	a household that observes well the practices of *misin*
moksin tongbŏp	목신동법 （木神動法）	wood imp
Momju	몸주 （主）	Body-governing God
mudang	무당 （巫堂）	shaman or priestess
mugam	무 （巫） 감	trance dance performed by ordinary women who wear the *mansin*'s costumes
mugŏri	무거리 （巫臣里）	shaman's divination
munbyŏng	문병 （問病）	visit the sick
Munhwa Yu (surname group)	문화유 （文化柳）	

musokchŏk	무속적　（巫俗的）	of or pertaining to *mudang* practices
myŏn	면　（面）	district
myŏngdari	명　（命）　다리	cloth bridge used to dedicate children to the Seven Stars
naerida	내리다	to descend
naerim kut	내림굿	*mansin*'s initiation *kut*
naerin saram	내린사람	destined shaman
namjon yŏbi	남존여비　（男尊女卑）	man is respected and woman lowly
nanggu moksin (dialect)	낭구　목신　（木神）	wood imp
nunŭl ttŭida	눈을　띄다	to open wide one's eyes
Obang T'ŏjŏn	오방　（五方）　더전	Five Direction Forces
orŭda	오르다	to ascend
pabŭl anmokŭmyŏn, siksaga andoenda	밥을안목으면　식사　（食事）가　안된다	if you don't eat rice, it's no meal
Paekche (kingdom)	백제　（百濟）	
paksu mudang	박수　무당　（巫堂）	male shaman
p'alcha	팔자　（八字）	the eight characters that determine one's fate
p'alchaga sanapta	팔자　（八字）가　사납다	to have a difficult fate
paltong hada	발동　（發動）　하다	to move about
pan mudang	반　무당　（半巫堂）	half shaman
panjang	반장　（班長）	hamlet chief
panmal	반　（半）　말	blunt speech
pansu	판수　（判數）	blind exorcist
para	바라　（哱囉）	brass cymbals
Pari (Princess)	바리　（鉢里）	(god)
Pari Kongju	바리공주　（鉢里公主）	Princess Pari

pon'gwan	본관 （本貫）	place of origin for a lineage
Ponhyang Sansin	본향산신 （本鄉山神）	Mountain God of one's ancestral home
pŏptang	법당 （法堂）	main hall in Buddhist temple
posal	보살 （菩薩）	bodhisattva, title for temple caretaker or diviner
p'udakkŏri	푸닥 거리 （臣里）	exorcism
pujŏk	부적 （符籍）	charm, talisman
pujŏng	부정 （不淨）	pollution
pujŏng ŏmnŭn saram	부정 （不淨） 없는사람	one who is free from pollution
pujŏngmul	부정 （不淨） 물	water to cleanse pollution
Pulgong	불공 （佛供）	Buddhist mass
Pulgyo	불교 （佛教）	Buddhism
Pulsa	불사 （佛師）	Buddhist Sage
Pulsŏk Puch'ŏnim	불석 （拂石？） 부처님	Pulsŏk Buddha
Pyŏlsang/-sŏng	별상/ 성 （別星）	Special Messenger (god)
pyŏngwŏn	병원 （病院）	hospital, clinic
Pyŏnso Kakssi	변소각씨 （便所閣氏）	Toilet Maiden (god)
sadaebongsa	사대봉사 （四代奉仕）	honoring the ancestors of four ascendant generations
Saemaŭl Undong	새마을 운동 （運動）	New Village Movement
Saja	사자 （使者）	Death Messenger (god)
Sajik	사직 （社稷）	Altar to Land and Grain
sal	살 （煞）	invisible arrow
sallim halttae put'ŏ	살림할때부터	from the time one sets up housekeeping

Salyuk Taegam	살육대감 (殺戮大監)	Massacring Official (god)
salp'uri	살 (煞) 푸리	exorcism to remove *sal*
sam	삼	placenta
samch'on	삼촌 (三寸)	relative within three degrees of relationship, uncle
samhon	삼혼 (三魂)	three-part soul
Samsin	삼신 (三神)	Birth Spirit (god)
Samsin Chesŏk	삼신제석 (三神帝釋)	Birth Spirit (god)
Samsin Halmŏni	삼신 (三神) 할머니	Birth Grandmother (god)
Samsin Me	삼신 (三神) 메	ritual honoring Birth Spirit
Samsin padŭngŏt	삼신 (三神) 받은것	receiving the Birth Grandmother
sangmun	상문 (喪門)	death humor
sangnom	상 (常) 놈	commoner, base born
Sangŏp Taegam	상업대감 (商業大監)	Commerce Official (god)
Sangŏri, Sangsangŏri	산거리 (臣里), 상산거리	War God's segment of a *kut*
Sansin Kak	산신각 (山神閣)	Mountain God's shrine
Sansinje	산신제 (山神祭)	ritual honoring the Mountain God
sanŭl ssŭda	산 (山) 을 쓰다	to use the mountain
seda	세다	to be strong, vigorous
shinrui (Jp)	親類	ego-centered group including cognates and affines
Shugendo (Jp)	修験道	folk Buddhism with many Shinto elements
sian-si:-ma (Ch-Hokkien)	先生媽	female healer who specializes in restoring children's souls
sijo	시조 (時調)	vernacular poetry form

sikkŭrŏun kkumjari	시끄러운 꿈자리	noisy dream, night-mare
Silla (kingdom, dynasty)	신라 (新羅)	
sillyŏng	신령 (神靈)	spirit, god
sin	신 (神)	spirit, god
sinbyŏng	신병 (神病)	possession sickness of a destined shaman
sindang	신당 (神堂)	god hall, *mansin*'s shrine
sini ollatta	신 (神) 이 올랐다	the god ascended
Sinjang	신장 (神將)	Warrior (god)
Sinjang Taegam	신장대감 (神將大監)	Warrior Official (god)
sinŏmŏni	신 (神) 어머니	spirit mother, i.e., initiating *mansin*
sinsik	신식 (新式)	new style
sinttal	신 (神) 딸	spirit daughter to *sinŏmŏni*
sinwi	신위 (神位)	wood or paper marker for ancestor
son	손 (損)	ominous force
Sŏnang/Sŏnghwang	서낭/성황 (城隍)	village Tutelary God
Sŏnang/Sŏnghwang Tang	서낭당/성황당 (城隍堂)	Village Shrine
sŏngjo	성조 (成造)	creator
Sŏngju	성주 (城主 or 聖主)	House Lord (god)
Sŏngju padŭngŏt	성주 (城主) 받은것	receiving the House Lord
Sŏngju tae naerinŭngŏt	성주 (城主) 대 내리는 것	descent of the House Lord on a branch
sŏpsu	섭수 (攝受)	distant dead
su	수 (數)	fate
sul kosa	술 고사 (告祀)	offer wine to house-hold gods
Sumun	수문 (守門)	Door Guard (god)

Sumun Taegam	수문대감 （守門大監）	Door Guard Official (god)
Taegam	대감 （大監）	Official (god)
taeju	대주 （大主）	master of the house
Taesang	대상 （大祥）	Great Send-off (of deceased)
Taesin Halmŏni	대신 （大神） 할머니	Great Spirit Grand-mother (god)
Taesin Taegam	대신대감 （大神大監）	Great Spirit Official (god)
Taewang	대왕 （大王）	King (god)
Taewang Kut	대왕 （大王） 굿	*kut* to honor King deity
tanggol mudang	당골무당 （堂骨？巫堂）	hereditary priestess
tang-ki (Ch Hokkien)	童乩	shaman
tangnaegan	당내간 （堂內間）	relatives within eight degrees of relation-ship
tan'gol	단골 （丹骨）	regular client
Tano	단오 （端午）	lunar 5.5, holiday
Todang	도당 （都堂）	community Tutelary God
Todang Kut	도당 （都堂） 굿	*kut* honoring Tutelary God
todungnyŏ	도둑녀 （女）	robber woman
T'ŏju Taegam	터주대감 （…主大監）	House Site Official (god)
Tokkaebi Taegam	도깨비대감 （大監）	Goblin Official (god)
tol	돌	first birthday
tongje	동제 （洞祭）	village offering
tongbŏp	동법 （動法）	imp
tongja	동자 （童子）	child
Tongja Pyŏlsang/-sŏng	동자별상 / 별성 （童子別星）	Child Messenger (god)

tongnae halmŏni	동내 （洞內） 할머니	neighborhood grandmother
tongt'o	동토 （動土）	harm attributed to dislodged earth spirit
Tongyang Saram	동양 （東洋） 사람	East Sea Person, Oriental
T'osinje	토신제 （土神祭）	ritual honoring the Earth God
ttŏk kosa	떡 고사 （告祀）	offering rice cake to household gods
Twitchŏn	뒷전	final segment of *kut*
uhwan kut	우환 （憂患） 굿	healing *kut*
uhwani ŏppta	우환 （憂患） 이 없다	to be free of anxiety
Ŭlhwa (novella)	을화 （乙火）	
ŭm	음 （陰）	*yin,* dark, cold, female forces
ŭmnae	읍내 （邑內）	county seat
ŭmsa	음사 （淫祀）	lewd rites
ŭp	읍 （邑）	county seat
wang	왕 （王）	king
wŏn	원 （圓）	principal unit of currency
Yaksa Puch'ŏnim	약사 （藥師） 부처님	Healing Buddha
yang	양 （陽）	bright, hot, male forces
yangban	양반 （兩班）	high-born, hereditary elite
yangban ch'ulsin	양반출신 （兩班出身）	of *yangban* stock
Yangban? Musŭn yangban?	양반 （兩班） 무슨 양반 （兩班）?	*Yangban?* Him a *yangban?*
ye	예 （禮）	rite, propriety
yesikchang	예식장 （禮式場）	commercial wedding hall
Yi (dynasty)	이 （李）	
Yŏmna Taewang	염라대왕 （閻羅大王）	King of Hell (god)

yomu	요무 （妖巫）	wicked shamans
yŏngsan	영산 （靈山）	ghost
yŏngsandari	영산 （靈山） 다리	ghost bridge, cut to sever their influence
yŏ-/yet'am	여 / 예탐 （豫探）	feast food given to the ancestors before a wedding or *hwan'gap*
Yugyo	유교 （儒敎）	Confucianism
yuji	유지 （有志）	local elite

Bibliography

Ahern, Emily M. 1973. *The Cult of the Dead in a Chinese Village.* Stanford: Stanford University Press.

———. 1975. The Power and Pollution of Chinese Women. In *Women in Chinese Society,* ed. M. Wolf and R. Witke, 193–214. Stanford: Stanford University Press.

———. 1978. Sacred and Secular Medicine in a Taiwan Village: A Study of Cosmological Disorder. In *Culture and Healing in Asian Societies,* ed. A. Kleinman, et al., 17–40. Cambridge, Mass.: Schenkman Publishing Co.

Akamatsu, Chijo, and Akiba Takashi. 1938. *Chōsen fuzoku no kenkyū* (Study of Korean shamanism). 2 vols. Tokyo: Osakayago Shōten.

Akiba, Takashi. 1957. A Study on Korean Folkways. *Folklore Studies* (Tokyo) 14:1–106.

Allen, H. N. 1896. Some Korean Customs: The Mootang. *Korean Repository* 3:163–168.

Beuchelt, Eno. 1975. Die Ruckrufung der Ahnen auf Chejudo (Süd Korea) Ein Ritual zur Psychischen Stabilisierung (Calling back ancestors in Chejudo, a ritual of psychic stabilization). *Anthropos* 70:10–179.

Biernatzki, William E. 1967. Varieties of Korean Lineage Structure. Ph.D. diss., St. Louis University.

Bishop, Isabella Bird. 1897. *Korea and Her Neighbors.* New York: Fleming H. Revell.

Blacker, Carmen. 1975. *The Catalpa Bow.* London: George Allen and Unwin.

Bogoras, Waldemar. 1907. *The Chukchee.* Memoir of the American Museum of Natural History, Vol. 7. Publication of the Jessup North Pacific Expedition. New York: American Museum of Natural History.

Brandt, Vincent. 1971. *A Korean Village: Between Farm and Sea*. Cambridge: Harvard University Press.

Chang, Chu-gün. 1973. *Kankoku no mingan shinkō* (Korean folk beliefs). Tokyo: Kinkasha. (English summary, 2–15.)

———. 1974. Mingan sinang (Folk beliefs). In *Han'guk minsokhak kaesŏl* (Introduction to Korean ethnology), 128–197. Seoul: Minjung Sŏgwan.

Ch'oe, Kil-sŏng. 1978. *Han'guk musok ŭi yŏn'gu* (Research on Korean *"mu"* practices). Seoul: Asia Munhwasa.

———. 1981. *Han'guk musongnon* (Essay on Korean shamanism). Seoul: Hyŏngsŏl Ch'ulp'ansa.

Ch'oe, Kil-sŏng, and Chang Chu-gün. 1967. *Kyŏnggido chiyŏk musok* (Shaman practices of Kyŏnggi Province). Seoul: Ministry of Culture.

Chung, Bom-mo, Cha Jae-ho, and Lee Sung-jin. 1974. *Boy Preference and Family Planning in Korea*. Seoul: Korean Institute for Research in the Behavioral Sciences.

———. 1977. Boy Preference Reflected in Korean Folklore. In *Virtues in Conflict: Tradition and the Korean Woman Today*, ed. S. Mattielli, 113–127. Seoul: Royal Asiatic Society.

Clark, Charles Allen. [1932] 1961. Religions of Old Korea. Reprint. Seoul: Society of Christian Literature.

Cohen, Myron L. 1976. *House United House Divided: The Chinese Family in Taiwan*. New York: Columbia University Press.

Colson, Elizabeth. 1969. Spirit Possession among the Tonga of Zambia. In *Spirit Mediumship and Society in Africa*, ed. J. Beatie and J. Middleton, 69–103. New York: Africana Publishing Corp.

Curley, Richard T. 1973. *Elders, Shades, and Women: Ceremonial Change in Lango, Uganda*. Berkeley and Los Angeles: University of California Press.

Deuchler, Martina. 1977. The Tradition: Women during the Yi Dynasty. In *Virtues in Conflict: Tradition and the Korean Woman Today*, ed. S. Mattielli, 1–48. Seoul: Royal Asiatic Society.

———. 1980. Neo-Confucianism: The Impulse for Social Action in Early Yi Korea. *Journal of Korean Studies* 2:71–112.

———. n.d. Neo-Confucianism in Action: Agnation and Ancestor Worship in Early Yi Korea. In Religion and Ritual in Korean Society, ed. L. Kendall and G. Dix. Unpublished MS.

Dix, Griffin M. 1977. The East Asian Country of Propriety: Confucianism in a Korean Village. Ph.D. diss., University of California, San Diego.

———. 1979. How to Do Things with Ritual: The Logic of Ancestor Worship and Other Offerings in Rural Korea. In *Studies on Korea in Transition*, ed. D. McCann, J. Middleton, and E. Shultz, 57–88. Honolulu: Center for Korean Studies, University of Hawaii.

———. 1980. The Place of the Almanac in Korean Folk Religion. *Journal of Korean Studies* 2:47–70.

———. n.d. The New Year's Ritual and Village Social Structure. In Religion and Ritual in Korean Society, ed. L. Kendall and G. Dix. Unpublished MS.

Douglas, Mary. 1966. *Purity and Danger: An Analysis of Concepts of Pollution and Taboo.* New York: Praeger.

Durkheim, Emile. [1915] 1966. *The Elementary Forms of the Religious Life.* Reprint. New York: Free Press.

Eberhard, Wolfram. 1967. *Guilt and Sin in Traditional China.* Berkeley and Los Angeles: University of California Press.

Eliade, Mircea. 1964. *Shamanism: Archaic Techniques of Ecstasy.* New York: Pantheon.

Evans-Pritchard, E. E. [1937] 1976. *Witchcraft, Oracles, and Magic among and Azande.* Reprint, abr. Oxford: Clarendon.

Ewha Women's University, Woman Studies Project (EWUWSP). 1977. *Women of Korea: A History from Ancient Times to 1945,* ed. and trans. Y. Kim. Seoul: Ewha Woman University Press.

Fairchild, William P. 1962. Shamanism in Japan. *Folklore Studies* (Tokyo) 21:1–122.

Feuchtwang, Stephan. 1974. Domestic and Communal Worship in Taiwan. In *Religion and Ritual in Chinese Society,* ed. A. Wolf, 105–129. Stanford: Stanford University Press.

Fortes, Meyer. 1957. *The Web of Kinship among the Tallensi.* Oxford: Oxford University Press.

Freedman, Maurice. 1958. *Lineage Organization in Southeastern China.* London: Althone.

———. 1966. *Chinese Lineage and Society: Fukien and Kwangtung.* London: Althone.

———. 1974. On the Social Study of Chinese Religion. In *Religion and Ritual in Chinese Society,* ed. A. Wolf, 19–41. Stanford: Stanford University Press.

———. 1979a. Rites and Duties of Chinese Marriage. In *The Study of Chinese Society: Essays by Maurice Freedman,* ed. G. W. Skinner, 255–272. Stanford: Stanford University Press.

———. 1979b. Ritual Aspects of Chinese Kinship and Marriage. In *The Study of Chinese Society: Essays by Maurice Freedman,* ed. G. W. Skinner, 273–295. Stanford: Stanford University Press.

———. 1979c. Ancestor Worship: Two Facets of the Chinese Case. In *The Study of Chinese Society: Essays by Maurice Freedman,* ed. G. W. Skinner, 296–312. Stanford: Stanford University Press.

Gale, James S. [1913] 1963. *Korean Folk Tales: Imps, Ghosts, and Fairies.* Reprint. Tokyo: Charles E. Tuttle Co.

Gifford, D. L. 1892. Ancestral Worship as Practiced in Korea. *Korean Repository* 1:169–176.

———. 1898. *Everyday Life in Korea: A Collection of Studies and Stories.* New York: Fleming H. Revell.

Gluckman, Max. 1954. *Rituals of Rebellion in Southeast Africa.* Manchester: Manchester University Press.

Gould-Martin, Kathrine. 1976. Women Asking Women: An Ethnography of Health Care in Rural Taiwan. Ph.D. diss., Rutgers University.

Griffis, William Elliot. 1911. *Corea, the Hermit Nation.* New York: A.M.S.

deGroot, J. J. M. [1892–1910] 1967. *The Religious System of China,* vol. 6. Reprint. Taipei: Ch'eng-wen.

Guillemoz, Alexandre. 1983. *Les Algues, Les Anciens, Les Dieux.* Paris: Le Léopard d'Or.

Hahm, Pyung-Choon. 1967. *The Korean Political Tradition and Law: Essays in Korean Law and Legal History.* Seoul: Hollym.

Han, Chungnim Choi. 1949. Social Organization of Upper Han Hamlet in Korea. Ph.D. diss., University of Michigan.

Han, Sang-bok. 1977. *Korean Fishermen: Ecological Adaptation in Three Communities.* Seoul: Population and Development Studies Center, Seoul National University.

Harris, Grace. 1957. Possession "Hysteria" in a Kenya Tribe. *American Anthropologist* 59:1046–1066.

Harvey, Youngsook Kim. 1976. The Korean *Mudang* as a Household Therapist. In *Culture-Bound Syndromes, Ethnopsychiatry, and Alternate Therapies,* ed. W. P. Lebra, 189–198. Honolulu: University of Hawaii Press.

———. 1979. *Six Korean Women: The Socialization of Shamans.* St. Paul: West Publishing Co.

———. 1980. Possession Sickness and Women Shamans in Korea. In *Unspoken Worlds: Women's Religious Lives in Non-Western Cultures,* ed. N. Falk and R. Gross, 41–52. New York: Harper and Row.

Henderson, Gregory. 1968. *Korea: The Politics of the Vortex.* Cambridge: Harvard University Press.

Hori, Ichiro. 1968. *Folk Religion in Japan: Continuity and Change.* Trans. J. Kitagawa and A. Miller. Chicago: University of Chicago Press.

Hulbert, Homer B. [1906] 1970. *The Passing of Korea.* Reprint. Seoul: Yonsei University Press.

The Independent (Tongnip Sinmun). 1896–1898. Seoul.

Janelli, Dawnhee Yim. 1977. Logical Contradictions in Korean Learned Fortunetelling: A Dissertation in Folklore and Folklife. Ph.D. diss., University of Pennsylvania.

Janelli, Roger L. 1975a. Anthropology, Folklore, and Korean Ancestor Worship. *Korea Journal* 15:34–43.

————. 1975b. Korean Rituals of Ancestor Worship: An Ethnography of Folklore Performance. Ph.D. diss., University of Pennsylvania.

Janelli, Roger L., and Dawnhee Yim Janelli. 1978. Lineage Organization and Social Differentiation in Korea. *Man,* n.s. 13:272–289.

————. 1979. The Functional Value of Ignorance at a Korean Seance. *Asian Folklore Studies* 38 (1): 81–90.

————. 1982. *Ancestor Worship and Korean Society.* Stanford: Stanford University Press.

Jones, George Heber. 1902. The Spirit Worship of the Koreans. *Transactions of the Korea Branch of the Royal Asiatic Society* 2:37–58.

Jordan, David K. 1972. *Gods, Ghosts, and Ancestors: Folk Religion in a Taiwanese Village.* Berkeley and Los Angeles: University of California Press.

Kawashima, Fujiya. 1980. The Local Gentry Association in Mid-Yi Dynasty Korea: A Preliminary Study of the Ch'angnyŏng Hyangan, 1600–1839. *Journal of Korean Studies* 2:113–138.

Kendall, Laurel. 1977a. Caught Between Ancestors and Spirits: A Korean *Mansin*'s Healing *Kut. Korea Journal* 17 (8): 8–23.

————. 1977b. *Mugam:* The Dance in Shaman's Clothing. *Korea Journal* 17 (12): 38–44.

————. 1977c. Receiving the *Samsin* Grandmother: Conception Rituals in Korea. *Transactions of the Korea Branch of the Royal Asiatic Society* 52:55–70.

————. 1981. Wood Imps, Ghosts, and Other Noxious Influences: The Ideology of Afflication in a Korean Village. *Journal of Korean Studies* 3:113–145.

————. 1984. Korean Shamanism: Women's Rites and a Chinese Comparison. In *Religion and the Family in East Asia,* ed. T. Sofue and G. DeVos, 57–73. Senri Ethnological Studies, vol. 11. Osaka: National Museum of Ethnology.

Kessler, Clive S. 1977. Conflict and Sovereignty in Kelantanese Malay Spirit Seances. In *Case Studies in Spirit Possession,* ed. V. Crapanzano and V. Garrison, 295–332. New York: Wiley Interscience.

Kiester, Daniel. 1980. Korean Mudang Rites for the Dead and the Traditional Catholic Requium: A Comparative Study. In *Customs and Manners in Korea,* ed. S. Chun, 45–54. Seoul: International Cultural Foundation.

Kim, Kwang-iel [Kim Kwang-il]. 1972a. Sin-byŏng: A Culture-Bound Depersonalization Syndrome in Korea. *Neuropsychiatry* (Seoul) 11:223–234.

————. 1972b. Psychoanalytic Consideration of Korean Shamanism. *Neuropsychiatry* (Seoul) 11:121–129.

————. 1973. Shamanist Healing Ceremonies in Seoul. *Korea Journal* 13 (4): 41–47.

Kim, T'ae-gon. 1966. *Hwangch'ŏn muga yŏn'gu* (A study of shaman songs of the Yellow Springs). Seoul: Institute for the Study of Indigenous Religion.

———. 1970. A Study of Shaman's Mystic Illness During Initiation Process in Korea. *Journal of Asian Women* (Seoul) 9:91–132.

———. 1971. *Han'guk muga chip* (Anthology of Korean shaman songs), vol. 1. Iri: Folklore Research Institute, Wŏn'gwang University.

———. 1972a. The Influence of Shamanism on the Living Pattern of People in Contemporary Korea. In *The Modern Meaning of Shamanism,* ed. T. Kim, 71–80. Iri: Folklore Research Institute, Wŏn'gwang University.

———. 1972b. Components of Korean Shamanism. *Korea Journal* 12 (12): 17–25.

———. 1972c. Etude du Processus initiatique des Chamans Coréans. *Revue de Coreé* 4 (2): 53–57.

———. 1978. Shamanism in the Seoul Area. *Korea Journal* 18 (6): 39–51.

Kim, T'aek-kyu. 1964. *Tongjok purakŭi saenghwal kujo yŏn'gu* (A study of the structure of social life in a lineage village). Seoul: Ch'onggu.

Kim, Tu-hön. [1948] 1969. *Han'guk kajok chedo yŏn'gu* (Study of the Korean family system). Reprint. Seoul: Ulyu.

Kim, Tŭk-kwang. 1963. *Han'guk chonggyosa* (History of Korean religion). Seoul: Haemunsa.

Kim, Young-key, and Dorothea Sich. 1977. A Study on Traditional Healing Techniques and Illness Behavior in a Rural Korean Township. *Anthropological Study* (Seoul) 3 (June): 75–108.

Kinsler, Arthur W. 1976. A Study in Fertility Cult for Children in Korean Shamanism. Ph.D. diss., Yonsei University, Seoul.

———. 1977. Korean Fertility Cult for Children in Shaman Ritual and Myth. *Korea Journal* 17 (2): 27–34.

Knez, Eugene. 1959. Sam Jong Dong: A South Korean Village. Ph.D. diss., Syracuse University.

Korean Mudang and Pansu. 1903. *Korea Review* 3:145–149, 203–208, 257–260, 301–305, 342–346, 383–389.

Lebra, William P. 1966. *Okinawan Religion: Belief, Ritual, and Social Structure.* Honolulu: University of Hawaii Press.

Lee, Du-hyun [Yi Tu-hyŏn]. 1969. *Han'guk kamyŏn'guk* (Korean Mask-Dance Drama). Seoul: Ministry of Culture, Bureau of Cultural Properties Preservation.

Lee, Hyo-chae. 1977. Protestant Missionary Work and Enlightenment of Korean Women. *Korea Journal* 17 (11): 33–50.

Lee, Jung-young. 1975. Shamanistic Thought and Traditional Korean Homes. *Korea Journal* 15 (11): 43–51.

———. 1981. *Korean Shamanistic Rituals.* Mouton: The Hague.

Lee, Kisuk [Yi Ki-sŏk]. 1967. Kuŭp ch'wirake kwanhan yŏn'gu: Kyŏnggi chi-bangŭl chungsimŭro (A Study of *Ku-eup* [Former Local Administrative Town] Settlements in Kyŏnggi Province). M.A. thesis, Seoul National University.

Lee, Kwang-kyu [Yi Kwang-gyu]. 1974. Kwan, hon, sang che (Passage rites). In *Han'guk minsokhak kaesŏl* (Introduction to Korean ethnology), ed. C. Chang, D. Lee, and K. K. Lee, 59–87. Seoul: Minjung Sŏgwan.

———. 1975. *Han'guk kajok ŭi kujo punsŏk* (Analysis of Korean family structure). Seoul: Ilchisa.

———. 1977. *Han'guk kajok ŭi sajŏk yŏn'gu* Historical study of the Korean family). Seoul: Ilchisa.

———. n.d. Ancestor Worship and Kinship Structure in Korea. In *Religion and Ritual in Korean Society,* ed. L. Kendall and G. Dix. Unpublished MS.

Lee, Man-gap [Yi Man-gap]. 1960. *Han'guk nongch'onŭi sahoe kujo* (The social structure of Korean villages). Seoul: Han'guk Yŏn'gu Tosŏg-wan.

LeVine, Robert A. 1962. Witchcraft and Co-wife Proximity in Southwestern Kenya. *Ethnology* 1:39–45.

Lewis, I. M. 1966. Spirit Possession and Deprivation Cults. *Man,* n.s. 1 (3): 307–329.

———. 1969. *Ecstatic Religion.* Harmondsworth: Penguin.

Lowell, Percival. 1886. *The Land of the Morning Calm.* Boston: Tickman and Co.

McBrian, Charles D. 1977. Two Models of Social Structure and Manifest Personality in Korean Society. *Occasional Papers on Korea* (Seattle) 5:1–7.

McCann, David R. 1983. Formal and Informal, Korean Kisaeng Songs. In *Korean Women: View from the Inner Room,* ed. L. Kendall and M. Peterson, 129–137. New Haven: East Rock Press.

McCune, Evelyn. n.d. Queen Rule in Korea. Unpublished MS.

Marwick, Max. 1967. Sociology of Sorcery in a Central African Tribe. In *Magic, Witchcraft, and Curing,* ed. J. Middleton, 101–126. Garden City, N.Y.: Natural History Press.

Meskill, John. 1965. *Ch'oe Pu's Diary: A Record of Drifting Across the Sea.* Tucson: University of Arizona Press.

Messing, Simon D. 1958. Group Therapy and Social Status in the Zar Cult of Ethiopia. *American Anthropologist* 60:1120–1126.

Mills, John E., ed. 1960. *Ethno-Social Reports of Four Korean Villages.* San Francisco: United States Operations Mission to Korea.

Ministry of Culture and Bureau of Cultural Properties Preservation (MCBCPP) 1969–. *Han'guk minsin chonghap chosa pogosŏ* (Report on the cumulative investigation of Korean folk belief). Cum. vols.

arranged by province. Seoul: Ministry of Culture, Bureau of Cultural Properties Preservation.

Mischel, Walter, and Francis Mischel. 1958. Psychological Aspects of Spirit Possession. *American Anthropologist* 60:249–260.

Moose, Robert J. 1911. *Village Life in Korea*. Nashville: Methodist Church, Smith and Lamar, Agents.

Morioka, Kiyomi. 1968. Religion, Behavior, and the Actor's Position in His Household. *Journal of Asian and African Studies* 3 (1–2):25–43.

Murayama, Chijun. 1932. *Chōsen no fuken* (Korean shamanism). Kiejō: Chōsen Sōtokufu.

———. 1938. *Shakuson, kiu, antaku* (Commemoration, rain invocations, and house rituals). Keijō: Chōsen Sōtokufu.

Murphy, Yolanda, and Robert F. Murphy. 1974. *Women of the Forest*. New York: Columbia University Press.

Nadel, S. F. 1952. Witchcraft in Four African Societies: An Essay in Comparison. *American Anthropologist* 54:18–29.

Nakane, Chie. 1967. *Kinship and Economic Organization in Rural Japan*. London: Althone.

Norbeck, Edward. 1965. *Changing Japan*. New York: Holt, Rinehart, and Winston.

Onwuejeogwu, Michael. 1969. The Cult of the *Bori* Spirits Among the Hausa. In *Man in Africa,* ed. M. Douglas and P. Kaberry, 279–306. London: Tavistock.

Osgood, Cornelius. 1951. *The Koreans and Their Culture*. New York: Ronald.

Pak, Ki-hyuk, and Sidney D. Gamble. 1975. *The Changing Korean Village*. Seoul: Shin-hung.

Pak, Pyŏng-ho. 1974. *Han'guk pŏpchesa ko* (Reflections on Korean legal history). Seoul: Pŏbmunsa.

Palais, James B. 1975. *Politics and Policy in Traditional Korea*. Cambridge: Harvard University Press.

Peterson, Mark. 1983. Women without Sons: A Measure of Social Change in Yi Dynasty Korea. In *Korean Women: View from the Inner Room,* ed. L. Kendall and M. Peterson, 33–44. New Haven: East Rock Press.

Pillsbury, Barbara. 1982. Doing the Month: Confinement and Convalescence of Chinese Women after Childbirth. In *Anthropology of Human Birth,* ed. M. A. Kay, 119–146. Philadelphia: R. A. Davis.

Plath, David W. 1964. Where the Family of God is the Family: The Role of the Dead in Japanese Households. *American Anthropologist* 66:300–317.

Potter, Jack M. 1974. Cantonese Shamanism. In *Religion and Ritual in Chinese Society,* ed. A. Wolf, 207–231. Stanford: Stanford University Press.

Pyun, Young-tai. 1926. *My Attitude toward Ancestor-Worship.* Seoul: Christian Literature Society of Korea.

Rhi, Bou-yang. 1970. Psychological Aspects of Korean Shamanism. *Korea Journal* 10 (9): 15–21.

———. 1977. Psychological Problems among Korean Women. In *Virtues in Conflict: Tradition and the Korean Woman Today,* ed. S. Mattielli, 129–146. Seoul: Royal Asiatic Society.

Rutt, Richard. 1971. *The Bamboo Grove: An Introduction to Sijo.* Berkeley and Los Angeles: University of California Press.

Sakurai, Tokutaro. 1968. The Major Features and Characteristics of Japanese Folk Beliefs. *Journal of Asian and African Studies* (Special issue on the Sociology of Japanese Religion) 3 (1–2): 13–24.

Shigematsu, Mayumi. 1980. Saishin ni mirareru josei no shakai kankei (The women's social sphere in the Korean *mansin*'s *kut*). Minzokugaku Kenkyū: 93–110.

Sich, Dorothea. 1978. Some Aspects of Traditional Medicine and Illness Behavior in Korea. *Korea Journal* 18 (3): 30–35.

———. 1981. Traditional Concepts and Customs on Pregnancy, Birth and Post Partum Period in Rural Korea. *Social Science and Medicine* 15B:65–69.

Sich, Dorothea, and Kim Young-Key. 1978. A Study on the Childbearing Behavior of Rural Korean Women and Their Families. *Transactions of the Korea Branch of the Royal Asiatic Society* 53:27–55.

Smith, Robert J. 1974. *Ancestor Worship in Japan.* Stanford: Stanford University Press.

Sofue, Takao. 1965. Childhood Ceremonies in Japan: Regional and Local Variation. *Ethnology* 4:148–164.

Sorensen, Clark Wesley. 1981. Household, Family, and Economy in a Korean Mountain Village. Ph.D. diss., University of Washington.

Spiro, Melford E. 1967. *Burmese Supernaturalism.* Englewood Cliffs, N.J.: Prentice Hall.

Strathern, Marilyn. 1972. *Women in Between—Female Roles in a Male World: Mt. Hagen, New Guinea.* London: Seminar Press.

Turner, Victor. 1967. *The Forest of Symbols: Aspects of Ndembu Ritual.* Ithaca: Cornell University Press.

Van Gennep, Arnold. [1909] 1960. *The Rites of Passage.* Reprint. Chicago: University Press of Chicago.

Wagner, Edward W. 1983. Two Early Genealogies and Women's Status in Early Yi Dynasty Korea. In *Korean Women: View from the Inner Room,* ed. L. Kendall and M. Peterson, 23–32. New Haven: East Rock Press.

Wang, Sung-hsing. 1974. Taiwanese Architecture and the Supernatural. In *Religion and Ritual in Chinese Society,* ed. A. Wolf, 181–192. Stanford: Stanford University Press.

Welch, Holmes. 1970. Facades of Religion in China. *Asian Survey* 10 (7): 614–626.

Werbner, Richard P. 1964. Atonement Ritual and Guardian-Spirit Possession among the Kalanga. *Africa* 34:206–222.

Wilson, Brian. 1983. The Korean Shaman: Image and Reality. In *Korean Women: View from the Inner Room,* ed. L. Kendall and M. Peterson 113–128. New Haven: East Rock Press.

Wolf, Arthur P. 1974. Gods, Ghosts, and Ancestors. In *Religion and Ritual in Chinese Society,* ed. A. Wolf, 131–182. Stanford: Stanford University Press.

Wolf, Margery. 1972. *Women and the Family in Rural Taiwan.* Stanford: Stanford University Press.

———. 1974. Chinese Women: Old Skills in a New Context. In *Women, Culture, and Society,* ed. M. Z. Rosaldo and L. Lamphere, 157–172. Stanford: Stanford University Press.

Yang, C. K. 1961. *Religion in Chinese Society.* Berkeley and Los Angeles: University of California Press.

Yangjugun t'onggye yŏnbo (YTY) (Statistical yearbook of Yangjugun). 1965, 1975. Üijŏngbu: Yangjugun.

Yi, Nŭng-hwa. 1976. *Chosŏn musok ko* (Reflections on Korean shamanism). Translation of the 1927 ed. by Yi Chae-gon. Seoul: Paengnŭk.

Yim, Suk-jay [Im Sŏk-chae]. 1970. Han'guk musok yŏn'gu sŏsŏl (Introduction to Korean "*mu*-ism") *Journal of Asian Women* (Seoul) 9:73–90, 161–217.

Yoon, Hong-key. 1976. *Geomantic Relationships between Culture and Nature in Korea.* Taipei: Orient Culture Service.

Yoon, Soon-young. 1976. Magic, Science, and Religion on Cheju Island. *Korea Journal* 16 (3): 4–11.

———. 1977a. Occupation, Male House Keeper: Male and Female Roles on Cheju Island. In *Virtues in Conflict: Tradition and the Korean Woman Today,* ed. S. Mattielli, 191–208. Seoul: Royal Asiatic Society.

———. 1977b. Su-Dong Project Report. Unpublished MS.

Yoshida, Teigo. 1967. Mystical Retribution, Spirit Possession, and Social Structure in a Japanese Village. *Ethnology* 6 (3): 237–62.

Young Barbara. 1980. Spirits and Other Signs: An Ethnography of Divination in Seoul, R.O.K. Ph.D. diss., University of Washington.

———. 1983. City Women and Divination: Signs in Seoul. In *Korean Women: View from the Inner Room,* ed. L. Kendall and M. Peterson, 139–157. New Haven: East Rock Press.

Yu, Tong-sik. 1975. *Han'guk musokŭi yŏksawa kujo* (Korean shamanism's history and structure). Seoul: Yonsei University Press.

Index

Adultery, 71–72, 76, 131
Affines. *See* Women, and patrilocality
Agnates. *See* Family; Lineage
Agriculture, 45–46
Ahern, Emily M., 174–176
Ajŏn (functionary at magistrate's court), 42, 191 n. 2
Akiba, Takashi, 193 n. 1
Almanac, 97–98, 192 n. 4
Altar to Land and Grain (Sajik), 41
Ancestors *(chosang, chusang malmyŏng):* and affliction, 89, 91, 94–100, 148–152, 197 n. 2; in *chesa,* 147; of Chŏn family, 6–8, 20–21; in East Asian societies, 122, 170–172, 177–178; as gods, 3, 50, 55, 68, 132–134, 139; guilt toward, 44; husband as, 151; husband's first wife as, 90–91, 96, 100, 102, 142, 148–149; husband's parents as, 100, 126, 148, 197 n. 2; in *kut,* 36, 38, 100, 144, 147–151, 156–160; of lineage, 41, 133–134; and *mansin,* 73–74, 142; pre-Confucian ancestors, 29; village ancestors, 119; wife's kin as, 100, 148–150, 157–163, 168–169. *See also* Dead, the; Ghosts; Souls; Spirit possession
Ancestor worship. *See* Chesa
An family *kut,* 136–138, 161–162

Bell Mansin, 67
Biernatzki, William E., 150
Birth Grandmother (Samsin Chesŏk), 12–14, 113, 115, 189 n. 2, 194 n. 6; and women, 124–127, 165
Bishop, Isabella Bird, 152

Blacker, Carmen, 171
Body-governing God (Momju), 66, 81, 117, 135–139, 142 143, 166. *See also* Mugam
Bogoras, Waldemar, 23
Boil-face Mansin, 58–59, 133
Brandt, Vincent, 30
Brass Mirror Mansin, 105–106
Brothers, 26, 162, 171–172. *See also* Family
Buddhism: and the dead, 149–150, 152, 155; in Japan, 171; and *mansin,* 12–13, 29, 36, 83–85, 126, 191 n. 7; monks, 176; in Okinawa, 178; temples, 40, 81, 83–85, 152
Buddhist Sage (Pulsa), 12, 17, 53, 55, 68, 131–142. *See also* Buddhism, and *mansin*

Chatterbox Mansin, 58–59, 63, 67, 69–70, 133. *See also* Chŏn family *kut*
Chesa (ancestor worship): and ancestors, 99, 149–150, 163, 195 n. 3; as Confucian ritual, 29–30, 144–147, 195 n. 2; and death humors, 103–105; and kinship, 25, 42, 156, 167–168; mock *chesa,* 154–155; and women, 26, 145–147, 167, 195 n. 1, 196–197 n. 1
Childbirth: death in, 8, 158–159, 162; and ritual danger, 105–107, 118, 125, 175; sources on, 194 n. 7. *See also* Birth Grandmother; Conception; Seven Stars
Child Messengers (Tongja Pyŏlsang), 134–135, 138, 141–142, 195 n. 9
Children: anxieties caused by, 72, 75–76, 105–106; ritual protection of, 80–81,

84, 102, 115, 128, 165. *See also* Child Messengers; Ghosts, children as; Seven Stars

China: family organization in, 25–26, 171–172; folk religion in, 34, 122, 152, 155, 170–176

Chinsuk's Mother, 131–132, 143, 148–149

Chip. See Family; House; Household

Ch'oe Kil-sŏng, 38, 190 n. 5; and Chang Chu-gŭn, 51, 61, 189 n. 6

Cho family, 98, 133

Chŏn family *kut,* 1–22, 139–140, 189 n. 5

Cho Yŏng-ja, 61

Christianity: in Enduring Pine Village, 39, 53; and *mansin,* 34, 56–57, 77–78, 82–84, 94, 167; missionary attitudes, 32

Ch'usŏk (lunar holiday), 145–147

Clark, Charles Allen, 150

Clear Spring Mansin, 33, 57, 66–71, 83, 105, 130

Clown (Ch'angbu), 17

Cohen, Myron L., 196 n. 14

Cold wind (*ch'an param*), 126, 194 n. 7

Community rituals, 31–32, 41, 47, 171, 174, 191 n. 3. *See also Kut,* for Tutelary God; Mountain God; Tutelary God

Conception, 34–35, 38, 125, 127–128, 173, 194 n. 7. *See also* Birth Grandmother; Childbirth; Seven Stars

Confucianism, 25–36, 62, 124, 164, 167–168, 178; Confucian shrine (*hyanggyo*), 39, 41

Cosmology, 23, 38, 97–99, 109–110

Costumes, 6–8, 132–137, 142–143. *See also Mugam*

Credit associations (*kye*), 47

Dance, 62. *See also Mugam*

Daughters, 26, 73–74, 125, 149–150; and mother's rituals, 21, 74–75, 82, 85, 88. *See also* Women

Daughters-in-law: and ancestral affliction, 96, 121; and co-residence, 72, 131, 137; and mother-in-law's traditions, 11, 82, 85, 138; senior daughter-in-law, 146

Dead, the, 20, 65, 87–88, 100, 155–156, 163. *See also* Ancestors; Ghosts; *Kut,* for the dead; Souls

Death: in childbirth, 8, 158–159, 162; death fate, 96; pollution from, 5, 104–106, 118, 130; supernatural factors in, 91, 103–104, 106–107, 130–131, 138–139, 156; violent or untimely, 19, 99, 192 n. 1, 196 n. 10. *See also Kut,* for the dead

Death humors (*sangmun*), 103–105

Death Messenger (Saja), 67, 69, 87, 104, 153–155, 195 n. 4

Divinations: and child gods, 195 n. 9; in China, 172–173; by horoscope reading, 94–95, 192 n. 2; and illness, 3, 86, 93, 158; by *mansin* (*mugŏri*), 38, 66–67, 70–79, 109, 148–152, 166–167. *See also* Chŏn family *kut;* Fate

Dix, Griffin, 38, 192 n. 4

Door Guard Official (Sumun Taegam), 18, 114

Dreams, 37–38, 56, 60, 68, 80, 116

Drum, 4, 68, 121

Durkheim, Emile, 24–25

Earth God (T'osin), 124. *See also* House Site Official

Earth imps (*chisin tongbŏp*), 90–91, 97–99, 192 n. 4

East Town Mansin, 83

Eight Characters (*p'alcha*). *See* Fate

Emigration, 120

Exorcism: of affliction (*p'udakkŏri*), 68, 71, 77, 108, 149, 158; description of, 51, 87–105; divine intervention during, 60; of invisible arrows (*salp'uri*) 106; during other rituals, 5, 14–15, 19, 80, 143

Family: as ritual unit, 21, 74, 137–138, 155–157, 161–163, 165–168; social organization of, 25–26, 145, 171–172, 197 n. 4. *See also* Gods, and family traditions; Household

Fate, 15, 75–76, 87, 94–98, 102–103, 108–109. *See also* Divination

Feasts, and ritual danger, 76, 100–101, 103, 107, 109. *See also* Food offerings

Feuchtwang, Stephan, 172

Filial piety (*hyodo*), 30, 167. *See also Chesa*

Financial trouble, 17, 32, 71, 121

Five Direction Forces (Obang T'ŏjŏn), 114

Food offerings: for the dead, 87, 146–147, 153, 159, 195 nn. 2, 4; for gods, 1–19, 114–117, 119–123, 141. See also Feasts
Fortes, Meyer, 167
Foundation God (Chisin), 1, 18, 114
Freedman, Maurice, 171–172
Funerals, 47, 151, 163, 191 n. 3; mock funerals, 87, 104; and ritual danger, 76, 102–103, 105–107, 109

Gale, James S., 64–65
Genealogies, 26, 41
General (Changgun), 14, 133, 142–143
Geomancy, 40, 119, 151–152; Geomancer, 152, 192 n. 5
Ghosts: and affliction, 76, 87–89, 91, 95–102, 142, 156–157; children as, 134–135, 157, 159, 173, 195 nn. 4, 9; in kut, 19–20; and women, 157–162, 168–169. See also Ancestors; Dead, the; Exorcism; Kut, for the Dead; Souls
Gifford, D. L., 34, 150
God-descended person (naerin saram), 71. See also Mansin, calling of
Gods: and affliction, 4, 26–27, 95–96, 168; in East Asian societies, 170–177; and family traditions, 20–21, 55, 73–74, 127–129, 131–132, 137–143; household gods, 38, 105, 113–124, 193 n. 1; of mansin, 29, 55–57, 63–64, 73, 81, 142–143. See also Death, supernatural factors in; Kosa; Kut
Grain God (Köllip), 18
Grandchildren, 72, 101–102, 106
Graves, 6, 151. See also Geomancy
Great Send-off (Taesang), 155
Great Spirit Grandmother (Taesin Halmöni): of Chön family, 3, 6–8, 20–21, 139; and mansin, 72–73, 132–133, 139, 142; of Song family, 137–138, 156–157
de Groot, J. J. M., 150
Guillemoz, Alexandre, 38

Hallucinations, 37, 60
Han, Sang-bok, 192 n. 5
Hangil's Mother, 76–77, 95
Harvey, Youngsook Kim, 37–38, 60, 190 n. 3, 191 nn. 1, 6, 192 n. 8
Healing Buddha (Yaksa Puch'önim), 84

Healing kut. See Kut, healing kut
Health system. See Illness; Medicine
Hell, 13, 87–88, 151–156, 174
Hongsu Megi. See New Year, Hongsu Megi at
Horoscope. See Fate
House, 1, 20, 108–110, 168. See also Gods, household gods
Household, 26–27, 81–82, 108–109, 117, 121–124, 164–168. See also Family
Household gods. See Gods, household gods
Household head, 115, 118, 147, 165
House Lord (Söngju), 16, 113–118, 124, 194 n. 4
House Site Official (T'öju Taegam), 17–18, 113–115, 119–121, 123
Husband: as ancestor, 151; anxieties concerning, 55, 71–72, 76, 105, 121, 132; rituals on behalf of, 32–33, 78, 102, 148. See also Chön family kut; Pyön, Mr.; Yangja's Father; Yi, Mr.
Hwang, Lucy, 196 n. 7

Illness: and health-seeking process, 1–3, 47–48, 86–91, 191 n. 5; and mansin, 32–33, 38, 71–73, 77–79, 90–94, 108; and mansin's calling, 37; and the supernatural, 20–21, 91–110, 119–120, 138–139, 156–158
Inheritance and succession. See Family, social organization of
Invisible arrows (sal), 105–107, 192–193 nn. 7, 9, 10

Janelli, Dawnhee Yim, 192 n. 2
Janelli, Roger L., and Dawnhee Yim Janelli, 38, 50, 150, 195 n. 1, 197 n. 2
Japan: colonization by, 42–43; ritual roles in, 122, 170–171
Jones, George Heber, 193 n. 1
Jordan, David K., 173–174, 176

Kendall, Laurel, 38
Kiester, Daniel, 196 n. 7
Kim, Mrs., 95–96, 148, 160
Kim, Young-key, and Dorothea Sich, 38
Kim Kwang-iel, 36–37
Kim T'ae-gon, 37, 189–190 n. 6, 196 nn. 7, 9
Kindred, 163, 169, 196 n. 13

King (Taewang), 50, 133–134, 138, 141, 143
King of Hell (Yŏmna Taewang,), 151–152
Kisaeng (female entertainer), 61, 63
Kitchen God (Chowang), 113, 122, 124, 171–172
Korean War: experiences during, 40, 43–44, 60, 158; and the supernatural, 100, 131–132, 149, 196 n. 11
Kosa, 17, 114–117, 119–120, 123–124, 134, 193–194 n. 2
Kut: characteristics of, 20–21, 36, 189–190 n. 6; for the dead *(chinogi kut),* 69, 153–156, 196 nn. 7, 9, 10; flower-greeting *kut (kkonmaji kut),* 56, 81, 142–143; healing *kut (uhwan kut),* 4–21, 60, 89, 93–94, 105, 121; initiation *kut (naerim kut),* 58, 65–66; for King deity (Taewang Kut), 50, 134; location of *kut,* 32–33, 81, 120; in public buildings *(kwanch'ŏng kut),* 41; for rain *(kiu che),* 41; for Tutelary God *(Todang kut, Sŏnang kut),* 41, 47, 119, 123–124, 194 n. 5; and women, ix–x, 21–22, 38, 165. *See also* Ancestors, in *kut;* An family *kut;* Chŏn family *kut;* Song family *kut;* Yu family *kut*
Kwanyin Buddhist Sage (Kwanseŭm Pulsa), 84

Landlady, of anthropologist, 33, 85, 88, 103–104, 115–116
Lebra, William P., 28
Ledyard, Gari K., 191–192 n. 7, 194 n. 4
Lee Du-hyun, 50–51
Lewis, I. M., 23–25
Lineage, 25, 41, 50. *See also* Pae family
Lotus Paradise (Kŭngnak), 87, 151–156, 195–196 n. 6

McCune, Evelyn, 190 n. 7
Madness, 37, 57–59, 93, 95–96, 100, 148
Magistrate, 31–33, 40–41, 49, 65
Mann saeg phox (Cantonese shaman), 173, 195 n. 9
Mansin (shaman): Appointed Mansin (An Mansin), 41; attitudes toward, x, 30–34, 106, 108, 176; calling of, 27, 37–38, 57–60, 63, 139; clients of, 21, 52–55, 67, 76–79, 81–85; initiation of, 58, 65–66; *mansin* teams, 3–4, 16, 18,

69–71; *mansin*'s shrine, 54–57; nick-names of, xi; powers of, 21, 147–150, 164–167, 175–177; prevalence of, 190 n. 3; as shamans, xi, 27–29; status of, 4, 60–65; studies of, 34–38, 189–190 n. 6; training of, 67–68. *See also* Gods, of *mansin;* Illness, and *mansin; Mudang;* Shaman; *Tan'gol* relationship; *and names of individual* mansin
Mansin from Within the Wall, 69–70
Marriage, 48, 163, 168; and divination, 73, 76, 78, 95, 109; remarriage, 138; and the supernatural, 101, 106, 134–135, 138–141, 159. *See also* Weddings
Mask dance, 50–51
Medicine, 18, 47–48, 90–93, 192 n. 8. *See also* Illness
Medium, 171, 195 n. 9. *See also* Shaman
Men: ritual roles of, 26–30, 118, 122–124, 144–147, 167–169; and women's rituals, 10–11, 32–34, 61–62, 82, 165–166
Menstruation, 66, 84, 105, 129–130, 175
Migration, 44–45
Ministry of Culture, Bureau of Cultural Properties Preservation, 189–190 n. 6
Mirŭk Buddha (Maitreya), 133
Mischel, Walter, and Francis Mischel, 23–24
Moose, Robert J., 155
Mothers. *See* Ancestors, wife's kin as; Daughters; Women, and natal kin
Mothers-in-law, 72, 89, 105, 125–127, 141; and ritual transmission, 121–122, 128, 130–131, 137, 146
Mountain God (Sansin, Ponhyang Sansin), 6, 14, 84, 113, 130; annual offering to, 41, 47, 191 n. 3; mountain *kami,* 171; powers of, 55, 60, 130–131, 146–147
Mountain pilgrimage *(sanŭl ssŭda),* 66, 127–131
Mourning, 66
Mudang (shaman, priestess), xi, 23, 28, 31–34, 64–65; *tanggol mudang,* 38, 191 n. 3. *See also Mansin*
Mugam (trance dance), 10–12, 16–17, 38, 59, 143, 165. *See also* Body-governing God
Munae's Mother, 96, 148–149

Neo-Confucianism. *See* Confucianism
Nephews, 137–138, 151–152
Netherworldly guards *(kamang)*, 6
New Village Movement (Saemaül Undong), 39, 47, 48, 105
New Year: *chesa* at, 145–147; divinations at, 74–76, 109; Hongsu Megi at, 80, 101–102, 105, 141–142
Noxious influences, 4–5, 20, 95–110

Official (Taegam): as Body-governing God, 81, 117, 136, 143; as household god, 114; portrayals of, 8–10, 14–16, 42, 69, 117, 141–143; possession by, 95–96. *See also* Door Guard Official; House Site Official: Soldier Official
Okinawa, 28, 177–178
Okkyŏng's Mother, 12–13, 67–68, 70, 121, 137, 191 n. 4. *See also* Chŏn family *kut*

Pae family, 133, 135, 138–139, 141, 143
Paksu mudang (male shaman), 27, 36, 139
Pansu (exorcist), 23
Plath, David W., 171
Pollution *(pujŏng)*, 66, 84, 118, 132, 168, 175–177. *See also* Childbirth; Death; Menstruation; Purification
Posal (bodhisattva), 126, 132
Priestess, 28, 177
Princess (Hogu), 13, 134–135, 138
Princess Pari (Pari Kongju), 154, 196 n. 8
Pulsŏk Buddha (Pulsŏk Puch'ŏnim), 84
Purification, 5–6, 20, 80, 129, 141, 189 n. 1. *See also* Pollution
Pyon, Mr., 86–92, 96, 100, 148

Red disaster *(hongaek)*, 102–103, 117, 192 n. 7
Rhi Bou-yang, 36–37
Rice Shop Auntie, 79–80, 105, 136, 141–143

Saudi Arabia, 45, 105
Scapegoat, 19–20, 87, 96
Seven Stars (Ch'ilsŏng): as Body-governing God, 66, 136–138, 143; and Buddhism, 84, 126, 189 n. 2; and the Chŏn family, 11–12, 15, 20, 139; as protectors of children, 80–81, 115, 127–128,

142–143; rituals honoring, 81, 113, 116, 165, 194 n. 3
Shaman, 23–24, 27–38, 171–175. *See also Mansin*
Shaman ritual, scholarly views of: by anthropologists, x–xi, 24–25, 37–38; by folklorists, 20, 35; by Korean Institute for Research in the Behavioral Sciences, 34; by psychiatrists, 36–37; by religious historians, 28, 36
Shigematsu Mayumi, 38
Shinto, 171
Sich, Dorothea, 38, 192 n. 1
Singbyŏng (shaman's possession sickness), 37
Sixty-first birthday *(hwan'gap)*, 17, 76, 107, 109, 134, 193 n. 11
Soldier Official (Kunung Taegam), 4–5, 19
Son: anxieties due to, 71, 77–78, 94, 101, 106, 151; and domestic cycle, 26; son preference, 25, 34–35, 154. *See also* Children; Family
Song family *kut*, 77–78, 137–138, 156–157
Sorcery, 31
Souls, 13, 87–88, 150–152. *See also* Ancestors; Dead, the; Ghosts
Special Messenger (Pyŏlsang), 14, 189 n. 3. *See also* Child Messengers
Spirit daughter *(sinttal)*, 58–60. *See also* Okkyŏng's Mother
Spirit mother *(sinŏmŏni)*, 58–60, 67, 133. *See also* Chatterbox Mansin; Clear Spring Mansin
Spirit possession: in Japan, 171; and madness, 58, 93, 95–96, 105; types of, 65–66, 135–136; and women's status, 24–25. *See also* Body-governing God; *Mansin,* calling of
Spirit Warrior (Sinjang), 14–15, 68–69, 93, 133, 142–143
Stepchildren, 132, 148, 190 n. 7
Stepfather, 139, 141
Stove God. *See* Kitchen God
Suicide, 19
Superstition *(misin)*, 28, 33

Tanggol mudang. See mudang
Tang-ki (Taiwanese shaman), 172–175
Tan'gol relationship, 79–81, 141–143, 167. *See also Mansin,* clients of

Tano Festival, 32, 123
Taoist priests, 174–176
Toilet Maiden (Pyŏnso Kakssi), 113–114
Town Mansin, 4, 16
Trance, x, 21, 24–25, 28, 34, 38. *See also* Body-governing God; Spirit possession
Transvestitism, 24, 27, 36
Tutelary God (Todang, Sŏnang), 31–32, 40, 118–119, 194 n. 5. *See also Kut,* for Tutelary God

Visions, 21, 72–73, 108, 139

Waterfall Valley Auntie, 132, 141–142
Weddings: and affines, 163; in Enduring Pine Village, 33, 47–48, 191 n. 3; and ritual danger, 107, 109, 134–135, 159, 193 nn. 11, 12. *See also Yŏt'am*
Werbner, Richard P., 162
Widows, 51–52, 59, 91, 95, 196–197 n. 1
Willow Market Auntie, 132, 138, 142
Wine House Auntie, 134–135, 141–142
Witchcraft, 190 n. 2
Wolf, Arthur P., 194 n. 4
Women: in Enduring Pine Village, 44, 46–47; in other ethnography, 23–25; as informants, x–xii, 30; marginal women, 63; and natal kin, 74, 145, 157–160, 168–169, 196 n. 11; palace women, 31; and patrilocality, 21–22, 26, 169–179; ritual roles of, 26–28,

30–31, 34–38, 122–124, 144, 164–170; Song of a Mediocre Woman, 164; status of, ix–xi, 34, 164–165. *See also* Ancestors, wife's kin as; Ghosts, and women; Gods, and family traditions; *Kut,* and women
Wood imps *(nanggu moksin, moksin tongbŏp),* 90–91, 97–99

Yangban, 41–42, 49–50, 133. *See also* Pae family
Yangja's Father, 102, 143
Yangja's Mother, 85, 116–117, 136, 141–143, 169
Yi, Mr., 105, 169
Yim Suk-jay, 28, 192–193 n. 9
Yongsu's Mother: bad fate of, 95; calling and initiation of, 59–60, 66–69; at *chesa,* 167; divinations by, 76; gods of, 54–57, 120, 128–131, 142–143; parents of, 131; and the Pyon family, 86, 89–92; relationship with anthropologist, 4, 51–53, 55, 73, 81–82, 101–103; relationship with other *mansin,* 16, 18, 68–71, 83; status as *mansin,* 61–62. *See also* Chŏn family *kut; Tan'gol* relationship
Yoon, Soon-young, 38, 191 n. 5
Yŏt'am, 17, 33, 56, 135, 159
Young, Barbara, 192 n. 2, 195 n. 9
Yu family *kut,* 161 fig.2, 162

About the Author

Laurel Kendall holds a Ph.D. in anthropology from Columbia University. Her study of Korea and its people began with a three-year stint in the Peace Corps. She returned again as a fellow of the Fulbright Foundation and the Social Science Research Council, spending nearly two years in a rural Korean community researching *Shamans, Housewives, and Other Restless Spirits*. Dr. Kendall is assistant curator in charge of Asian Ethnographic collections at the American Museum of Natural History. She is the author of several articles on Korean religion and women's lives and is co-editor, with Mark Peterson, of *Korean Women: View from the Inner Room*.

Studies of the East Asian Institute

The Ladder of Success in Imperial China, by Ping-ti Ho. New York: Columbia University Press, 1962.

The Chinese Inflation, 1937–1949, by Shun-hsin Chou. New York: Columbia University Press, 1963.

Reformer in Modern China: Chang Chien, 1853–1926, by Samuel Chu. New York: Columbia University Press, 1965.

Research in Japanese Sources: A Guide, by Herschel Webb with the assistance of Marleigh Ryan. New York: Columbia University Press, 1965.

Society and Education in Japan, by Herbert Passin. New York: Teachers College Press, 1965.

Agricultural Production and Economic Development in Japan, 1873–1922, by James I. Nakamura. Princeton: Princeton University Press, 1966.

Japan's First Modern Novel: Ukigumo of Futabatei Shimei, by Marleigh Ryan. New York: Columbia University Press, 1967.

The Korean Communist Movement, 1918–1948, by Dae-Sook Suh. Princeton: Princeton University Press, 1967.

The First Vietnam Crisis, by Melvin Gurtov. New York: Columbia University Press, 1967.

Cadres, Bureaucracy, and Political Power in Communist China, by A. Doak Barnett. New York: Columbia University Press, 1968.

The Japanese Imperial Institution in the Tokugawa Period, by Herschel Webb. New York: Columbia University Press, 1968.

Higher Education and Business Recruitment in Japan, by Koya Azumi. New York: Teachers College Press, 1969.

The Communists and Peasant Rebellions: A Study in the Rewriting of Chinese History, by James P. Harrison, Jr. New York: Atheneum, 1969.

How the Conservatives Rule Japan, by Nathaniel B. Thayer. Princeton: Princeton University Press, 1969.

Aspects of Chinese Education, edited by C. T. Hu. New York: Teachers College Press, 1970.

Documents of Korean Communism, 1918–1948, by Dae-Sook Suh. Princeton: Princeton University Press, 1970.

Japanese Education: A Bibliography of Materials in the English Language, by Herbert Passin. New York: Teachers College Press, 1970.

Economic Development and the Labor Market in Japan, by Koji Taira. New York: Columbia University Press, 1970.

The Japanese Oligarchy and the Russo-Japanese War, by Shumpei Okamoto. New York: Columbia University Press, 1970.

Imperial Restoration in Medieval Japan, by H. Paul Varley. New York: Columbia University Press, 1971.

Japan's Postwar Defense Policy, 1947–1968, by Martin E. Weinstein. New York: Columbia University Press, 1971.

Election Campaigning Japanese Style, by Gerald L. Curtis. New York: Columbia University Press, 1971.

China and Russia: The "Great Game," by O. Edmund Clubb. New York: Columbia University Press, 1971.

Money and Monetary Policy in Communist China, by Katharine Huang Hsiao. New York: Columbia University Press, 1971.

The District Magistrate in Late Imperial China, by John R. Watt. New York: Columbia University Press, 1972.

Law and Policy in China's Foreign Relations: A Study of Attitudes and Practice, by James C. Hsiung. New York: Columbia University Press, 1972.

Pearl Harbor as History: Japanese-American Relations, 1931–1941, edited by Dorothy Borg and Shumpei Okamoto, with the assistance of Dale K. A. Finlayson. New York: Columbia University Press, 1973.

Japanese Culture: A Short History, by H. Paul Varley. New York: Praeger, 1973.

Doctors in Politics: The Political Life of the Japan Medical Association, by William E. Steslicke. New York: Praeger, 1973.

The Japan Teachers Union: A Radical Interest Group in Japanese Politics, by Donald Ray Thurston. Princeton: Princeton University Press, 1973.

Japan's Foreign Policy, 1868–1941: A Research Guide, edited by James William Morley. New York: Columbia University Press, 1974.

Palace and Politics in Prewar Japan, by David Anson Titus. New York: Columbia University Press, 1974.

The Idea of China: Essays in Geographic Myth and Theory, by Andrew March. Devon, England: David and Charles, 1974.

Origins of the Cultural Revolution, by Roderick MacFarquhar. New York: Columbia University Press, 1974.

Shiba Kokan: Artist, Innovator, and Pioneer in the Westernization of Japan, by Calvin L. French. Tokyo: Weatherhill, 1974.

Insei: Abdicated Sovereigns in the Politics of Late Heian Japan, by G. Cameron Hurst. New York: Columbia University Press, 1975.

Embassy at War, by Harold Joyce Noble. Edited with an introduction by Frank Baldwin, Jr. Seattle: University of Washington Press, 1975.

Rebels and Bureaucrats: China's December 9ers, by John Israel and Donald W. Klein. Berkeley: University of California Press, 1975.

Deterrent Diplomacy, edited by James William Morley. New York: Columbia University Press, 1976.

House United, House Divided: The Chinese Family in Taiwan, by Myron L. Cohen. New York: Columbia University Press, 1976.

Escape from Predicament: Neo-Confucianism and China's Evolving Political Culture, by Thomas A. Metzger. New York: Columbia University Press, 1976.

Cadres, Commanders, and Commissars: The Training of the Chinese Communist Leadership, 1920–45, by Jane L. Price. Boulder, Colo.: Westview Press, 1976.

Sun Yat-sen: Frustrated Patriot, by C. Martin Wilbur. New York: Columbia University Press, 1977.

Japanese International Negotiating Style, by Michael Blaker. New York: Columbia University Press, 1977.

Contemporary Japanese Budget Politics, by John Creighton Campbell. Berkeley: University of California Press, 1977.

The Medieval Chinese Oligarchy, by David Johnson. Boulder, Colo.: Westview Press, 1977.

The Arms of Kiangnan: Modernization in the Chinese Ordnance Industry, 1860–1895, by Thomas L. Kennedy. Boulder, Colo.: Westview Press, 1978.

Patterns of Japanese Policymaking: Experiences from Higher Education, by T. J. Pempel. Boulder, Colo.: Westview Press, 1978.

The Chinese Connection: Roger S. Greene, Thomas W. Lamont, George E. Sokolsky, and American-East Asian Relations, by Warren I. Cohen. New York: Columbia University Press, 1978.

Militarism in Modern China: The Career of Wu P'ei-fu, 1916–1939, by Odoric Y. K. Wou. Folkestone, England: Dawson, 1978.

A Chinese Pioneer Family: The Lins of Wu-feng, by Johanna Meskill. Princeton: Princeton University Press, 1979.

Perspectives on a Changing China, edited by Joshua A. Fogel and William T. Rowe. Boulder, Colo.: Westview Press, 1979.

The Memoirs of Li Tsung-jen, T. K. Tong and Li Tsung-jen. Boulder, Colo.: Westview Press, 1979.

Unwelcome Muse: Chinese Literature in Shanghai and Peking, 1937–1945, by Edward Gunn. New York: Columbia University Press, 1979.

Yenan and the Great Powers: The Origins of Chinese Communist Foreign Policy, by James Reardon-Anderson. New York: Columbia University Press, 1980.

Uncertain Years: Chinese-American Relations, 1947–1950, edited by Dorothy Borg and Waldo Heinrichs. New York: Columbia University Press, 1980.

The Fateful Choice: Japan's Advance into Southeast Asia, edited by James William Morley. New York: Columbia University Press, 1980.

Tanaka Giichi and Japan's China Policy, by William F. Morton. Folkestone, England: Dawson, 1980; New York: St. Martin's Press, 1980.

The Origins of the Korean War: Liberation and the Emergence of Separate Regimes, 1945–1947, by Bruce Cumings. Princeton: Princeton University Press, 1981.

Class Conflict in Chinese Socialism, by Richard Curt Kraus. New York: Columbia University Press, 1981.

Education under Mao: Class and Competition in Canton Schools, by Jonathan Unger. New York: Columbia University Press, 1982.

Private Academies of Tokugawa Japan, by Richard Rubinger. Princeton: Princeton University Press, 1982.

Japan and the San Francisco Peace Settlement, by Michael M. Yoshitsu. New York: Columbia University Press, 1982.

New Frontiers in American-East Asian Relations: Essays Presented to Dorothy Borg, edited by Warren I. Cohen. New York: Columbia University Press, 1983.

The Origins of the Cultural Revolution: 2, The Great Leap Forward, 1958–1960, by Roderick MacFarquhar. New York: Columbia University Press, 1983.

The China Quagmire: Japan's Expansion on the Asian Continent, 1933–1941, edited by James William Morley. New York: Columbia University Press, 1983.

Fragments of Rainbows: The Life and Poetry of Saito Mokichi, 1882–1953, by Amy Vladeck Heinrich. New York: Columbia University Press, 1983.

The U.S.-South Korean Alliance: Evolving Patterns of Security Relations, edited by Gerald L. Curtis and Sung-joo Han. Lexington, Mass.: Lexington Books, 1983.